THE MYSTERY

The Mystery

A Scriptural Discourse on the Believer's Identification with Christ

Richard E. Mallette, TH.D.
Dwayne Norman

The Mystery Col. 1:25-27
A Scriptural Discourse on the Believer's Identification with Christ
Richard E. Mallette, TH.D.
Dwayne Norman

Unless otherwise indicated, all scripture quotations are taken from the King James Version of the Bible.

The Mystery
ISBN 978-0-88144-520-6
Copyright c 1998
Living Word Ministries
All rights Reserved

Published by
Yorkshire Publishing Group
9731 East 54th Street
Tulsa, OK 74146
www.yorkshirepublishing.com

Table of Contents

Acknowledgments   vii

Dedications   ix

Preface   xi

Chapter 1   The Power of The Gospel   1

Chapter 2   The Gospel of Calvary's Cross   19

Chapter 3   The Identification Principle (Part 1)   33

Chapter 4   The Identification Principle (Part 2)   51

Chapter 5   It's All Yours in Christ   61

Chapter 6   The First Adam and The Last Adam   75

Chapter 7   Seven Identifications with Christ   89

Chapter 8   Some Important Facts About Your Redemption   103

Chapter 9   More Important Facts About Your Redemption   117

Chapter 10   The Old Man is Dead   133

Chapter 11   Did Jesus Die Spiritually? (Part 1)   145

Chapter 12   Did Jesus Die Spiritually? (Part 2)   159

Chapter 13   Did Jesus Die Spiritually? (Part 3)   171

Chapter 14   Did Jesus Die Spiritually? (Part 4)   181

Chapter 15   Did Jesus Die Spiritually? (Part 5)   191

Chapter 16   Made Alive with Christ   205

Chapter 17   Conquering and Raised with Him   219

Chapter 18   Seated with Christ   231

Chapter 19   In Him Through Covenant Loyalty   247

Chapter 20   In Him   259

              About the Authors   271

Acknowledgments

For all the hours of typing, correcting, and transforming a complicated bunch of notes and tapes into something readable and understandable, Wendy Carpenter, we thank you for all those tiring hours that you gave to make this book possible. Only time will attest to the many who will read this book and walk up into higher level of faith and trust in the finished work of Calvary. All of these victories to come will be, in part, because of your contribution.

We choose not to observe the rules of grammar with respect to our adversary. He deserves no such privilege. Therefore, we acknowledge satan and the devil in lower case only, since he is, after all, under our feet.

Dedications

To my dear family, my wife Adrienne, my daughter, Lauren, my son, Richard Jr. my daughter-in-law, Paloma and my dear grandchildren, Juliana and Nathaniel. May this book inspire all of you to hunger and thirst to know who you are in Christ, and the rights and priveleges you have as a partaker of His Divine nature.

Richard Mallette

To my precious children, Julianne and Daniel, that they may embrace the principles found in this book to bring joy, peace, and victory to their lives.

Dwayne Norman

Preface

Most people like a good mystery, as long as it's understandable and they know how it ends. According to the Bible, there was a time when God's mystery, his plan for man in Jesus Christ, was not revealed. There was a time when this mystery was truly a mystery. That time has come to an end.

Let us rejoice that our redemption is complete in Christ! Now, is the light and knowledge of the mystery of the gospel of Jesus Christ made manifest to the people of God! This book is about the mystery of God, which is centered in our identification with Christ.

Within the pages of this book get ready to embark on a wonderful journey, from the crucifixion of Christ unto the ascension of Christ at the Father's right hand. The vehicle that will provide our transportation is called "in Him".

Romans 16:25,26 says, "Now to him that is of power to establish you according to my gospel, and the preaching of Jesus Christ, according to the revelation of the mystery, which was kept secret since the world began, but now is made manifest, and by the Scriptures of the prophets, according to the commandment of the everlasting God, made known to all nations for the obedience of faith."

The Apostle Paul gives us more light in Colossians 1:25 – 27: "Whereof I was made a minister, according to the dispensation of God which is given to me for you, to fulfill the word of God even the mystery which hath been hid from ages and from generations, but now is made manifest to his saints; to whom God would make known what is the riches of this mystery among the Gentiles; which is Christ in you, the hope of glory."

This book is about the riches of the glory of *the mystery* of Christ (the Anointed One and His Anointing) <u>in you,</u> and all that the Lord Jesus did <u>for you</u> from the cross to the throne.

The revelation of the Word, or mystery of God, gave us a solid foundation upon which to establish our lives, Jesus Christ being the Rock and foundation that the church is built upon. We later learned that a correct and firm foundation (in Christ) can sustain and empower a believer to triumph over all the storms of life.

When the Spirit of God began to reveal in us this mystery of Christ, and all that He did for us at Calvary, it transformed our lives. It changed our way of believing. It changed our way of thinking. It changed our way of speaking. And, it changed our way of living.

So, get ready to be revolutionized, changed and transformed forever for the glory of God the father and His son, Jesus Christ.

Your Authors,
Richard Mallette, Dwayne Norman

1

THE POWER OF THE GOSPEL

As you begin to study along with us in this book, and that is what it is a study, you will soon discover what your redemption is all about. Much of what we are going to say will be foreign to many. But our request of you is that once you start, do not stop until you have completed this book. We will constantly review things we've previously said so that important principles will be grasped.

In Matthew 22:29, Jesus said, "Ye do always err, not knowing the scriptures, nor the power of God." So if we know the scriptures, we will be less apt to err. The Prophet Hosea said, "My people are destroyed for the lack of knowledge..."

So if it's the lack of knowledge that destroys the people of God, then the accumulation of God's Word (knowledge) will be the thing that will prevent destruction.

We will be setting before you in this book God's Word on redemption – and we will be carefully setting before you all the details involved in Jesus' labor on our behalf to bring about that redemption. Indeed it was labor, a labor of love. This book tells of the two most important men in all history, Adam and Jesus. These men are what we will term *representative men*. You will see clearly what this means in the pages ahead; you will understand it and grasp its significance. We will unfold for you what a substitute is, because that is what Jesus became. He became our substitute – his sacrifice was substitutionary. And because Jesus became our substitute, He was able to identify with us concerning every facet of our lives that needs redemption.

Our identification with Christ is only made possible because Jesus identified with us first. The Epistles of Paul speak about this ever so much, and in a clearly stated manner.

Our identification with Christ is what the Apostle Paul refers to as "the mystery of Christ". He explains in Ephesians, chapter 3, about the knowledge that the Lord gave him in "the mystery of Christ". He continues in verses 9-11, to explain what this mystery is about, and how we (the church) are to participate in it. It all starts with understanding the Gospel of the Lord Jesus Christ and who we are in Him.

Most of the true believers in Christ have never had a revelation of who they are in Christ, and consequently they have been held hostage to the devil, if he has not already destroyed them for the lack of knowledge. A lack of biblical knowledge has kept the Body of Christ in bondage for centuries.

In this book, we will give every effort to help you see who you are *in Christ and* what you have become *in Christ*. We will carefully speak about Jesus' crucifixion, death, burial, His new life, His conquest, His resurrection and His final place of glory— being seated next to the Father. We will endeavor to show you how all of us fit into each phase of Jesus' redemptive, substitutionary work of first identifying with us, and then our identification with Him. We will see why we call Jesus our *Substitutionary Sacrifice*.

When we understand all this, it will give us such a reality of who we are IN CHRIST, that we will no longer be dominated by our circumstances, sin and the lies of demonic suggestions. We will have the ability to rise, IN CHRIST, above all adverse circumstances and situations that may hinder that abundant life that Jesus came to give us.

So enter into the pages ahead with the idea that you *can* understand what is being written, and with this prayer, "Father, open up my spiritual eyes and let me see the revelation of your Word that you want me to have." You will rise up victorious and your life will change! Once you understand what is being said, you'll begin to live it.

Over the years, we have seen so many people close their spirits because they thought they had reached a point where they couldn't be taught anymore. Many pastors and teachers hear the same individuals make comments like, "oh, that was just a confirmation of everything I already know." And you know, when anyone has the attitude that they know it all, that person will probably not learn anything. Do you know someone like this?

As we began to mediate on this one subject, we realized that those certain individuals who are "Gospel-hardened," who have hardened their hearts and think they know everything, are the same ones who have not attained the level of spirituality they think they have. Their lives show a lack of spiritual depth.

They quote scripture without any understanding of what they've quoted. There is a lack of stability in their lives, and from day to day they are on a roller coaster ride, Today one of these individuals may be down in the gutter—"I don't think God loves me. I'm guilty: I feel condemned. I don't feel saved." The next day we see that same person, way up high, and we think, "What in the world happened to him overnight? Yesterday we were talking to him and he looked like he had lost his last friend. He told us he was guilty; he was condemned; he didn't know whether he was saved. And today he's going around preaching the Gospel, back up on a straight walk with the Lord. Then tomorrow, back down he goes." No stability, no evenness, no straight walk with the Lord. And we have to ask ourselves, "Why?"

We believe that we have to go further in the basics than we have ever been before. The Lord showed us that His people don't have a good understanding of their identification with Christ, and that when they get more established in this foundational teaching from God's Word they will quit experiencing a roller coaster walk. What it boils down to is, they never really understood the Gospel.

There is exciting good news for all of us in the gospel – but do we really understand what the gospel is all about? Maybe, but perhaps not.

Know Where You're Going

Now here's a little story that is not ours originally. We first heard it ten years ago. It's the story of an Arab father who carefully and diligently raised his son over a number of years. Finally this son arrived at an age where he came to his father and said, "Dad, I'm going to leave home. I'm going out on my own into the world."

And of course the father didn't get upset, because he had been training his son properly. He knew his son was well equipped to face the world out there; but he said, "I'm just going to give you some information, Son, as you depart from the household. And if you'll hear this and learn what I'm going to say, it will help you out."

He said, "Son, when you are away from home, out in the world, you will encounter different kinds of people. First of all, and listen very carefully —

3

there are those who don't know what they don't know. These people are stupid. Avoid them."

He continued, "Then there are those who don't know, and they know they don't know. These are asleep. Son, you ought to wake those people up. And then there are those who know, but they don't know that they know. They are asleep also, and you must wake them up."

Then he said, "There are those that know and are sure they know; these are the ones, Son, you should follow."

Now think about those words the father said to his son. Have you always wanted to follow people who were sure about themselves? Wouldn't you want to follow a Christian leader who says, "This is the way we are going. I'm following the dictates of Scripture." That's a wise leader.

When people first become Christians, most hold their pastors in high esteem, especially if they're leaders who seem to know where they're going, leaders who have an understanding of what the Scriptures command for their own lives. We were no different. We wanted to follow such men who had good knowledge of God's ways.

But over the years, we have come to the conclusion that the average Christian just does not know which way he is going. The average Christian has little idea what his life is all about. Those who know where they are going, if you look around in the body of Christ, do great exploits for the Lord. They seem to always be on top of things, winning souls for Christ, getting people delivered, and giving godly counsel to people. Their knowledge is not just purely intellectual, head knowledge, but rather a knowledge that is ever deepening. They have a bigger hope and capacity for faith than many other Christians. Where did these that know, and are sure that they know, get this assurance? From a disciplined, continuing study of God's Word, and applying it to their daily lives.

Do you want to be among those followers of Christ who know God's Word and are sure they know? If so, let us take you back to your future, because your future begins at the cross of the Lord Jesus Christ.

Word-of Faith People Are Not Ashamed of the Gospel

Let's look at Romans 1:13-17: "Now I would not have you ignorant, brethren, that oftentimes I purposed to come unto you, (but was let hitherto) that I might have some fruit among you also, even as among other Gentiles."

*I am debtor both to the Greeks, and to the Barbarians; both
to the wise, and to the unwise.
So, as much as in me is, I am ready to preach the gospel to
you that are at Rome also.
For I am not ashamed of the gospel of Christ: for it is the
power of God unto salvation to every one that believeth; to
the Jew first, and also to the Greek.
For therein is the righteousness of God revealed from faith
to faith: as it is written, The just shall live by faith.*

Focus on verse 16: "For I am not ashamed of the gospel of Christ…" (Listen carefully to what he says he is not ashamed of):

"…I am not ashamed of the gospel of Christ: for it is the power of God unto salvation to everyone that believeth; to the Jew first, and also to the Greek. For therein (in the gospel that is) is the righteousness of God revealed from faith to faith: as it is written, The just shall live by faith."

Now it totally baffles the mind how any pastor can get up in the pulpit and say, "Folks, I want you to know that I am not a word-of-faith man." This was said recently in a local church. The pastor said, "I want you to be sure you know that I am not a word-of-faith man."

So we have to ask ourselves, "Well, what is he? A word-of-unbelief man?" Now just let your mind reflect a little bit. What did he really say to his people? In other words, he really said, "I don't want to get hooked up with that 'faith' movement, so to speak. I'm not part of that. I'm not a word-of-faith man."

Do you know what it says in Romans 14:23? "…whatsoever is not of faith is sin." Also in Hebrews 11:6: "But without faith it is impossible to please him…" One theme runs through the entire New and Old Testaments, one thread that you cannot pull out of there. It is in everything, and that is the word **faith.** God says, "Without *faith* you cannot please me." The just shall live by faith. Faith is the trademark of every Christian, every believer in God. And when a man stands up and says, "I'm not a word-of-faith man." He is telling us how ignorant he is about the Word of God. He may be trying to not identify with a certain group, but man did not start faith, that was God's idea. Don't miss out on how God wants you to live!

We cannot please God without faith. The reason we say we are "Word-of-faith people is because our faith is in the Word of God; not in someone's organization. What else do we put our faith in? Naturally, we can put our faith in things other than the spiritual.

When you cross the Quinnipiac Bridge in New Haven, CT., your faith has to be in the engineer who put that thing up. You're not so sure you have that much faith in him, but you have enough to cross the bridge. We can have faith in natural things, but when we discuss faith in this context, we're referring to faith in God. When we're talking about faith in God, we're talking about faith in His Word. There is no other way to know God but through His Word. So my faith in Almighty God is through my belief in His Word.

The Gospel Is Power Unto Salvation

So what did Paul just tell us through these verses? Remember, all this is given by inspiration of the Holy Spirit. It isn't something we're making up. Paul said that within the Gospel is power. And that power can produce, he said, one very important thing—salvation. The Gospel is for everyone who believes, and it doesn't activate unless you believe. It's in there. The power is in there, but the power in the Gospel is for those who believe.

And when you believe the Gospel, the power of God has an energy. *Energia* is the Greek word. The Gospel has an energy that causes something to happen. When you say, "I believe it," you receive salvation. Your belief activates salvation for you.

The Gospel also reveals God's very own righteousness. We receive a revelation of God's righteousness through the Gospel. And all of this is made available to anyone who believes, anyone who has faith in what God has spoken through His Word. If you believe this, it will work for you.

The Gospel is a revelation of God's righteousness. It has to do with His just dealings with a fallen race of people. If God is going to deal with a fallen race of people, He is going to do it through His written word—it will be seen in the gospel. So it must all begin on Golgotha's Hill. If God is going to deal with fallen man's sin, it must begin at the cross of Calvary. No other place. Right there on Mount Calvary. So let us pursue the Gospel. Let us begin at the cross and look for the power God is speaking of in the Gospel.

If you get a hold of your identification with Jesus Christ like you grasp many other subjects in the Bible (but this one is even more important), your life will no longer be a roller coaster. If you can fully understand your identification through the substitutionary work of Jesus Christ, you will walk in victory. No matter what your circumstances, your mind and heart will be in line with God's Word, which says that when he triumphed, you were In Him, *so you triumphed with Him.*

Let's say this; you may think this is a teaching on evangelism. At this point, you may be saying, "You keep talking about the Gospel." Yes, that's where we're going back to, the Gospel. We've never learned about the Gospel. We don't know what is contained in the Gospel. We go out and preach to people but we don't preach the Gospel. We preach what we think is the Gospel.

Someone may say, "Well, I'm a little surprised. I don't agree with that." Well, you will, because when we show you what the Gospel is really all about, many are going to say, "Oh my goodness, we were missing it by a country mile!"

First Corinthians 1:17 says, "For Christ sent me not to baptize, but to preach the gospel: not with wisdom of words, lest the cross of Christ should be made of none effect." Now don't misunderstand what Paul is saying here. Let's not major in the minors.

That's the problem in the body of Christ today—too many major in the minors. For years theologians were arguing about the first chapter of the Book of Ephesians, regarding election and predestination, when Paul wasn't really even concerned about that. His concern was, "God, why have You showered us with all these blessings? Why have You given us all other things? I have searched myself; I have searched other human beings. We're not worth it. We're not worth a plug nickel (without Jesus' Blood). Why God?"

God answers, "Because I love you." And here are the other guys, many theologians, arguing about something that really is not that important compared to the grace of our Lord Jesus Christ. So let's not major in the minors.

Paul is not saying, "It's wrong to water baptize." Rather, Paul says the emphasis is on preaching the Gospel. This is where he puts the emphasis, on preaching the Gospel. Paul has done some baptizing. Look at 1 Corinthians 1:13-15, just so you won't misunderstand this:

> Is Christ divided? Was Paul crucified for you? Or were ye baptized in the name of Paul? I thank God that I baptized none of you, but Crispus and Gaius; lest any should say that I have baptized in my own name.

So Paul is not saying that it is wrong to baptize. He was baptized. That is not his point. He is not preaching about water baptism here but is telling us that when he preaches the Gospel, it's not under his own ability, not under his own mental prowess; nor through his rabbinical education. Rather, he says, it is as Peter taught, that the Holy Spirit came down from heaven upon him, and he spoke under the power and influence of the Holy Spirit-the Gospel of the Lord Jesus Christ.

It is the Gospel message itself that is empowered by the Holy Spirit, not what we think the Gospel is. You have to preach the Gospel message in order to have power in it. There are a lot of people preaching what they call the Gospel message. Then you look around and you say, "Well, where's the power? Nobody ever gets saved, healed or delivered." Just go into some of your denominational churches. They read the Gospel every week-at least what they think it is. They get up and give book reports out of *Reader's Digest,* and they can't understand why nobody comes to the altar, nobody ever gets saved. Well, they're not preaching the Gospel. The Holy Spirit has to be in this. And when He comes, He will convince the world of what? Sin, righteousness and judgment (John 16:8-11). But that won't happen until you preach the Gospel.

You see if you want people saved, you can't preach your opinions. You have to preach the Gospel.

When He came, Jesus spoke of the Holy Spirit saying, "He is going to show everything of Mine unto you (John 16:14)." How many can say they know everything about Jesus? The Holy Spirit has revealed it *all* to them? You know, we often think that we have to stop our learning when we get to a particular place. Many think Paul wrote it all. Why should we ask for any more revelation than what Paul received? Well, do you think everything Paul got was the total revelation of God? Just because Paul wrote it, are you going to say that all we need to learn is what Paul wrote? It will be wonderful if we learn what Paul wrote. We haven't even done that yet. But can't God open up more for us if we ask him?

We want you to know something-we should strive to go even beyond what Paul wrote. We're not suggesting that we write another chapter or book of the Bible. (That's all completed by the inspired writers.) But you know, we limit God. Why can't we get more revelation than Paul? Is there any reason why we can't? It is only our thinking that holds us back, because we think, "Well we can't possibly go on beyond the great Apostle Paul." Well, who said that?

Don't you think God says, "I want you to know everything about Me?" Why stop with just this? Why can't God take this and open more to you? I know that everything He knows and all His wisdom is not in this Book. You know that. This is only a portion, a small portion. God is unfathomable. Why can't each of us say, "God, I want everything I can get from You that is possible, Everything." Don't you want that, more and more from God each day? We don't want to stop at any particular place and think, that's it. We want to get all we can from God, and about God.

But you know what, if we would grasp what Paul wrote, we would have something. Those other disciples who stood beneath the cross of the Lord Jesus Christ had no idea of what Jesus was doing on that cross. Did you know that? They were looking right up at Jesus. They heard every word He said. They watched the blood drip from Him until He had no more blood in Him. They watched as He was being scourged, and they watched Him as He was being beaten. And all they thought was, "This poor friend is being beaten and crucified, and He's dying."

Paul came along and got all that they didn't get, through revelation knowledge. And he wrote it down for us because he said, "I want you to be victorious in your life. I want you to be walking in victory over satan all the time." And what he wrote, if we grasp it, can change all our lives.

And yet, we in the body of Christ say, "Well, we don't have to learn anything else. We have it all together. We're Spirit-filled. We speak in tongues. We've been washed in the blood. We come to church every week. We pay our tithes. What more do you want from us?" Can any Christian say that they are experiencing the full manifestation of who they are in Christ and don't need any more training or teaching? No. We all have a lot more growing and developing to do.

But you know something, if we all had a hold on our identification with Jesus and applied that in our lives we would experience much more of our redemption and freedom. If we just understood this one subject. We're going to share some things with you that will transform your lives forever! This is one area the devil fights with all his might. He'll try to make you sleepy. He doesn't want you to learn this. He'll try to keep blinders on you and stop up your ears.

A lot of the evangelical community talk against all of this and they don't have the faintest idea what identification with Christ is all about. One of the big problems they have, that the devil fed them a long, long time ago is, "Well you see, God is sovereign. You can't overrule God. You can't do anything on your own. God is sovereign. And any time sickness comes on you, it's because God is sovereign, and He gets glory out of that. He put it on you to teach you something."

You see, we agree that God is sovereign. But God is only sovereign in line with His Word. He is only sovereign as far as His Word tells us He's sovereign. That means He will never do anything contrary to His Word! In other words, there are times when God says, "It's your move. I'm sovereign, but it's your move." And if you don't make the right move, you could go to

Hell. Did you know that? If you don't make the right move according to God's Word, you could have sickness on your body all your life and die a premature death.

God simply says, "it's your move, I told you what it says in My Word, but you don't want to believe it. There is nothing I can do about your situation, because it is faith that pleases Me. Without faith you cannot please Me." So our faith has to be included in our identification with Jesus Christ.

But if we don't know what our identification with Jesus Christ is, what are we going to put our faith in? How can we have faith for something we don't even understand? Look at 1 Corinthians 1:18: "For the preaching of the cross is to them that perish foolishness; but unto us which are saved it is the power of God." What is required here is that you believe something. And when you believe, the energy that is in the Word of God goes into you. That power is there; it's just there. It's ready like the atom bomb. It's powerful; it's ready to do something for you. But if you don't believe it, it won't do a thing. And you'll just walk away and say, "That's foolishness." Much of what this book is about will be foolishness to many.

Spiritual things are not going to be determined through your head, through your intellect. They are determined through your spirit man. Spiritual things are discerned spiritually.

So you ask, "Well, what is this power of God you keep referring to?" The power of God, friends, is the preaching of the cross. Let that sink in because you will discover that these phrases are interchangeable; the preaching of the Gospel and the preaching of the cross are the same thing. That's where it is, at the cross of Calvary. The Gospel starts at the cross of Calvary.

Notice that the preaching of the Gospel, or we might say the Gospel itself, is the power of God. (See Romans 1:16-17.) The Gospel is the power of God. "For I am not ashamed of the gospel of Christ: for it is the power of God unto salvation…" Paul is talking about the preaching of the cross being the power of God.

Preach the Gospel/Preach the Cross-They Are the Same

When we preach the Gospel, could we then say we have to always include the cross of Calvary? Yes. So if we're going to preach a gospel message that does not include the cross, is there any power in it? "If you're going to preach a gospel that does not include the cross of Calvary, there is no power." That is why people don't get saved. We stop the power of God from flowing with what we think is the Gospel.

It is obvious that Paul understood the Gospel, and he knew that the preaching of the Gospel message had to include the cross of Calvary. He said, "I preach the Gospel. I'm not ashamed of it. I preach the cross." He said there is power in both. He put them together. "Oh, we know about the cross. Why do you have to teach us about the cross again?" Because you didn't get it the first time. We didn't get it the first time. We haven't thoroughly understood it yet. We're working on it. We're meditating on it. We're beginning to grasp it.

Well, let's add a category number five that the Arab father could have said to his son. He could have said this: "There are people who think they know, but they do not know that they don't know. These have to be awakened to the things they don't know. Son, go out and wake these people up." In essence, that's what God said to us. "Wake them up. Show them what the cross is all about." Teach them the true gospel.

What Paul is talking about is our identification with Christ. The cross is the place where our identification took place. Not totally, but some of it took place at the cross. But to most Christians "identification" is a mystery. You say to people, "Have you studied yet on identification with Christ?" They'll say, "What do you mean by that?" This is the most important thing you can learn early in your Christian walk.

In fact, it is also obvious that Paul knew what his purpose was while he was here on this earth. The Lord probably gave Paul some advice when He sent him into the world just like the Arab father gave to his son. He might have said to Paul, "There are people out there who think they are here to get a degree. Others say they are here to get married. Someone else may say, "Well, I'm here to get ahead in life."

Paul said, "I understand totally why I'm here. To preach the Gospel."

You may be thinking as you are reading, "Well, I don't know if that's my purpose in life." Oh yes, that is your purpose in life. Paul knew his purpose, and you must know your purpose. God didn't exclude any one of us. He said, "You're here: to preach the Gospel." God sent us into the world to preach the Gospel. He sent you into the world to preach the Gospel. In fact, He gave us what we call "The Great Commission." He said, "…Go ye into all the world, and preach the gospel to every creature," (Mark 16:15). That's our command! Yes, we all have many natural responsibilities to fulfill everyday, but in the midst of them we should look for every opportunity to preach the Gospel, heal the sick, cast out demons and set the captives free! (Mathew 10:7,8)

There are those who know but don't do anything about it. They know about the Great Commission, but they don't go out and preach it. Our number-one priority while on earth is to preach the Gospel. It is absolutely wonderful that we pray and praise the Lord. But have you noticed that neither of these wonderful things is listed in the Great Commission?

God didn't say go into all the world and sing Godly songs. That's a wonderful thing to do. He didn't say (in the Great Commission) go into all the world and praise Me every day. That's wonderful to do, and we should praise God everyday. He didn't say go into all the world and fellowship with other Christians every day, did He? Even though we should have continual fellowship with the saints. He said, "… Go ye into all the world, and preach the gospel…" That's our number-one priority and command, and who is doing it? Not many. "Doesn't He want me to praise Him anymore?" Yes, keep praising Him, but go and preach the Gospel. "Doesn't He want me to fellowship with my brothers and sisters?" Yes, keep doing it; it's wonderful. But go and preach the Gospel because therein is the power of God.

"Well, I thought this book was going to be on my identification. Sounds to me like you're writing an evangelistic book." No, we're going to look at our identification with the Lord Jesus Christ; but our main goal is to preach the Gospel. And along with that priority, we are told to make disciples out of those who become Christians so they can go out and display the power of the Gospel also. God wants His people to be fully conformed to the image of Christ (Romans 8:29), to be on fire for Him, then to go out and set everyone else on fire (Mathew 28:18-20)!! But can we go out and preach the Gospel if we don't understand what the Gospel is? How can we? Can a man say, "I'm going to be a doctor without any training in the medical field". He can't do it. Well, it's no different here. We must first understand what the gospel is all about.

Many of us who say we have been preaching the Gospel have not. You see, in some churches they say, "Oh yes, we preach the Gospel." But just listen to what's being said. They're teaching psychology, human ideologies, humanism and opinions. But where is the Gospel? If you are preaching things that are contrary to what God did for us in Christ at Calvary then you are not preaching the Gospel!

Go into a lot of churches on Sunday and listen to what is being proclaimed. You won't hear the Gospel preached. You see, we said that the Gospel has power. But just look in those churches. They are preaching a powerless Gospel, because it's not the gospel at all.

Do you want to learn something about the Gospel? Study the Book of Acts. That's the demonstration of the Gospel. It is a book of power. Why?

Because it *is the* Gospel. Everywhere those disciples of Jesus went there was power, miracles, signs and wonders. Why aren't we seeing them today? Because too often we are not preaching the Gospel. Didn't Paul say the power of God was in the Gospel? Well, if that's the truth, and we happen to believe it is, then why are we not seeing signs, wonders and miracles like we see in the Book of Acts? "But we are preaching the Gospel!" you may say. No, we can't be. God said the power is in the Gospel. *If we're preaching the Gospel, where is the power?*

In the chapters ahead, we are going to look at Calvary's cross. That's where we need to start again. We're going to tell you what went on at that cross. You see the power unto salvation is in the cross, as Paul said, the preaching of the cross.

Do you know what the word "salvation" is in the Greek? *Soteria*, or if you prefer, *sozo*, meaning "deliverance, preservation, rescue, prosperity, healing and general well-being." Somebody may say, "Well, I thought salvation was eternal life." That's part of it but not all of it. We'll see this later on.

"So what are you saying?" Well, we're saying simply this: the Gospel is the power of God unto life eternal, preservation, deliverance, prosperity, health and victory over satan every day of your life. But how many of us have those things? How many of us walk in divine health? How many of us have victory over satan every day of our lives? How many of us constantly feel like we're delivered? Not that many.

We also saw that the preaching of the cross is the power of God. We've said this over and over. And the preaching of the Gospel must always contain the preaching of the cross of Jesus Christ. You cannot preach the Gospel without preaching the cross. If you preach the cross, you are preaching the Gospel. If you're preaching the Gospel, you have to preach the cross. No matter what subject you are preaching on from the Bible it should always be in line with the death and resurrection of the Lord Jesus.

The Holy Spirit Brings Understanding and the Rhema of the Word

The Word of God is not complex. Many individuals say, "Oh, the Word of God is so difficult for me to understand. I just can't get it, no matter how much I try. I don't understand it." It is because you haven't made up your mind that it's not complex. God says the Kingdom is made of little children. Do you think He's going to write a Gospel for little children that they cannot understand?

The reason you think its complex is because you've made up your mind to think it is. "I don't understand it." You don't want to understand it. And when we begin to teach it, you say, "Oh it's too complicated for me. I'll never follow this; Ill never get it." Yes, you will. Make up your mind. Say, "I will get it." Don't keep saying, "I don't get it. I can't get it. I'm confused." We hear this all the time. What are you confused about? You're confused because you keep saying you're confused. You're going to get what you say. You're snared by the words of your mouth.

Before beginning any study, a person should say to the Holy Spirit, "I am not a confused person because the Word of God says that confusion is of the devil. I'm not of the devil; I'm of the living God." That settles it right there, doesn't it? The devil has no way to bring confusion to you when you say, "Greater is He that is in me than he that is in the world. Devil, you can try to confuse me but you can't. I'm of God. I'm made of the substance of God. I've been made with the incorruptible seed of God. God's very image and likeness is in me. The very seed of life, the incorruptible, ever-living seed of the Word of God has generated me. I'm of God, and I don't get confused."

"Well you don't understand. You're just very fortunate that you never get confused." No, no, there was a time when we were all confused—before we met Christ. Each of us used to walk around thinking, "Boy, I'm confused." That was life before Christ. We were *all* confused. We didn't know where we were going, but we were going there fast. We were on our way to Hell just as fast as we could go and didn't even know it.

You don't have to be confused. You don't have to think the Word of God is complex. It is not. The Holy Spirit wrote it for you to understand, and He's saying, "I'll open it up to you. I'll help you understand it, if you want to understand it."

In 1 Corinthians 1:23, Paul says, "But we preach Christ crucified…" Now we said you can't preach the Gospel without preaching the cross. So Paul again is emphasizing: "But we preach Christ crucified…" Now he's getting even more detailed about it.

First he says, "I preach the cross." With that, you get a certain word picture in your mind. But now he says, " I preach Jesus Christ crucified." That gives you a better picture, doesn't it? All of a sudden you zero in a little bit more. "Oh, do I have to think about Jesus being crucified in order to preach the Gospel? To preach the cross? Yes, that's important.

Now look at 1 Corinthians 2:2: "For I determined not to know any thing among you, save Jesus Christ, and him crucified." How important do you think that was to Paul? He said, "… I determined for me not to know *anything* among you, except Jesus Christ, and him crucified." That was his obsession. Why? Is it important for me to know Jesus Christ and Him crucified? Yes. This is the crux of the Gospel. This is the foundation of Christianity! Calvary was the focal point of history. Everything in the Old Testament pointed to Calvary. Everything in the New Testament points back to Calvary. That's why the Gospel has the power of God. "I don't want to know anything, but Jesus Christ, and Him crucified." Sounds like Paul knows something important. Shouldn't we find out what he determined to know?

Let's go to 1 Corinthians 15:1: "Moreover, brethren, I declare unto you the gospel…" Well, here goes Paul again. Seems like that's all he wants to talk about, the Gospel. He says, "Moreover, brethren, I declare unto you the gospel which I preached unto you, which also ye have received, and wherein ye stand…" Do you wonder what he meant by that? He says, "… I declare unto you the gospel which I preached unto you…" He must be referring to 1 Corinthians, chapters 1 and 2, where he was speaking about Jesus being crucified at the cross.

Now look at chapter 15, verse 3: "For I delivered unto you first of all…" Oh, you mean there's nothing that comes *before* this? We guess not. He says, "For I delivered unto you *first* of all that which I also received, how that Christ died for our sins according to the scriptures." We just can't get away from this, can we? Paul is preaching the Gospel. He is preaching the cross; he is preaching Jesus Christ crucified. And over here he's talking about Jesus dying. And in verse 4, "…and that he was buried and that he rose again the third day according to the scriptures."

Well, we can't get away from it. The Scriptures are replete with it. Paul can't get away from it. How are we going to get away from it? And he said, "First of all I do this." This must be very important. Isn't this amazing? That's why Paul says, "First of all, I'm going to teach you about Jesus Christ's death, burial and resurrection." How important is it? It must be very important.

Everywhere we have looked so far, Paul has said, "I'm going to preach the Gospel. I'm going to preach the cross. I'm gong to preach Jesus Christ crucified. I'm going to preach Jesus Christ dying." Let's really drive this point home. We're deliberately doing this. He preached the Gospel. And it included the death, burial and resurrection of Jesus Christ. If this is what should be preached, shouldn't we be able to find some examples of this in the Book of Acts? Sure we should! This Book is the beginning of the early church under the leadership of the Holy Spirit.

The death, burial and resurrection of our Lord Jesus Christ mean so little to most Christians. They have such a small understanding of its total significance. All that a lost person needs to believe are simply the facts that Jesus died, shed His Blood and arose from the dead to become a Christian. But, as a Christian, we need to have a greater understanding of the significance of those facts to grow spiritually.

It's so important that we understand how we're identified with the Lord Jesus Christ! Do you believe that Jesus died, was buried and was resurrected? "Yes." You'll say. Why was He? Why did He have to be crucified? Why did He have to die? Why was He buried? Why was He given new life? Why was He resurrected? Can you answer that? Let's think about it. How many Christians really could answer that? Probably even many pastors, once a year on Easter Sunday, go back through and refresh their memories before they teach it. Why isn't it so fresh in our minds that it's rolling off our tongues every time somebody asks us about it? It's that important, isn't it?

> Acts 2:22-24 states:
> *Ye men of Israel, hear these words; Jesus of Nazareth, a man approved of God among you by miracles and wonders and signs, which God did by him in the midst of you, as ye yourselves also know:*
> *Him being delivered by the determinate counsel and foreknowledge of God, ye have taken, and by wicked hands have crucified and slain:*
> *Whom God hath raised up, having loosed the pains of death...*

Let us ask you something. When you're in death, is there any pain? So why would He have to be loosed from the pains of death? This is part of the Gospel. What are we talking about here? That He had to be loosed from the pains of death. Is there pain in death, physical pain? Don't people say, "R.I.P., rest in peace. They're dead." Isn't it true that once you die, there is no more pain? Well what could he mean by this? He was loosed from the pains of death. Could that be something other than a physical death?

Ah ha! Little bells go off. Then if He's being released from something other that physical death and there is pain to that other something, what does this mean? If we're going to unite ourselves and identify ourselves totally with the substitutionary work of Jesus, we had better find out. Are there some pains in certain kinds of death from which we need to be released also?

Someone may be thinking, "Well, I wonder what that's about." In these chapters, you're going to find that you have an identification with Jesus, and as we said in the beginning, the identification is a complete union. You cannot have identification with Jesus unless it's a complete identification. There is no partial identification. Everything that Jesus went through, He went through so you could identify with it. Or let's say it this way—so that He could identify with you.

He became sin that you might become the righteousness of God in Christ Jesus. Are you understanding that? He was made to be sickness that you might be able to have health. This is part of our identification. He was buried: so were we buried. He was raised again: so were we raised again. Ephesians 2 tells us that we're seated, not "going" to be seated, but we *are* seated in heavenly places in Christ Jesus.

If you believe you can be identified with that, and once you are identified with that, you don't have to walk around thinking, "I'm just a little old worm." Someone might ask, "You dare to say you're seated in heavenly places with Christ Jesus?" Yes. "Why?" It is not something you did; it's something He did. The Word says so.

If He became sickness for you so that you could have health, then why, if He was your substitute, do you continue to walk around sick? Doesn't a substitute take another person's place? If He took your place, then why do you still have it? Because you haven't identified with Him. You don't fully understand the Gospel. You haven't understood the cross. We all need to go back to the cross and start all over again. So let's do that in the chapters ahead.

2

THE GOSPEL OF CALVARY'S CROSS

Some rudimentary things are basic to an understanding of the Gospel. In this chapter, we will cover truths that will liberate your thinking. You will see once again how, for too long, many have been majoring in the minors rather than in the majors of the Bible, and that's why so many struggle in many areas of their lives We believe if we get a hold of this, grasp it, meditate on it, act upon it and keep on rehearsing it, we will understand, as never before, what the Gospel message is all about.

In Romans 1:16, Paul is speaking to the Church of Rome and he says, "For I am not ashamed of the gospel of Christ…" Notice right up front that he calls it the Gospel of Christ. He says, "For I am not ashamed of the gospel of Christ: for it is the power of God unto salvation to every one that believeth; to the Jew first, and also the Greek."

We want to tell you that to remain focused takes discipline. We want to stir up your thinking. What you're going to be thinking about is going to change the direction of your life. Those who shun the truth often find themselves in the counseling room wondering why their marriage is not going right, why they can't get healed, why they can't pay off their debts. This teaching is important, especially to those who constantly need counseling.

So Paul, once again, says, "For I am not ashamed of the gospel of Christ: for it is the power of God…" Notice *the Gospel of Christ is the power of God.*

"For I am not ashamed of the gospel of Christ: for it is the power of God unto salvation to everyone that believeth: to the Jew first and also to the Greek. For therein is the righteousness of God revealed..." Where? In the Gospel of Christ. "...For therein is the righteousness of God revealed from faith to faith: as it is written, the just shall live by faith."

If there is one thing that we drove home in the first chapter, it was this very thought: the Gospel of the Lord Jesus Christ, or the preaching of the Gospel, must include the cross. The cross and the Gospel are synonymous and go together. When we talk about preaching the cross of the Lord Jesus Christ as Paul was commanded, we're talking about what took place in the death, burial and resurrection of our Lord Jesus Christ. This is all synonymous. The power of God, the Gospel, the cross, and Christ-all go together in one plot. You cannot separate any of it. So when you say, "I am preaching the Gospel," you are preaching what took place on Calvary's cross in Jesus Christ. This is very important.

Defining the Gospel

Yet friend, if you were to ask many Christians what the Gospel is or what is the Gospel all about, they probably would not know for sure. Some might say, "Is it the new birth?" Indeed, most of us think that the Gospel is only about the new birth or going to Heaven. Well that's part of it, and a very important part. It is a piece that goes into the puzzle that you can't do without, because the new birth gives you the eternal life that's spoken about, that is, life in the presence of God. The new birth gives you the righteousness of God, which we have spoken about, but that's not all. The Gospel is much, much more than being born again.

Let's say for example that you get saved at 15 years old, and you live to be 80 years old. Friends, there's 65 years in between the time you get saved to the time you go home to be with the Lord. Now listen, the *Amplified Bible* says that the preaching of the cross is the manifestation of the power of God. Do you want the power of God in your life? Or do you want to spend 65 years in what we would call a powerless life? You could get saved at 15, but if you really don't understand the Gospel you may never make it to 80. How would you like to have a powerless church for 65 years? How would you like to have a powerless family for 65 years? How would you like to be powerless on the job for 20 or 30 years or even 65 years?

If you want power in your life, in your church, in your family and in your job, then find out about the Gospel's power. There is power in the Gospel. Paul said, "I am not ashamed of the gospel of Christ: for it is the power of God unto salvation to everyone that believeth…: To all who believe. That doesn't leave anyone out. *If you believe, there can be power for you.* Well, you can't believe something until you know about it. Isn't that right? So we're going to teach you about that power. We're going to teach you about what's inherent. The Gospel, friends, is potent: it's powerful: it's energized with something that God put in it. That's why Paul said, "I am not ashamed of the Gospel." He's saying, "There's great power in the Gospel." He knew about the power. He knew what he was talking about. He knew what it did for His life.

Being a Doer of the Word

Of course faith comes by hearing the Word, but faith is also released by acting on God's Word. Therefore, understanding is essential to obeying and doing the Word. Your existence, if you don't understand the Gospel, is a powerless existence.

Just think of your life right now. Do you think you are operating in the power of God the way He wants you to operate? Do you think God just wants you to preach every week and not see lives changed? Do you think God wants you to live this kind of life day in and day out without power? Of course not!

God wants you to be powerful. He says there is one way that you can be powerful and that is to learn about the Gospel. There is a power to usward who believe (Ephesians 1:19), and the Gospel of our Lord Jesus Christ is the power of God. We have not studied that. So the church is powerless for the most part. We need to preach the cross. We need to preach Christ. We need to preach the Gospel. When we preach the genuine, true Gospel of Jesus Christ, we are preaching power. When you get a hold of it, you're going to have an understanding of that power. The Bible tells us that.

Some people think the Gospel message is foolish: they don't know what took place at the cross. And as we said in the previous chapter, some of those disciples stood right beneath the cross, kneeling, looking at the Lord Jesus Christ hanging there and they did not see a thing except the man Jesus hanging on the cross with blood dripping off His body. If that's not true then why didn't some of those disciples at the cross talk in more detail about what went on there? They didn't know. They didn't understand it. All they saw was a man who they loved, hanging on a cross. It took the Apostle Paul many years to get a direct revelation from Jesus about what took place on the cross (Galatians 1:11,12).

Even the apostle Peter said this about Paul's writings, "…some things are hard to be understood,…" II Peter 3:15,16 (paraphrased by writer).

So it's not going to be effortless, but that doesn't mean you have to check out and say, "Well I won't be able to learn this because it's going to take a lot of effort." Well, it's going to take some effort, but we're going to make it easy for you. We've done a lot of the homework. We're going to present it to you, and all you need to do is check it out in the Bible, read it, meditate on it, and act upon the knowledge you receive; and your life will stop being powerless. You will not only experience more of God's power, but also a greater depth of His love for you! Because Calvary was the greatest demonstration of God's Love that mankind will ever experience!!

The Power Delivers

You can have electric power. You can have atomic power. But they do not even compare—they don't even begin to compare to the power of God that's in the Gospel. Electric power can't give you salvation. Atomic power can't bring you into righteousness, nor deliver you. But the power of God, which is the Gospel, can give you your righteousness and bring you into a place of salvation. The power of God can do that. Not atomic power. It doesn't matter how powerful it is. It can't give you your salvation, your deliverance. It can't give you riches and wisdom and victory over the devil. But the Gospel can. Atomic power can't seat you in heavenly places and cause you to reign and rule with Christ, but the power of the Gospel can do that.

That's why we don't have to be ashamed of the Gospel. Some people think it's foolishness. Do you? We're not ashamed of the Gospel, because it is the power of God unto salvation. Paul had a hold of something, didn't he? If we preach about the cross, if we preach Christ and Him crucified, we don't have to sweat; we don't have to exaggerate. We don't have to work something up. Why? Power is inherent in the Gospel. All we do is preach it and the power goes out. We don't have to do anything. We don't have to get into hype. We don't make the Gospel powerful by how we act in the flesh. It's already powerful! Paul said it: "I am not ashamed of the gospel because it is the power of God unto salvation." Let's look again at some of the power inherent in the Gospel.

Preach the Gospel/Preach Christ – Then Watch the Power!

Acts 8:5 says, "Then Philip went down to the city of Samaria, and preached Christ unto them." Isn't that statement amazing? He's been commanded to go out and preach *the Gospel* to every creature, yet he goes out and preaches *Christ* to them. Well, could we then say that preaching Christ is synonymous with preaching the Gospel? Of course we can. So Philip understood it. He went down to Samaria and preached Christ unto them. Preaching Christ means preaching the Gospel. We know this now.

Look at verse 6: "And the people with one accord gave heed…" We wish we could say that about the Church of Jesus Christ of the 21th century. The Church of Jesus Christ today does not, for the most part, take heed to what's being taught. Most of the time there is diverging thought going through the crowd when the Word is being taught. Some people believe the Word and some people don't.

But in verse 6, they said in one accord, "We believe it." And in fact, one of the words that's being used here, *prosecho*, means "to hold in mind" Don't let it leave your mind; continuously be applying what you're hearing. That's what the word "heed" means. They took heed unto those things which Philip spake, hearing and seeing the miracles, which he did. What did he preach unto them? **Christ.** What did he preach unto them? **The Gospel.** What did he preach unto them? **The Cross.** And look what happened. These people were paying attention. They were taking heed, and they believed what Philip said.

The Results of Preaching Christ and His Cross

Now look what happened in verses 7 and 8, the results that followed the preaching of Christ:

For unclean spirits, crying with loud voice, came out of many
that were possessed with them: and many taken with palsies
and that were lame, were healed.
And there was great joy in that city.

Phillip preached Christ. He preached the Gospel. He preached the Cross. We cannot deny the power that came out of the Gospel he preached. If we deny it, we're fools. There were miracles. Unclean spirits were kicked out. Those with palsies and the lame were healed. And great joy came to that city. Why? Because he preached Christ.

A person may go around today saying, "I'm preaching the Gospel." Well, why aren't these things happening? Perhaps he is really not preaching the Gospel. Maybe he *thinks* he's preaching the Gospel. Our Bibles say that God will follow the preaching of the Gospel, the Word of God, with signs and wonders (Mark 16:17,18). Well, why aren't we seeing that in the body of Christ? Why aren't we seeing that when we go out to the world? Either God's Word is accurately true or it isn't. He said, "I will give you signs and wonders following the preaching of the Gospel." Well, why isn't it happening? Who wants to answer that question?

Why isn't the power going out? Why isn't something happening? Why aren't there miracles and signs with lame people walking and blind eyes opening everywhere we preach the Gospel? Why isn't it happening very much? It happened in the Book of Acts, didn't it?

Friends, Philip preached Christ. That means he preached about the death, burial and resurrection of the Lord Jesus Christ. "Well I preach that, "someone will say. Well, something must be missing, because Philip preached Christ and all kinds of things happened-and there was great joy in that city.

The Missing Ingredient

What is lacking today? What is wrong? We're asking you as Christians. You say you preach the Gospel, but are you having these signs and wonders? Is there inherent power in what you're saying so much so that demons are leaving people, and lame people are getting healed with great joy in our cities? The answer is, it's not happening, is it? Then maybe Christ is not being preached. You're preaching something that somebody told you was the Gospel, but you're not preaching Christ. You're not preaching the cross. God is no respecter of persons, and He said, "I will follow with signs and wonders the preaching of the cross, the preaching of the Word, the preaching of the Gospel." Did He not say that? Then what is wrong? A lot of us are very conscience of what we eat. We go into restaurants and we're so careful. "We've got to eat this; this is good for us. And we'd better eat chick peas and this lettuce and this okra and this and that." We are very picky about what we put into our bodies.

But in the Church of Jesus Christ, we just pick up on any old thing, stuff it into our mouths, and think we get the Gospel. We think we are being fed spiritual food. If the body of Christ would become as conscious about their spiritual diet as they are about their physical, they would be dynamite today. We're not.

Did you know in God's Word there is food for babies? It says it in 1 Peter 2:2, "As newborn babes, desire the sincere milk of the word..." But you see, God doesn't stop there. He knows that when you're a baby you can't eat solid meat because you'll choke on it. So He says, "Eat baby food when you're a baby in Christ." But He also says, in Hebrews 5:14, that as you begin to grow "...strong meat belongeth to them that are of full age, even those who by reason of use have their senses exercised to discern both good and evil."

Yet, many in the body of Christ have no discernment whatsoever. They pick up anything. "Oh, that looks good. Let' read that." They're in the book-store spending $20 or $30, and they don't even know what they have picked up. In every bookstore they visit they have to get books. But they don't care what they pick. "Oh, this looks good. That's a nice-looking cover. Let's buy that one."

But when you go to a restaurant to eat that food for your physical bodies, you're so careful. "Oh, that upset me the last time I ate that. I won't eat that this time." But do you ever say that in the spiritual realm? "Man, I ate of that and it turned my spirit upside down. I better not read that kind of stuff anymore."

When are we going to wake up and begin to discern good from evil? When is each of us going to wake up in the body of Christ and say, "Wait a minute. I need to get a real good diet of God's food. I need to grow up strong and healthy spiritually." When are we going to do that in the body? We are so careless. And the body of Christ keeps walking around with pain, suffering, bills mounting higher and higher. Yet, we're so careless when it comes to spiritual things.

Someone will say, "Oh, but I thought that the Gospel was for those who were not saved." Well, that's true in part. But let's go over to 1 Corinthians 15. Let us show you something here. It says a whole lot to us.

In 1 Corinthians 15:1-6a, we read: "Moreover, brethren..." Whom is he talking to? The church. "Moreover, brethren, I declare unto you the..." The what? Oh, we just can't seem to get away from that word can we?

> ...I declare unto you the **gospel** which I preached unto you, which also ye
> have received, and wherein ye stand; By which also ye are saved, if ye

keep in memory what I preached unto you, unless ye have believed in vain.
For I delivered unto you first of all that which I also received, how that
Christ died for our sins according to the scripture; and that he was buried,
and that he rose again the third day according to the scriptures:
And that he was seen of Cephas, then of the twelve: After that, he was
seen of about five hundred brethren at once;...

Notice what he says: "I got saved by the Gospel that was preached." He was saying to these people, "You got saved because I preached the Gospel to you." Then he talks about keeping it in memory. What did he preach to them? The Gospel. He said, "By that Gospel you got saved: What else did he say? He said, "You got saved because you received it. You stand in it." He said in verse 2, "By which also ye are saved if you keep in memory what I preached unto you unless ye have believed in vain."

Now he tells you what he preached. He preached Christ-the death, burial and resurrection of Jesus. Then he goes on to talk about keeping something in memory. If you never go beyond the salvation message of the cross, then your memory would be limited only to salvation. If you don't go beyond this, your memory will only bring back that concerning salvation. That's good; that's wonderful. But salvation or being born-again is only part of the Gospel.

There is More—Much More!

Yes, you are saved, but there is more you need to know about the Gospel. And it is at this point every time in the teaching of this that somebody says, "Look, I know this is important, but it seems to me you're driving at something I'm not going to understand." Now if you're thinking that, the devil has already worked on your mind. There is nothing in this Gospel that you cannot understand. We want you to get that straight. If the devil or your head or your flesh is saying, "I'll never understand this. It's too difficult for me. I know you're driving at something that's going to be very, very difficult for me, then either you're awfully used to hype and exaggeration and everything to do with the flesh, or you've just never trained yourself to listen.

This material is not difficult. As the chapters go by, we're going to spell it out for you so clearly that even children will understand it, because the Gospel is made for children. You will learn how to have a life of power. Don't you want that?

This teaching is for those who want to grow. Do you want to grow? Do you want to grow out of your bondages? Do you want to grow out of your financial woes? Do you want to grow out of your lack of victory? Do you want to grow up into Christ in all things? Then you have to study Christ, the power of God.

Just watching miracles won't cause you to grow up spiritually, will it? Does watching people go out under the power of God (and we believe in that) cause you to grow spiritually? No. Does it teach you how to have God's power working in your life? No. Does it help you pay your bills? No. Does it get you healed? No. Does it improve your marriage relationship? No. But the Gospel will, if you understand what the Gospel is all about. It is more far-reaching than you ever imagined.

Laying the Proper Foundation is Important

In 1 Corinthians 3:10-11, we read: "According to the grace of God which is given unto me, as a wise master builder, I have laid the foundation, and another buildeth thereon. But let every man take..." What? There's that word again, *prosecho*. What does that mean? "To be continuously making application of what you hear." Take heed Christian believer.

"...But let *every man*...(that means you)"...*take heed* how he buildeth thereupon.

"For other foundation can no man lay than that is laid, which is Jesus Christ...:

Well, we just can't get away from Jesus either, can we? Talking about the Gospel means we're talking about Jesus. When we talk about the cross, we're talking about Jesus. We can't get away from Jesus Christ. We can't get away from the Gospel. We can't get away from the cross.

Your foundation, friends, is Jesus Christ. There's no other foundation. The Scripture says that "other foundation can no man lay." So if you think you're going to lay a different kind of foundation, you're deceived. You are grossly mistaken.

In the natural we all agree that we have to put in a foundation in order to assure a structure's stability and endurance. But when it comes to spiritual issues, it's too much work or we just don't care. Just look around and see the spiritual structures we've all tried to build without the proper foundation. Look, there's one that's down. There's one that's leaning and about to fall. There's one that's bruised. There's another—oh, it's crushed. Haven't you noticed that many of Christianity's spiritual buildings are not all standing? Why? No foundation. Or a foundation other than Jesus Christ.

The Gospel's foundation is the cross—the death, burial and resurrection of Jesus Christ. We have the Holy Spirit who will lead us into all truth, including our foundational truths. Do you think you're a wise master builder? Do you realize how important a spiritual foundation is to your Christian walk? Let's say you're going to church regularly. You're a good, steady tither. You witness, you study, you pray and you're always in the Word of God. Yet, you are not seeing the victory that you would like, the victory that Jesus provided for you. What you need to do is study the death, burial and resurrection of Jesus Christ.

"Oh, but that's going to take a lot of work." But does anything worthwhile come cheap? Do you get anything at all worthwhile for nothing? No. "I thought if I needed healing I would just get some good healing tapes. Doesn't it say that faith cometh by hearing the Word of God?" Yes. And it is very important to listen to healing tapes. But how many times have we listened to healing tapes and read all the healing books we could get our hands on, and yet we still didn't get healed? We have probably all asked the same question: "Where did I go wrong?"

Well, we found out where all of us went wrong. We have spent too much time on things that were not wrong to study, but we failed to build a solid foundation and give our attention to the major issues. We argue too much. How do we baptize? In the name of the Father, Son and the Holy Ghost or in Jesus' only? We're busy arguing if tongues is for today or not, or whether miracles ended in the year 70 AD. We're talking about minors when we should be studying the death, burial and resurrection of our Lord Jesus Christ. That's major! Those other issues are important, but they're not the foundation of Christianity.

In other words, if our foundation has been properly laid, we can listen to those tapes, meditate on them and erect spiritual buildings on a solid foundation. And the Scripture says, "For other foundation can no man lay than that is laid, which is Jesus Christ." And when the building goes up on a firm foundation there will be lasting victory.

Understanding Your Source

Healing, deliverance, victory over sin, prosperity are all merely by products of Calvary. Let's repeat that. Healing, deliverance, victory over sin and satan, prosperity are merely by-products of Calvary. These are some of the wonderful benefits of the death, burial, and resurrection of Jesus Christ. We've been spending all our time studying the by-products and the benefits of Calvary and not the *source of the benefits*. That's where we're making our mistake. And without understanding the source of the by-products, we will always have a hard time receiving and maintaining the benefits.

We're not saying tapes on healing are bad for you to listen to. Studying all those benefits and by-products of Calvary are very good. We do a lot of teaching on them. But if you put all your time into studying the by-products and little or no time studying the source, then you'll always struggle. You cannot get the by-products of Calvary without going through Calvary itself. You have to study Calvary.

If you think we're mistaken, then just think for a moment about all the Christians who have told you that they've been through "Life-changing" seminars, read all the healing books on the shelves, heard all the tapes on prosperity and healing and deliverance and yet, you see that their lives are unstable. They are not well, and financially, they are in a mess. Why? They've been putting all their energy into <u>studying the by-products without taking time to go to Calvary itself.</u>

Christians are not alone when it comes to the study of by-products. You have all seen the ads on television where motivational speakers teach you how to have a fulfilled life. But what's missing from what these speakers are saying and offering is that they don't go through Calvary.

Anytime you hear of a get-rich-quick scheme, that's all it is, a scheme. We don't care if they put the name Christian on it. There's no such thing in God's Word as getting rich quick. Don't fall for that scheme where someone says, "I can make you wealthy almost overnight. Just buy this product. Give me $3,000 and I guarantee you're on your way to riches." These people know just whom to appeal to. The people who get sucked into that are greedy. God's Word says, "Work, and Apply My principles. You are not going to get rich quick." You'd better start thinking about your motives. God is not going to bless anything done in greed.

You Can't Bypass Calvary

Furthermore, if you don't go through Calvary, you're not going to get it. If you think you can separate Jesus Christ from your finances, you will see sorrow. Some Christians, who were sucked into programs by other Christians, have felt the sorrow of their investment already. Their garages, their basements and their cellars are filled with products, they've never sold. You can't bypass Calvary.

Jesus Christ is the One who said, "I have come that you might have life and have it more abundantly." You can't have the abundant life without the One who came to give it. You can't separate yourself and say, "I'm going to have an abundant life, but I don't want to go through Calvary." It won't work. It may work for a period of time, but it won't work for long. He's also the same One who says, "I have come with a purpose. I have been manifested that I might destroy the works of satan." (I John 3:8)

If you want an abundant life, you have to get the works of satan out of your life. You have to go through Jesus. He says, "I give you the abundant life, but I'm also the One who has a purpose in coming to destroy the works of the devil." You see how the two work together? He came with a purpose, to destroy the works of satan: sickness, disease, eternal death and poverty. When those things have been taken out of the way, your life becomes abundant, full, complete in Christ. It becomes easier to fulfill God's purposes for your life. Your life was given to you to serve God, His plans and purposes. To make disciples of all the nations. And He knows you must have power to accomplish His will.

The Gospel is good news. The good news is that Jesus removed the curse so the blessing of Abraham might come upon all who believe. But you can't believe something you don't know. We must see those by-products through the eyes of Calvary, and when we do, our struggles will be over. We'll enter into God's rest.

Unfortunately, many keep struggling to get into the rest because their focus is on the by-products and not on Calvary's cross. Once you go to the cross and understand the Gospel, you then enter into God's rest. Your life will become abundant, without sweat, hype, exaggeration or trying to work something up. You will just sit back and praise the Lord for what Jesus has done for you through His redemptive acts. (Hebrews 4:9,10).

Through Atlanta to Wherever

We have all flown to many destinations. Let us give you an illustration of people who fly, especially people who fly down south. Almost every time you fly down south, you have to go through Atlanta. Have you ever noticed that? If you're flying from Florida to Chicago you will probably go through

Atlanta. If you're just flying to North Carolina, you go through Atlanta. In fact, someone once said when the Rapture takes place; we'll have to go through Atlanta!

Calvary is the same, speaking spiritually. If you want to go to healing, you must first go through Calvary. Someone will say, "Oh, but I have this great travel agent. He's teaching me that I can get to my destination of health without going through Atlanta." Well, maybe you'll go directly to health, but don't be surprised if you have to be re-routed through Atlanta later on because your sickness came back. Remember, it's all through the complete redemption of our Lord Jesus. No matter how you twist it, you cannot go to any of the benefits unless you make a layover at Calvary. Everything must go through Calvary. We hope this fact is now real to you.

And for all those who talk against the by-products, the ones who are saying, "I don't believe in this for today," all we can say is that they need to have a lengthy layover at Calvary. They'll change their minds when they begin to understand what took place on Calvary's cross, through His death and His resurrection.

CHAPTER
3

THE IDENTIFICATION PRINCIPLE
(PART 1)

It is of the utmost importance that we understand the foundation we have laid up to this point. The Word of God tells us to build line upon line, precept upon precept. If we don't put the first block in its proper place and comprehend what the first block is all about, we can't put the next block on the top of it. We must understand why that first block was put down and have complete understanding of why we are doing what we are doing. Then when we put the second block, the third, and so on before we know it, we begin to build a fine Christian edifice, one that will stand the winds of time. (Mathew 7:24-27)

As we look at 1 Corinthians 1, we want to reemphasize a very important truth by looking at verse 17: "For Christ sent me not to baptize, but to preach the gospel: not with wisdom of words, lest the cross of Christ should be made of none effect."

Up to this point, Paul has talked about the fact that he was called to preach the Gospel. Then he goes on and says he is not going to do it with his own wisdom, prowess, or intellectualism. He says, "I'm not going to use the wisdom of words of men, but I'm going to use what God gives me by revelation so that the cross of Christ should not be voided out or made of none affect."

Now look at verse 18: "For the preaching of the cross is to them that perish foolishness: but unto us which are saved it is the power of God." Now notice what Paul is saying as we look at Romans 1. Paul is saying, "I was called to preach the Gospel. I was called to preach Jesus Christ. And I was called to preach the cross." In Romans 1:16, he states,

> *For I am not ashamed of the gospel of Christ: <u>for it is the power of God unto salvation to everyone that believeth;</u> to the Jew first, and also to the Greek. For (therein the gospel, therein the cross, therein Jesus Christ) therein, is the righteousness of God revealed from faith to faith: as it is written, the just shall live by faith.*

We must understand what salvation is and how our faith works with God's power when we believe the Gospel.

Now what is Paul talking about? He is talking about the power of God. He is talking about the power of God manifested through the Gospel—the preaching of the Gospel, the preaching of the cross, and the preaching of Jesus Christ. He says there is power in the Gospel to all who believe. He says, "I'm not ashamed of it. I'm with understanding of this, and I know that there is such power in it that it reveals the righteousness of God."

Now many people criticize what we call the "faith movement" today. We don't like to refer to it as the faith movement because you see; it is a way of life, not a movement. A movement is something that comes and goes. Faith is not going to go. God says, "I am a faith God. Have faith in Me." (Mark 11:22) In other words, use faith like I use faith. Anyone who says he doesn't believe in this "word of faith" stuff, needs to ask himself this question: "If I don't believe in it, how am I going to fulfill the command over here that the just are to walk in faith, live by faith, act and think in faith?' According to God's Word, faith must be used in every aspect of our lives.

We need to recognize that we are going to be completely in disobedience to God if we refuse to walk in faith(II Cor. 5:7). God says we are faith people. He says, "I am a faith God. You are going to respond and react with Me, and I am going to respond and react with you in the realm of faith."

Galatians 2:20 says, "I am crucified with Christ; nevertheless I live, yet not I, but Christ liveth in me, and the life which I now live in the flesh, I live by the faith of the Son of God, who loved me and gave himself for me." Do you think Christ will live in you without requiring you to use the faith He gave you?

Paul says, "I'm not ashamed of it (the Gospel) because it is the power of God." We have asked the following question many times in this book: "What kind of life would you have if you didn't know the Gospel?" First of all, you couldn't have been saved. You would have a powerless life. Now just think, people in churches all over are hearing things taught week after week, but few are hearing the real Gospel. How do we know that? Just look at the lives of average Christians—they are lives without power. In other words, there's no power to rule and reign with Christ. That means that what is preached in many churches today is not the Gospel, because when you preach the Gospel, it releases the power of God. It is the power of God unto health, deliverance, preservation, and prosperity. The Gospel is to help you live victoriously. Paul says, "I'm not ashamed of the Gospel, for it is the power of God unto what?" **Salvation.** Now when we are talking about salvation, are we simply talking about eternal life? Not at all. The Greek word for salvation is *sozo* (this is the root word) or *soteria*.

It is wonderful that we receive eternal life through the Gospel when we accept Jesus Christ. But some of us are going to live on this earth for the next 20, 30, 40 years, If Christ doesn't come back soon. And if we're going to live all those years, don't you think we want to live them with power and rule with Christ? And so, even though we have eternal life by receiving Jesus Christ, by hearing the Gospel, there is going to be a whole lot more to our lives than that one experience. So we have to find out what salvation means in the total revelation given to Paul.

Well, salvation does mean eternal life, but it also means preservation, as we just noted a few paragraphs ago. Don't you like to be preserved as you're going through life? Preservation means you are protected. Isn't it good that when salvation comes to you, you can have protection and you are preserved from certain things that could happen to you?

We also have freedom from our bondages. *Salvation means freedom from bondages.* It means, holiness. It means wholeness. It means deliverance. Are you listening to what this word means? It means prosperity. This is what salvation is all about and it is available to all who believe. When you have faith in what God has done through Jesus, when you believe, the power for all this is released. Faith activates God's power to bring to pass what you are believing God for.

So when we hear the word "salvation" mentioned in conjunction with our need for faith (that the just are to walk their lives out in faith) and someone begins saying, "Well, I don't believe in that faith stuff," that is the time we must take a good look at all he's going to miss. Why? Because a person cannot have those things we mentioned in the paragraph above, without faith. Salvation begins at the Cross. It begins with Jesus, who *is* the Gospel.

A lot of people out there are saying, "We're going to preach the Gospel of Jesus Christ." But you never hear one word about your identification with Christ and His identification with you. And if you don't know your identification with Christ, you are living a powerless life filled with defeat and discouragement.

And all the time God is saying, "Don't be satisfied with just living, so to speak. Get on top of things. Live a victorious life. Do things for me without being stymied and staggering every day of your life. Get with the program that I have ordained to take place on this earth. I have great plans for you!" God has blessed us and wants to use us in establishing His Kingdom on the earth! The Lord Jesus said that we are to pray and therefore expect God's will in Heaven to be done on the earth. (Mathew 6:9,10)

The Gospel is the power of God unto preservation, deliverance, freedom from sin, victory over satan, holiness, wholeness, and prosperity. And here's another—health. Physical health. It's all in the "salvation" Jesus obtained for us at the cross. But if you don't know the Gospel and understand what took place at the cross your life is going to be powerless. How? It will be powerless against the devil and all his lies and vicious attacks on you. You're just going to kowtow under the thing. Fall apart and say, "Well I guess being a Christian isn't too profitable, and I don't know why I ever became a Christian. I'm not any better off than I was before I became a Christian." (That's what *they* think and say. Please read on and see what God says about what he's planned for you.) In the previous chapter we noted the fact that in Christianity there are no direct flights to anything. Let's qualify that a bit more by saying that for baby Christians, there are no direct flights to any place. Remember our comment that no matter where you fly down south, it seems they somehow usually route you through Atlanta? Recently, someone flew to Florida. Guess where he went first when he left Hartford, Conn.? If you're up in Connecticut and you want to go to Florida, they route you through Atlanta, Georgia. It seems there are no direct flights and there is always a layover. He had a four-hour layover.

And in the natural we don't like layovers, do we? Every time you book a flight you probably say, "Is this a direct flight?"

"No there's a layover in Detroit."

"Well, I don't want that flight."

"Well if you want the other one, it's going to cost you."

See the same thing is true in our walk with the Lord. There are no direct flights for the baby Christian, and for the most part, most of us may still be baby Christians. A victorious life is not found in direct flights. We have to learn to layover. But one of the problems we find is that nobody wants to layover, to study God's Word thoroughly. We all want direct flights to healing. We all want direct flights to prosperity and victory over temptation. In essence, we want God to manifest everything for us right now, but we don't want to commit much of our time to the Word. God's first goal for us is to be conformed to the image of Christ (Romans 8:29), and to learn how to walk and live on this earth as the people He created us to be.

Someone may say, "Come on now, I just want to be healed."

"I'm sorry, you'll have to layover at spiritual Atlanta."

"I can't have a direct flight?"

"No, you can't have a direct flight. You have to layover at spiritual Atlanta. That's Calvary." That's where you'll find the Cross.

"Come on, aren't there any direct flights anywhere?"

"No, not yet. You're still a baby Christian. You have to layover at Calvary."

"I don't want to do that. Don't you understand that I want all my needs met right

Now?"

"O.K., but first you have to go to Calvary." Are we getting the point across? Too many of us have never spent enough time at the Cross-we really haven't thought enough about the death, burial, and resurrection of Jesus Christ. Have you ever understood what happened at each one of these experiences Jesus went through?

"But you don't understand. I have some bills to pay!"

"We know, but first, you have to go to Calvary."

"Well, why can't I have a direct flight to get all my bills paid?"

"That's not the way it works. You must layover at Calvary for a while. There are no direct flights. Listen, if you don't understand what happened through Jesus' atonement as our Passover Lamb, you are a baby Christian."

"What do I do when I get to Calvary?"

"Just stay there and study all you can about the cross of Jesus Christ. Stay there long enough to get established in Christ's finished work. Let the Holy Spirit give you some *rhema*-some revelation. Yes, it's very true that God works lots of instant healings and miracles, and we expect to see more and more. But knowing that doesn't exclude us from growing up spiritually. Again, many have lost their healing and their victory because they were not strong enough in their faith in Christ and what He did for them to keep it. Mark 4:14-20 says that the devil comes with tests and trials to see if he can steal the Word of God out of your heart. Well, if you don't have any Word (who you are in Christ) established in you, you are going to be a push over!

The devil doesn't want us to spend time in the Word, because our strength is in Christ and His Word. Working out in God's Word is like physically working out with weights. You are going to get stronger and stronger and stronger! Therefore, you'll become a greater threat to the devil's kingdom and a greater blessing to God's Kingdom! We are not saying that you have to spend 3 hours studying the cross, every time, before you can ask the Lord for something. But, let us make a spiritual habit of always refreshing ourselves in our identification with Christ. Let's not forget the source of all the wonderful benefits!

"Look" at the Cross

In Numbers 21:8, we read the story of the murmuring Israelites. All of a sudden they were beginning to get bitten by the snakes around their ankles. They were beginning to get some annoyances.

"And the Lord said unto Moses, Make thee a fiery serpent, and set it upon a pole: and it shall come to pass, that everyone that is bitten, when he looketh upon it, shall live." Notice that word "looketh." That doesn't mean a casual glance at the serpent. "O.K. I see it. What do I do now?" No, the word "looketh" is from the Hebrew word, *raah*, meaning "to be occupied with and influenced by."

You are looking at the cross of Calvary, just as these people were made to look at the serpent. You are occupied with something, meaning you are not preoccupied with something else. Now what is it that the devil wants to do? What is this thing with which he wants to preoccupy you? He wants to preoccupy you with serpents biting your ankles-sickness, disease, circumstances, poverty. He wants to occupy you with that so you will not be occupied and influenced by the Word of God. He wants to keep your eyes on things other than the cross and what God wants you to understand about the Cross. What did Jesus experience at the Cross? Why did he have to die? Why did he have to shed his blood? Be occupied and influenced by these things.

Somebody may say, "Well, I don't know, it just seems like an awful lot of work to keep myself occupied with the cross." Oh yes, it's going to take a lot, believe us when we tell you. To become occupied with and influenced by the cross will require every bit of your effort and time, believe us. You cannot be totally occupied with TV and other things and be influenced by the Cross at the same time.

Be honest, since you have been reading this, how many times has your mind drifted to other things? Do you know what you have to do to bring your mind back to focus? You have to take charge. Your spirit man has to say to that body of yours, "Snap to! Wake up, body. Don't fall asleep. Mind, stay alert." Be occupied with the cross don't be occupied with tomorrow. Don't be thinking of mowing the lawn or what's on T.V., be occupied with what you are learning about the cross, because the cross is the power of God unto salvation.

Moses said, "He who looketh." He who is "occupied with and influenced by" shall live. Does that sound like some other parts of Scripture? Jesus said, "The words that I speak, they are life." (John 6:63) Do you want to live? Choose life. You cannot be occupied with anything else. You cannot be occupied with your bills. You cannot be occupied with the fact that you're unemployed. You have to be occupied with what has happened at the cross. Seek the Kingdom first, and all these other things will be added unto you (Mathew 6:33).

We preach Jesus Christ and Him crucified. We preach the Gospel. Paul said, "I'm not ashamed of the Gospel for it is the power of God." Do you want the power of God? Then you have to know about the cross. You have to know about Jesus Christ and Him crucified. You have to know about the death, burial and resurrection of the Lord Jesus Christ and what His experiences mean to you personally. Jonah 2:8 states: "They that observe lying vanities shall forsake their own mercy." You see the devil is going to keep you looking at lying vanities all the time. He's going to keep your attention on things it shouldn't be on. God says, "Get your eyes up on that serpent (the serpent represented Jesus becoming a curse for us) and you'll get your eyes off that serpent down there biting your ankles." Get your eyes off the adverse circumstances of your life-get them on the Cross.

If you will get your eyes on the cross, you won't be able, at the same time, to be occupied with something else. You see, you can't be occupied with Jesus Christ and Him crucified and your bills at the same time. If you're occupied with the bills, then you neglect the cross. If you neglect the cross, then you're not going to see what God wants you to see and receive the power of God unto salvation, which is <u>preservation, prosperity, wholeness, and victory over sin and satan.</u>

So the Word says, "look at it." Behold the Word of God. Behold means "to look into it". Don't just look on the surface: look *into* it and then meditate upon it. Meditate upon it. Understand it. Ask the Lord to show you what it all means.

Once you understand the cross, once you understand the Gospel, you will simply be able to say, "Father, I have a need, and I see that it's mine through the finished work at Calvary. I receive it now by faith. Thank you." Then just go about doing what God has told you to do in witnessing or preaching the gospel, and He will supply the need.

We make faith confessions because we believe what God has said is true. And it is true in our case. Therefore, we say the same thing God says.

<u>Your confession is concerning a fact that already is.</u> You find it in the Word. He says, "All your needs are met according to My riches in glory by Christ Jesus." If you have need of a car, it is a fact that the need has already been met if you understand what took place on Calvary's cross.

There's too much ignorance in the Body of Christ today. You don't have to work up a sweat, saying things over and over again, just to be repititous. Now, confession is very important. Philemon 1:6 says, "That the communication of thy faith may become effectual by the acknowledging of every good thing which is in you in Christ Jesus." But repetition itself doesn't make things come to pass. It's the power in the Gospel that does the work! So, just go, friends, to Calvary's cross. Layover there and see what Jesus did for you. But you will not find that out by making one quick stop and beating it out to the movies. As we said before, you have to *study* it. You can't surface Calvary. Get hungry! Get thirsty for more of God!!

The Word of the Cross Is Complete

Now we just mentioned having a need, maybe it's a car, but what you will learn at the cross will astonish you. There is forgiveness, healing, justification, deliverance, preservation, and prosperity. Remember, Jesus did a complete work there. It is finished. There is nothing more to do. It is a completed work. The Lord Jesus said, "It is finished, completed-perfectly perfect. Nothing more to do. It's done." When we say the Cross is a completed work, we are including all other aspects such as His death, burial, and resurrection.

The devil comes along and says, "Wait a minute! No, no, there are still some things for you *to do*. There's a lot for you *to do*. Don't believe that stuff. You have to work at this. In the kingdom of God you have to really work out your salvation." That's right; you have to work out your salvation with fear and trembling. But it's not talking about what was finished by Jesus Christ. His work is a finished work. He was crucified, died, was buried, raised up with new life, and seated in the highest place of authority-and He did it as *our* substitute. We don't have to work to make it true for us; we need to work at our faith; we need to believe that what He has done for us makes us more than victors. The devil wants you to believe that you have to earn and merit the blessings of God, that it is all based on your good works. There is a difference between works of faith and works of the flesh. Works of faith is believing and obeying God's Word. Works of the flesh is trying to do things and make things happen out of your own strength. As the saying goes, "trying to pull up yourself by your own boot strap". That's humanism. Humanism says that I don't need to believe in God. I'm my own god. I can do everything myself.

We are not perfected in the flesh. We are perfected through the Spirit. True maturity comes through the Spirit. If you will spend time and layover at Calvary, you will find that many of your struggles are really unnecessary. That's right. It's all right there at Calvary. If you think that Calvary is not an exciting subject, you have no idea what it's all about.

The foundation of any building is the least-noticed but most important part of that building. At construction sites in the city, when a new building is begun, a fence with a sign will be put up which says, "New Building Going Up." But you don't see anything behind that fence, do you? For weeks and weeks you wonder when that building is going up. But behind that fence, they are meticulously putting down the ditches, the forms and the wire so that when the concrete is poured, it just solidifies into a sold foundation that will hold the building up. All of a sudden after maybe five to eight weeks, the building goes right up. Why? Because the most important part was carefully laid down; the workers took their time. It was properly done so they could now put the building on that foundation. It will not topple. Many Christians don't take the time to put in foundations-and in a matter of weeks their beautiful Christian edifice crumbles.

But a lot of people say, "Well, wait a minute. That takes a lot of hard work." Be assured friends, if you take time to put down a foundation, you are going to find some of life's greatest rewards. Rewards which are lasting.

Someone will say, "Well, who cares about the foundation? No one sees it anyway. I just want to show everybody my nice healing edifice." So we look at you and you look pretty good today. You look pretty healthy. Your building looks real good. But we can assure you that even though it looks nice today, in about three or four weeks or in a month or in five years that building is going to topple, and the answer lies down at the bottom of the rubble. When you look for it, there will be no foundation. Are you listening?

Let's go to Matthew 13:23:" But he that received seed into the good ground is he that heareth the word, and…" There's a conjunction here that ties two thoughts together. That means one thought cannot be there without the other. You have to take both thoughts into consideration. He says, "But that received seed into the good ground is he that heareth the word, and understandeth it…" You can't just hear the Word; you have to <u>understand</u> the Word. Studying will bring understanding.

The scripture continues:"…which also beareth fruit, and bringeth forth, some an hundredfold, some sixty, some thirty." Did you notice that the word "understand" was in that sentence for a reason? You can't just hear and think that you're going to bear fruit. Look at your life. Have you heard something and just gone out automatically and bore some fruit over it? No, it doesn't happen that way does it?

The Spirit Must Be Fed

You need to hear, hear, hear and study, study, study. Then you will begin to understand what you have heard. That's why we emphasize points over and over. We are not trying to get you hyped up and excited and jumping up and down, "Hurrah! Hallelujah! I feel good." Hype leaves nothing in your spirit; it only excites the flesh. And later you will find yourself saying, "Wait a minute. What did they teach?" We taught nothing if we taught you how to jump and say, "Hallelujah!" Why? Because your spirit man was not fed. The spirit man must be fed. It must understand the principles and truths of God's Word.

It is going to take diligent effort. Crowds are not going to come running and knock down the door to hear this kind of teaching, because it requires study and effort on your part in order to grasp this. But it is going to be worth it.

Someone will say, "Well you know, I like to see miracles performed. That excites me."

"Well so do we. They're wonderful. They're great. They're wonderful to watch, but they don't pay your bills. They're not going to heal your marriage. They're not going to establish a foundation in your life." Has watching miracles healed your marriage-given you health?

"Oh well, I like to go to Christian concerts."

"Oh yes, they're good but they don't stabilize your life."

We're not against concerts, but concerts deal with the outward man, for the most part. At some concerts, people line up an hour-and-a-half ahead of time. Why? Because they know they won't receive any teaching requiring them to say, "Body, pay attention." In a concert you remain wide awake, but your spirit just sits there dormant and for the most part, is not fed, unless it's a concert where the emphasis is on God's Word and praising the Lord Jesus Christ. Too often we find we cannot understand the words being sung and are distracted from the message by the music and the loudness, not to mention the flashing lights.

Turn to Galatians 5:16-17: "This I say then, Walk in the Spirit, and ye shall not fulfill the lust of the flesh."

"For the flesh lusteth against the Spirit, and the Spirit against the flesh: and these are contrary the one to the other: so that *ye cannot do the things that ye would.*"

The flesh always wants to be pampered. The flesh is easy to take care of when it requires nothing of the spirit man's attention. It's easy. The spirit just sits there dormant, and the flesh just goes crazy. Do you know what is happening? There's a pulling back and forth. The spirit man says, "You know I really need something more than this."

And the flesh is saying, "Yeah, but it's much more fun this way."

The spirit is saying, "You're better off if you study."

But the flesh says, "Yes, but it takes a lot of effort to study. I like just listening to music."

The spirit man says, "Yes, but there's going to be great results if you get into the Gospel."

The flesh says, "I don't think its worth it to me."

And the spirit man answers, "Yes, I'm telling you, it's worth it to you."

We all go through this, don't we? The Holy Spirit says to you, "Why don't you just pick up your Bible tonight and shut off the television? Why don't you study on the subject of the Cross?"

How does our flesh react to that?

We start an argument on the inside of us. And we usually give in to the flesh. You know all the time the TV is on, your mind keeps telling you, "Boy, I probably should be studying the Word. I really should be."

But the flesh is saying, "But this is so comfortable. You don't have to do anything. Just sit here and be a blob on the couch."

Most of us are just Christian spectators.

So we are talking about a subject that requires the spirit man to be alert and to do battle. When it comes down to a subject like this, you must keep that spirit man awake, and the spirit man must keep that body alert too. If you understand the Cross, it could literally save your life.

Revelation through Christ Brings Understanding

Look at Galatians 1:11-12: "But I certify you, brethren, that the gospel..." Here it is again. Paul can't seem to get away from this word "Gospel." He says, "But I certify you, brethren, that the gospel which was preached of me is not after man. For I neither received it of man, neither was I taught it, but by the revelation of Jesus Christ."

Paul received this by revelation through Jesus Christ Himself, not by listening to other people's opinions. Not by books; not by tapes (even though there are a lot of good books and tapes available). He received it by revelation, and when you get a revelation, you get an understanding with it. It is not in your head, but rather, in your spirit man. Once you get something in your spirit, it becomes *rhema* to you. With rhema (when the Word is spoken into your spirit man like a light coming on in the dark) comes understanding. You may be able to quote some scriptures when we finish with this subject. You may know where they are in the Bible. That doesn't mean you understand them. You are going to have to study, meditate, and confess them, and let the Holy Spirit open them up to you. He will, through a revelation (revealing it to you in your heart or spirit), give you the understanding you need so it will become personal to you.

You see, God wants us to know as much as Paul knew. And you're not going to stop where Paul stopped. Aren't you going to go further than Paul went? Paul wasn't omniscient, was he? He wasn't God. He didn't know everything. We get some idea that we cannot go further than Paul does in our understanding. Who said so? We know God is not calling us to write another book of the Bible, but why can't we get more insight even than Paul? Don't ever be satisfied with what you know. Keep saying to God, "I want more, I want more. I want a deeper understanding. I want to have such an understanding that it will just flow out of my spirit. I want this to be first nature to me-just keep flowing out of me." Don't you want that? Wouldn't it affect your life and other people all around you? Go to Colossians 2:12: "Buried with him in baptism, wherein also ye are risen with him through the faith of the operation of God, who hath raised him from the dead." Now we haven't brought ourselves to the burial and resurrection of Jesus Christ. We are working ourselves to that point, but Paul speaks here about being risen with Him through faith in the operation of God.

It is important that we develop our faith in the operation of God in direct relation to His raising of Jesus Christ from the dead, because true spiritual growth and an understanding of this new life Jesus obtained, has a direct relationship to us. Now this doesn't mean that you couldn't grow up spiritually by studying other subjects. But every bit of your foundation comes from the true knowledge of what you get by understanding the death, burial, and resurrection of Jesus.

It is wonderful to understand all you can about the by-products, but know they are by-products. If we would take a long hard look at where the by-products come from, we wouldn't have to spend so much time studying them. The more you know and understand about Calvary the more solid your foundation is going to be. Then, your life can be what Jesus came to give you-abundant life.

First John 3:8 says, "... For this purpose the Son of God was manifested that he might destroy the works of the devil." Here's our question to you. Where did this defeat take place? On Calvary's cross. Do you know how this defeat came about? Do you know the particulars of this defeat? We have more questions. What works of satan were destroyed? Just some of them? All of them? Spiritual? Physical? Can you answer these questions? You will when we finish this study.

What took place on Calvary was merely a climax of what Jesus was teaching us all through His life. As Jesus was walking with His disciples, what was He telling them? What was He showing them? What was the important thing about His life? He was giving us examples of how to put down the works of satan. He says, "I'll give you My authority. In My name you cast out the devil. See how I do it. I walk up and say, 'O.K. devil, you come out of that person.' You say it with your mouth, 'Come out of that person.'" And when Jesus came into temptation, what did He say and how did He act? He said, "It is written. It is written." He then tells him what the Word says (Mathew 4). Jesus then goes up on the cross and in Colossians 2:14-15, says that He nailed the ordinances that were against us on the cross. He made an open show of satan, defeating Him utterly. Now take everything that Jesus said to do, "It is written. It is written. It is written." The devil comes along and he says, "I still have all the power. Not God. I have it all." And what do you do? You say, "Satan, you are a liar!

What was Jesus doing all during His life? He says, "I'm going to tell you how to defeat the devil. When I go to the cross I'm going to make it final. I'm not only going to take away sickness, I'm going to take away disease. I'm going to take away poverty. I'm going to take away everything that the devil brought in when the curse came. I'm utterly nailing it to the cross, making an open show of the devil publicly. He's defeated, and his head is crushed under the heals of my fee!"

Now Jesus says, "Christian, I've told you about your authority. I've told you about who you are in Me. I've told you what you can say and what you can do, and I'm telling you that every time you do this, the very throne of God will back you up."

You don't have to be confused! Either you believe the devil or you believe Jesus. You see? You have to look at the Word. Jesus said, "It is written." Your confession should be, "If it is written, it is so." There is nothing to argue about. Say, "Devil, you're lying to me."

"Oh no," he says, "I'm telling you the truth."

"No, you're a liar because it says in the Word, 'It is written that Jesus Christ made an open show of you and defeated you! You are defeated! You can't touch me! It is written!"

The works of satan were defeated. Not one of them. Not some of them. All of them. And spiritual growth can only come about when those things which prevent your growth can be permanently removed. What is going to prevent your growth? A lack of knowledge. "My people are destroyed for the lack of knowledge." Your growth will come as a result of your studying the death, burial and resurrection of Jesus Christ. When you can study, meditate and ask God to reveal to you those scriptures, which reveal the operation of God in raising Jesus from the dead, then you will see growth in your life. Faith is developed as we understand the operation of God in raising Jesus from the dead.

We want to study all we can to enhance our knowledge on our identification with Jesus. We listen to tapes and read books on the subject. We read commentaries along with our own personal study of the Word. We can't get enough of what is going on in the Epistles. We study in the Old and New Testaments, but the Epistles are letters from God written to the Church. So, we spend a lot of time in them. It's in the Epistles that the Holy Spirit gives us a "behind the scenes look" at Calvary. It's where He lays out for us much more detail of all that took place in the spirit realm when Jesus redeemed us. You see, God revealed the law to Israel through Moses in the Old Covenant, and He revealed the mystery of Christ to the Church through the apostles and prophets, but mainly through Paul in the New Covenant. Listen to what the Apostle Peter said in 2 Peter 3: 15-18;

"And account that the longsuffering of our Lord is salvation; even as our beloved brother Paul also according to the wisdom given unto him hath written unto you;"

"As also in all his Epistles, speaking in them of these things; in which are some things hard to be understood, which they that are unlearned and unstable (notice those two words, *unlearned* and *unstable*) wrest (or *wrestle with*) as they do also the other scriptures, unto their own destruction."

"Ye therefore, beloved, seeing ye know these things before, beware lest ye also, being led away with the error of the wicked, fall from your own steadfastness. But grow in grace, and in the knowledge of our Lord and Savior Jesus Christ."

Jesus is the Gospel. The Gospel is Jesus Christ. You cannot study Jesus Christ without studying Jesus Christ and Him crucified. You cannot study Jesus without studying the cross. And you cannot study Jesus being crucified on the cross unless you go into the Gospel. The heart of the Gospel is the death, burial and resurrection of our Lord Jesus Christ. It is the foundation and the center (focal point) of the Kingdom of God that was preached in the book of Acts.

Now you're going to need a revelation. You will not receive a revelation just because you are reading this book. Your pastor can write a book and have a revelation on the subject. You can read your pastor's book, but that doesn't mean that you're going to get the revelation of it. You get the revelation, or rhema, as you study and desire to know the truth, when you get hungry and start digging; like searching for gold. God will turn on the light inside of you.

What "Identify" Means

Because we are studying our identification with Christ, we ought to know what the word "identify" means. This is important. Memorize it. You will hear it over and over again. It is a theme, which runs through this entire book. Write it down and memorize it. It holds the key to understanding what Jesus did in His death, burial and resurrection, and how it affects your life.

Webster says that the word "identify" means to make identical and to consider or treat as the same. The second half of this definition really adds an explanation to the first half. You see, when some things are identical, you will consider and treat them the same. We like to make a faith confession in which we state, "I will respect God and His Word in the same manner." That means we treat them as being identical. We consider them the same and treat them the same. Whatever you think about God, you think about His Word. Whatever you think about His Word, you are actually thinking about God, because the Word is God (John 1:1). We treat them the same.

47

Now there are two sides to identification. We could not be identified with Christ Jesus our Lord until He was first identified with us. He had to identify with us before we could be identified with Him. The very reason why we can be identified with Christ is because He was first identified with us. The first part of this definition means to make identical. Christ became identified with us. Galatians 3:13 says, "Christ hath redeemed us from the curse of the law, *being made a curse for us…*"

Now we were lost, alienated from the life of God, bound by the curse of the law, so Jesus became identified with us in that He became a curse for us. So now we can say that Jesus became identical with us. He became one with what we were. He identified with our curse.

The second half of our definition says that we were considered and treated the same as. That means we were bound by the curse, under its influences and judged by Almighty God under that curse. Now that Jesus is identified with us, God must consider and treat Jesus the same as He treats us. He is under judgment and bound by the curse just as we were. Can you see that?

Under the curse we were spiritually dead and under this condition we were doomed to ultimately go to Hell. While we lived on this earth, we were doomed to be sick, poor, and defeated. That was the influence of the curse on our lives. So in order for God to be just, or fair, He had to consider Jesus and treat Him the same as He would us. In other words, this is where we get our word 'substitute,' which means that Jesus became all that we were in Him at Calvary. He identified with us and all that we were; and so we became one with Him. And God considered that and treated us the same way He treated Jesus. In other words, we participated in a sense, in His death, burial and resurrection. And that could have happened only after He participated in us. He was identified with us so we could be identified with Him.

Because Jesus rose from the dead and is at the Father's right hand God can treat us just as He treats Jesus Christ because Christ is identified with us and we are identified with Christ. You see, God sees Jesus and us as being identical. If you grasp this definition, you will find this is going to work for you. To identify means to make identical; to consider and treat the same.

As you go through this teaching with us, you are going to find we are going to say this over and over again. Jesus identified with me. We have the effects of the curse on us. Jesus comes along and says, "I am going to be made a curse for you." He identified with our condition. Under this condition of the curse, God says to us, "You're doomed." Jesus steps in and says, "I'm going to identify with you. I'm going to be your substitute." So everything that was due us is now going to be due Jesus, because if we are identical, God is going to treat us both the same.

The only difference is, Jesus becomes our substitute. Galatians 2:20 says, "I am crucified *with Christ*: nevertheless I live; yet not I, but Christ liveth in me: and the life which I now live in the flesh I live by the faith of the Son of God, who loved me, and gave himself for me." Another scripture says, "I am buried with Christ." Yet another says, "I am raised with Christ." Another scripture says, "I suffered with Christ." Another says, "I've become victorious with Christ." Do you see it? He identifies with us, so we can identify with Him.

And every time the Father looks at us and looks at Jesus, He considers us identical. So when Jesus goes through the crucifixion for you, you are crucified with Him. You are on that cross with Him. The Father says, "You're due to die because you're under the curse. You're going to die." So you go on the cross with Jesus and you're on the cross with Him. You are crucified with Christ. Crucifixion is not death in itself, but you died with Christ. You are crucified with Christ. You died with Christ. You are buried with Christ. You are risen with Christ. You are put in heavenly places with Christ. As the Father sees Jesus sitting in heavenly places, ruling as King of all, having full authority, He looks at you and He sees you identically. You are treated identically. This is your identification with Jesus. Because He is identified with us, you can now identify with Him. What the Father thinks of Him, the Father thinks of you (John 17:23; I John 4:17b). We all must see ourselves in this manner. This was real to Paul; it should be real to us. No, we're not Jesus, but we are joint heirs with Him. We are His Body, one spirit with Him (Romans 8:17; I Cor. 6:17; Ephesians 1;19-23)!

Once you grasp this truth, everything else is going to fall into place. You are going to be able to see who you are in Christ and see what the Father really thinks about you. Everything He thinks about Jesus, He thinks about you. He cannot think toward you any differently, because He identifies you with Christ. And He is going to treat you exactly the same as He treats Jesus.

Once this gets in your spirit, you are going to say, "Oh my goodness, that stinking, lying devil. He's fooled me, lied to me, and deceived me. How could I have been so dumb not to see it?" The devil doesn't want you to read this material, because he knows when you get through, you are going to say, "Hey, look you little worm, get under my foot. I'm going to squash you." And he knows he will have to obey you.

The Gospel is the cross. The cross and the crucifixion of Jesus are the Gospel. The heart of the Gospel is the death, burial and resurrection of

Jesus. You were identified with Jesus. God treats you and Jesus the same. He identified with you; you can identify with Him. When the Father looks at Jesus, He's looking at you. When the Father looks at you, He is seeing Jesus. God only sees us through Jesus' Blood! He only sees us in Christ!

The church today has been told a lot of gobbledygook. They spend a lot of time majoring in the minors, while the devil is kicking them around. God doesn't look on our outside. He looks at your spirit man. He wants you to take your authority in Christ. Are you standing victorious? His Son Jesus paid the price so that you could stand strong and defeat the devil every day of your life.

Let's get smart about the Word of God. God says His people are destroyed for lack of knowledge. We have to be so persuaded of our authority in Christ that the devil can say anything to us and we will immediately recognize his lies. It will ring a sour note and we will say, "Wait a minute, that's not true. The Word says…devil, who do you think you're fooling? I'm one of those smart Christians. I'm not one of those that majors in the minors. I major in the cross of Calvary. Who do you think you're talking to, devil? You think I don't know that what you're saying to me is a lie?"

Jesus said for us to say, "It is written." It is already a finished fact. Jesus defeated satan, annihilated him, and completely wiped him out. But satan comes along and puts some lie in your mind and you believe it. You get right back into the old curse syndrome again. You have to know what the Word says. It will give you victory in your life. What would you rather have? A flesh that is all hyped up or a victorious spirit, filled with the Word?

You know what it means to "look". Don't you? To be occupied with and influenced by the Word. Some people would say, "Oh, you people are too Word crazy." Let's hope we *are* Word-crazy. We're not into hype. We're into the Word. God wants the Word brought to His people because people are destroyed for the lack of what? Information, Knowledge is information. You might be getting information but you may be getting the wrong information. You need the right information. Knowledge that comes by revelation. When you get it by revelation, you get enlightenment. When you get enlightenment in your spirit, you understand what this is all about. That is our goal, for your spirit to be enlightened.

We want God's Word to become rhema to you. Let's go to the next chapter with a continued open mind. Your mind is part of your soul. Did you ever notice that God said in 3 John 2, "Beloved, I wish above all things that you prosper and be in health, even as your soul prospers"? Your soul *will* prosper-if given an education.

CHAPTER

4

THE IDENTIFICATION PRINCIPLE
(PART 2)

This chapter is going to show you what is already yours through Christ. You're perhaps going to find out why your faith isn't working the way you'd like it to. There are always reasons, maybe things we are not understanding, that hinder our faith.

This subject is spiritual, not thrilling in any physical sense. Your flesh is not going to like to sit and read this kind of teaching material because it is spiritual. We have to sometimes discipline ourselves in order to comprehend the more spiritual subjects in the Bible, because they have nothing to do with the flesh. Most Christians let their flesh lead them in life. What *feels* right they do?

We hope you remember what the words, "to identify," mean. We said "to identify" has two parts to it: 1) it means to make identical; and 2) to consider and treat the same. In other words, if something is identical, then it can be considered the same, and therefore, we can treat it the same.

Let's re-emphasize that before we could identify ourselves with the Lord Jesus Christ, He had to identify Himself with us. Now what do we mean by that? Well, we can bring you to two scriptures and show you where He identified with us in our plight before we were redeemed, and then we can show you the identification in terms of the exchange that Jesus made once He identified with us. Then, and only then, can we identify ourselves with Him.

Redeemed from the Curse

Galatians 3:13 says simply this; "Christ hath redeemed us from the curse…" Did you notice the tense of that sentence? Christ *has* past tense. Now here is the identification He makes with us, "…being made a curse for us…" He's identifying with the fact that all of us, as unredeemed people, were under the effects of the curse. He has to somehow get us out from under the effects of the curse.

In the Garden of Eden, God cursed the serpent. He cursed the ground. He cursed the days of man ahead of him and said they were going to be troublesome days. But Jesus Christ had to come and take us out from underneath the effects of the curse. In other words, we were bound by the effects of the curse. We were spiritually dead, and of ourselves, could do nothing. A slave can't redeem a slave.

Many people misunderstand what spiritual death is. Spiritual death is *not* a state of nonexistence. When someone is spiritually dead, he does not cease to exist. He just exists in another state-a state of alienation from Almighty God. The life of God is not being poured into that individual. When the light of God and the life of God is no longer coming into the individual, then he is in darkness. He has no way of getting life into him. He is alienated from God in his spiritual death condition. The Bible says that sin separates men from God.

In addition to being under the curse (and that's bad enough), we were sick, diseased or defeated; and we were on our way to Hell for an eternal punishment. Jesus identified with us in all that by becoming a curse for us. He became our substitute. He is your substitute; He is our substitute. And in taking our place, He became identified with all that we were and all that we were bound by.

So, as He became identified with us, God was obligated by justice, or we might call it fairness, to consider and treat Jesus the same as He would have treated us before the redemption. As soon as Jesus identified Himself with us in our sins, in other words, when He was made to be sin for us (He who knew no sin) II Cor. 5:21, then we gained the potential to become the righteousness of God in Him. Do you see the exchange here?

First of all, Jesus identified with each of us. He said, "You are in sin and I'm going to identify with that sin by taking that sin on me." Jesus didn't sin, mind you, and note that well. Jesus never sinned; He was made to be sin for us. As soon as He identified with our sin problem, then we gained identity with the righteousness of God. In other words, once Jesus had identified totally with us and had taken everything that was ours in our state of disobedience to God, then each of us can say to Jesus, "I'll take everything that you are, once I've been redeemed."

Jesus had to identify with us in our sins before we could identify with Him in everything that God gave Him, once He was raised from the dead. But in order for this redemption to be a complete redemption, a total work received by God as finished and perfect, <u>Jesus had to identify with us in every single aspect of the curse.</u>

Understanding Spiritual Death

One of the problems that comes out of this, and we will get into it a little later on, is that people do not understand spiritual death. Man was spiritually dead when he sinned against God. We might say that high treason took place in the Garden of Eden. People who do not understand what spiritual death is think that Jesus did not die spiritually, because they think that spiritual death is cessation of life. It is simply an alienation from God. As we said, the life of God is no longer coming into an individual who spiritually dies. He is still alive (he still exists), but not with the life of God.

That's why, when Jesus was hanging on the cross, He said, "My God, my God, why hast thou forsaken me?" Why did God forsake Him? Why did God turn His back on Him? Because Jesus was made to be sin for us. He who knew no sin was made to be sin so that the exchange could take place, and we could become the righteousness of God in Him.

Spiritual death is not a nonexistent state. It is simply an alienation from the presence of God. In fact He says, "Your iniquities have separated you from your God." If we want to put it that way, spiritual death is separation. In order for our redemption to be complete, Jesus had to go through everything; He had to identify with us in totality. Please take note that He had to become or take everything that would be ours under the curse. He was our substitute so that we could have everything He became through His death, burial, and resurrection.

He had to experience spiritual death because you experienced spiritual death. We were all alienated from God. He had to be alienated from God. Jesus became poor so that you could become rich. That's one of God's ultimate purposes. Jesus had to take on rejection so that you could be accepted with God (Ephesians 1:6). Jesus had to take depression and all oppression. Jesus had to take all sickness and disease because health is part of God's ultimate plan for all of us (Isaiah 53; Mathew 8:16,17).

And so Jesus had to experience and identify with us in every aspect of the fall. He had to become sick. He had to become poor. He had to become depressed. He had to become dejected and rejected. Remember all His disciples left Him. He must have experienced depression. You can't tell us He wasn't depressed on that cross. He had to experience everything that the fall brought upon man. He had to experience and to identify with it in order to take it from us as our substitute so the exchange could take place later when He was risen from the dead.

So, we are going to look at the death, burial and resurrection of Jesus, or the complete redemptive act of Jesus which took place about 2,000 years ago. But first we must have an understanding of why Calvary had to take place to begin with. "Why did Jesus have to be crucified?" Is the question we should be asking? If we don't know that, it will be more difficult to understand what took place behind the scenes of Calvary. So we are going to go back to the beginning and see what Adam did in the garden to some small degree. Then we are going to work our way back to Calvary.

In Adam/In Christ

First Corinthians 15:21, states: "For since by man came death, by man came also the resurrection of the dead, "Now what this is simply saying is-one man brought death; one man also brought the resurrection of the dead. Now we must remind you to keep the word "identify" in your mind. Don't lose that understanding. "To identify," once again, is to make identical, to consider and treat the same.

Now look at verse 22:For as in Adam all die, even so in Christ shall all be made alive." Now verse 22 tells you who those two men were. Adam brought death. Jesus brought life. Notice also that "in Adam" all died. Don't forget that phrase, "In Adam" all died and, don't forget, "in Christ" all shall be made alive. These phrases hold the key to understanding the whole subject of identification through Calvary's cross. We are preaching the cross. That was presented in the first two chapters. We are preaching Jesus Christ and Him crucified. We are preaching the Gospel. This is the heart of the Gospel.

Who are the two most important men in the entire Bible? We say Adam and Jesus. Someone might say, "Wait a minute, I know Jesus is the most important man in the Bible but what in the world did Adam ever do that you would call him one of the most important men in the Bible? It doesn't say anything about him performing miracles. He didn't ever cast out any devils. All I can see that Adam ever did was name a few animals. I mean if you had said Moses or Elijah or Abraham, but Adam and Jesus? I can see Elijah and Jesus, but Adam and Jesus? Yes, Adam and Jesus.

Why Adam and Jesus? Well, it's not because either one of them ever cast out devils or performed miracles. That's not why. They were the two most important men in the entire Bible *because their lives affected the entire human race.* In all history these two men affected *all* of humanity. Even though Abraham was a great man, his actions did not affect all humanity. Not even Paul's actions affected all humanity, even though he wrote a lot of the New Testament. But Adam's actions did and Jesus' actions did also. And so, we are curious to know why. Shouldn't we study about these two men? If the Word of God tells us that Adam caused us to die spiritually, then we should want to find out why. He affected your life. He affected our lives in a serious way. This is not something like figuring out some famous baseball player's batting average. Such things don't matter because they don't affect us. But what Adam did had an effect on all our lives. And of course what Jesus did affects us. So we want to learn all we can about it. We want to study it, read it, meditate upon it, and find out why these two men affected our lives so much.

Adam's action has an affect on people right now, 6,000 years later. We want to know what he did, don't you? We want to know why what Jesus did 2,000 years ago has had such an affect on our lives today. Major in what Adam and Jesus did. These two people affected all mankind, not just a few.

Humanity's Representatives

You see the reason why these two men are so important is that they are *representative men.* When you represent another person, your actions affect them. When you are a representative man or woman, no matter what you do, your actions are going to affect somebody else. For example, fathers and mothers are, to some degree, representative people to their children. The children look like them, smile like them, walk and talk like them. Their children seem at times to take on many of their characteristics, their habits, and we might even say, the mannerisms of their parents.

But it goes further. It goes deeper, much deeper with Adam and with Christ. In 1 Corinthians 15:22, once again we read: "in Adam all died…" Not some. "in Adam *all* died…" And it says "…in Christ all will be made alive." What they did affected all humanity-each one of us. "Now wait a minute. You say Adam represented the whole human race. What proof do you have that he did?"

"We just read it to you. God said he did.'...in Adam all died...in Christ all live.' God said it. He didn't say a few here and a few there. He said, "...in Adam all died..." All means everybody. Nobody is excluded. All died." There's no argument.

He was humanity's representative, wasn't he? And if, in Jesus, all were made alive, then He must have represented the whole human race. These are the only two men in the Bible who represent the whole human race. We can't find any other text which speaks about someone else taking the position of representing the whole human race, only Jesus and Adam.

If Adam represented all of us, we came out of Adam and whether we like it or not, we picked up his characteristics and traits. And so, the humans of the world are merely acting like their father. The world came out of Adam, who affected every single one of them. In other words, they came out of the one who represented them, and he most assuredly had an effect on every one of them. Just look around and you'll see Adam at work, killing, causing strife, etc.

We are speaking about a "representative." It is important that we understand this word. The dictionary defines a *representative* as "someone who stands in for someone else to serve as an official delegate or agent." Adam stood for all of humanity. He represented all of us. That's why 1 Corinthians 15:22 says, "For as in Adam all die...". In other words, Adam's sin became our sin. Everything he did, we did, so we were held accountable in God's eyes.

Look at what the *Living Bible* says about 1 Corinthians 15:21-22; "Death came into the world because of what one man [Adam] did, and it is because of what this other man [Christ] has done that now there is the resurrection from the dead."

The *Amplified Bible* makes it even clearer: "For just as (because of union of nature) in Adam all people die, so also (by virtue of their union of nature) shall all in Christ be made alive." Notice the expressions in there. The "union of nature." The union of nature with Adam is that all die. The union of nature with Christ is that all are made alive.

We were united in Adam. He was our representative in his willful disobedience against God Almighty. When he sinned against God, because we had union with him, we also sinned against God. Whether you think it's fair or not, that's just the way it is. How many times have you said, "But if I had been there I wouldn't have done that." Really? "Well it's not fair. It's just not fair." Well, I can't help it. That's just the way it is. Through Adam you and I were there. God says, "When Adam sinned, you sinned." Adam was our representative man. We were in Adam.

When we elect representatives, officials in our government, and they vote for a particular law, a piece of legislation to be enacted, they represent all of us. They are, by election, your representatives. They don't always do what you want them to, do they? But nonetheless, you are affected by their decisions and the way they vote. It may not be fair. They may not do what you would have done yourself, but as they gave their representative voice and vote, it affected you either positively or negatively. A representative stands in your place. He is your official delegate. He substitutes for you. He takes your place.

There was such a union of the human race in Adam that it was as though we were in the garden, in the flesh, and it was each of us who sinned against Almighty God. That's the way God sees it. It is just as though we took the very fruit of the tree from Eve as she handed it to Adam. When Adam tasted it, we tasted it. His sin became our sin. In Genesis 3:6, where we read that Eve took the fruit thereof and did eat and gave it also unto her husband and he did eat, we can each just slip our name in there. It was just like you were there. Listen carefully, God doesn't see it any other way. You were there. It was like you took the fruit and tasted it just as Adam and Eve did. God sees you there in Adam. You can say when Eve handed out the fruit, you got it and died with them spiritually. You tasted death with Adam. You were there in the garden in Adam's loins-God saw you there.

Do you realize that Adam committed high treason for us? We had nothing to say about it. If we don't like it, well, there's not a thing we can do about it. He was our representative man. When he sinned and died spiritually, we had the effect of his sin charged to our account. And when he suffered all the effects of the curse, we were also affected by that curse. Man's sin separated him from God. God promised that the day Adam ate of that fruit, he would surely die-not physically, because we know that Adam lived a long time after that-but spiritually (Genesis 2:17). His spirit man was immediately drained of the life of God. His spirit was darkened and alienated from the life of Almighty God. That's spiritual death! Not cessation of life as some think of dying spiritually. Isaiah 59:2 says, "But your iniquities have separated between you and your God..." Adam separated you from God when he sinned.

So, if Adam represented me, then God's life was drained from me also. I died spiritually along with Adam. And I know that's true because the Bible says so. The Bible says that by one man's sin death came upon all (Romans 5:12).

Are you considered part of all? Then you died spiritually when Adam died spiritually because he represented all. So all were affected. Now you've got it.

A positive side of this whole thing is that, "...in Christ shall all be made alive." We were just as much "in Christ" at Calvary as we were "in Adam" in the garden. Christ was the representative of all of mankind. That's what puts us in union with Christ. He was our official representative. He stood in our place. Paul understood this. It shouldn't be difficult for us to understand?

Remember in Galatians 2:20, Paul said, "I am crucified with Christ..." Paul understood it clearly. He is the one who wrote all about identification. "I am crucified *with* Christ..." When Jesus was on that cross as our representative, it was just as though those nails were driven straight into our hands. Now that might be something difficult to understand, but Paul understood it. He said, "*I'm* crucified with Christ..."

How was Christ crucified? He had nails driven into His hands. Paul must have imagined that those nails were driven into his hands also. Just as when Adam tasted the forbidden fruit, we also tasted it, and death entered the human race through our representative man. The Scriptures say that Jesus tasted death *for every man* (Hebrews 2:9).

Now you may have said, "Well, why wasn't I born in Florida, or Texas or some gorgeous place where we never see cold or the snow of winter?" Well, you didn't have a choice. Wherever your mother birthed you, that is the state you were born in. You didn't have a choice, did you? Likewise, you were birthed into whatever state Adam was in. He was in the state of "mortal sin," which simply means he was in the state of spiritual death. And all the results produced by that state of death began immediately to take effect on Adam's life. And because you were in Adam, those same effects will be produced in your life until you meet the One who brings life, the one who can free you from separation *from God* unto life *in God*.

By one man came death: by one man came life. Adam moved from the place of life to the place of sin and death. That's the place we were in when we were born. Well, Jesus came to get us out of that place into a new place called life. We were alienated from the life of God into a darkened position and Jesus came to bring us into a new position, a place called *righteousness*, a place where God's life reigns-where His grace is poured out.

Look at Romans 5:12-19:
Wherefore, as by one man sin entered into the world, and death by sin; and so death passed upon all men, for that all have sinned.

(for until the law sin was in the world: but sin is not imputed
when there is no law
Nevertheless death reigned from Adam to Moses, even over
them that had not sinned after the similitude of Adam's trans-
gression, who is the figure of him that was to come.
But not as the offence, so also is the free gift. For if through
the offence of one many be dead, much more the grace of
God, and the gift by grace, which is by one man, Jesus Christ,
hath abounded unto many.
And not as it was by one that sinned, so is the gift: for the
judgment was by one to condemnation, but the free gift is of
many offences unto justification.
For if by one man's offence death reigned by one; much more
they which receive abundance of grace and of the gift of
righteousness shall reign in life by one, Jesus Christ.)
Therefore as by the offence of one [Adam] judgment came
upon all men to condemnation; even so by the righteousness
of one the free gift came upon all men [that one is Jesus
Christ] unto justification of life.
For as by one man's disobedience [Adam] many were made
sinners, so by the obedience of one [Jesus Christ] shall many
be made righteous.

Notice the expressions one, many, one, many. Notice what this says. By *one*, condemnation came. By *one*, justification of life came unto *many*. One, many. One, all. All, many-they are repeated over and over. One, all. We want you to see the balance in this verse. We are talking about representative men-Adam and Jesus, the two most important men in the entire Bible, the only two who affected all humanity. Now you can understand representation. It is the same as a substitute. One who takes another's place? A stand in.

CHAPTER
5

IT'S ALL YOURS IN CHRIST

Understanding this teaching can make all the difference in whether or not we have a victorious life-the life Jesus stated that we can have. Jesus said that He came that we might have life and have it more abundantly. He wants us to have a full life-a life that experiences the fullness of the blessing of the Gospel of the Lord Jesus Christ! We don't ever want to take lightly what God's Son has done for us. We can consider it a privilege to study about what Jesus obtained for us and what the Bible says is ours. It should be our priority to understand what Jesus did for us and how He wants to use us as His representatives on the earth (II Cor. 5:20).

Sometimes if we look at the negative side of something, we are better able to see the positive aspects of it. Look again, at Romans 5:12-19:

> *Wherefore, as by one man sin entered into the world, and*
> *death by sin; and so death passed upon <u>all men,</u> for that <u>all have sinned:</u>*
> *(For until the law sin was in the world: but sin is not imputed when there*
> *is no law.)*
> *Nevertheless <u>death reigned from Adam to Moses,</u> even over them that had*
> *not sinned after the similitude of Adam's transgression, who is the figure*
> *of him that was to come.*
> *But not as the offence, so also is the free gift. For if through the offence <u>of one many</u>*

be dead, much more the grace of God, and the gift by grace, which is *by one man, Jesus Christ, hath abounded* unto many.

And not as it was by one that sinned, so is the gift: for the judgment was *by one to condemnation,* but the *free gift* is of *many offences unto justification.*

For if by one man's offence death reigned by one; much more they which receive abundance of grace and of the gift of righteousness *shall reign in life by one, Jesus Christ.)*

Therefore as by the offence of one [Adam] judgment came upon *all men* to condemnation; even so *by righteousness of one* [Jesus Christ] the free gift came upon all men

unto justification of life.

For as by one man's disobedience [Adam] many many were made sinners, so by the obedience of one [Jesus Christ] shall many be made righteous.

We must have an understanding of what Jesus Christ did at Calvary's cross. In other words, what was the purpose of Calvary? When we gain an understanding of this, we will see what our identification with Jesus Christ is all about. We must see that Jesus had to identify with the sinner first.

Let's focus on Romans 5:18-19: "Therefore as by the offence of one judgment came upon all men to condemnation; even so by the righteousness of one the free gift came upon all men unto justification of life."

"For as by one man's disobedience many were made sinners, so by the obedience of one shall many be made righteous."

One Affects All

Here we see how the actions of one affects all. And here lies the crux of the whole message. Everyone was affected by one man-either by his obedience or disobedience. Adam was a representative man and what he did affected all of us in a negative way. Jesus was a representative man and what He did affected all of us in a positive way. Paul is stating this over and over again. If one man did this, it affected all. One/all. So Adam and Jesus, as representative men, are the two most important men in Biblical history. They represented humanity in totality.

Verse 18 reveals that under Adam's name, we could write the word "judgment." This came about because of Adam's disobedience. The disobedience of one man, simply because he is a representative man, brought judgment upon every single human being on the face of this earth.

Under the name of Jesus we could put the word "justification." This came about because of Jesus' obedience. The obedience of One, Jesus, brought justification upon all. Again, we want you to see-one brought justification through obedience.

The *Williams translation* of the Bible states: "Through one offense resulted condemnation for all. Just through one act of righteousness resulted right standing for all." Do you see the comparison in what each man did for all humanity? What Adam and Jesus did affected us all-we may not totally understand this, but it's a biblical fact.

The *New English Bible* reads: "The issue of one misdeed was condemnation for all and the issue of one just act is acquittal and life for all." Do you like that translation?

The *Knox* translation says: "One man commits a fault and it brings condemnation upon all. One man makes amends, it brings to all justification." This is another great translation.

All through these translations we see that what Adam did was against us and was negative. It did not bless us. What Jesus did was a blessing for us and was good and positive. We have to know what Adam did. We have to know what Jesus did. They are representative men, and what they did affected every human being who has ever lived on the earth. We need to understand this early in our walk with the Lord. These are fundamental Bible truths.

Judgment Through Adam

Now let's go a step further in understanding the judgment that was upon us because of Adam, our representative man. In simple terms, we are talking about what Adam did and what it brought upon us-doom, condemnation and guilt. We became sin. Isaiah says that sin separates us from our God. All these things became ours because we were identified with Adam.

Remember the definition of what it means "to identify": to make identical, to consider and treat as the same. This is the theme of identification. Have you got this by now?

If we want to know what consequences came upon humanity in general, we look at what came upon Adam. What he got, we got.

But let's not focus entirely upon the consequences Adam brought upon the face of the earth. There was another Man involved here. His name is Jesus, and the same principle applies. What Jesus got at Calvary, we got.

Everything, God gave to Jesus because He went to Calvary's cross, we can have, because Jesus identified with us just as we were identified with Adam.

Blessing Through Jesus

The consequences of Calvary are justification, right standing with God, life, freedom, health, prosperity, success, victory over satan and sin. These are just *some of* the benefits Jesus acquired for us at Calvary's cross. Jesus represented us, so whatever He got, we got. Peace, preservation, wholeness and deliverance are some other benefits. This list is a wonderful reminder of how much more powerful God is over satan's attempt to be powerful.

Look at Romans 5:15: "But not as the offence, so also is the free gift. For if through the offence of one many be dead, much more the grace of God, and the gift by grace, which is by one man, Jesus Christ, hath abounded unto many.

Paul is contrasting these two men. Death came through Adam, but Paul said something greater came through Jesus Christ. In other words, what God did through Jesus was greater than what the devil did through Adam. We can all agree on that point.

The *Williams translation* says: "One offence caused the whole race to die. To a much greater degree, favor and God's gift overflowed for the whole race." Now it is obvious that what God did in Christ is much greater than what satan did in Adam. You can understand that there were no benefits to what satan did. There were absolutely no positive benefits to anybody in the human race. We can all agree with this with no hesitation.

But God surely blessed the entire human race through what Jesus Christ did on Calvary's cross. God purposed Calvary for our benefit and blessing through Jesus Christ. Did you notice we said God purposed Calvary for that reason? *Translators New Testament* states: "One man's sin brought death to all, but God's grace and gifts brought abundant blessings to all." That's awesome, praise God!

Look at Romans 5:16; "And not as it was by one that sinned, so is the gift: for the judgment was by one to condemnation, but the free gift is of many offences unto justification."

Every one of us, without exception, was condemned by one man's actions and ac-quitted by another man's actions. This is an outworking of the grace from God Himself. "By grace…" it says, "you were saved." Again, the word "saved," is *sozo* in Greek. It means <u>health, preservation, deliverance,</u>

wholeness, prosperity and protection. Grace and truth came by Jesus Christ. His grace acquitted you. You are no longer condemned. You have been made free, and His truth will keep you free, as you put your faith in God's truth which is His Word.

We need to be established in the facts of identification. We don't mean just a cursory look or overview. We must become established; because if there's one thing the devil will try to keep from the Church of Jesus Christ it is an understanding of what God did for us in Christ. He does not want us to know this. If he can keep us from understanding this teaching, he'll keep us in a place where we will never see victory. We will never break free from his dominion if we fail to see our identification with Christ.

Maybe this is a small point, but we want you to know that the cults don't like to discuss the Epistles. Anytime they come to your door. They will either talk about the Gospels or quote an Old Testament Scripture. Start talking to them about the Epistles of Paul, and watch how quickly they change the subject. Why? Because, there are some important truths in the Epistles that contradict their beliefs, their unbiblical beliefs.

For example, in the Epistles we find that Jesus Christ is Deity. It is written all over the Epistles.

You would have to be spiritually prejudiced not to see it. So cults would rather quote the Gospels and Old Testament Scripture. There's to much in the Epistles they would rather avoid. Take them to the Epistles and see for yourself.

The Epistles have been written to the Body of Christ. Do you know why cults don't want to hear them? Because they don't belong to the Body of Christ.

You Look Just Like Your Father…

We really don't need the Bible in order to know that Adam is still very much alive in many people today. The Bible confirms it, however. Just look around at people and you can see what they got from Adam. What he got, they got. You can walk up to anyone who is not in Christ and say, "I know who your father is. Your father is Adam."

"Oh, really, how do you know that?"

"Well, just look at the way you act. You act like him. You cheat; you lie; you're sick; you're poor; you're depressed; you're down and out. You look just like your father. Now that I've looked at you, I've seen a spitting image of Adam, and I'm now positive Adam was a representative man. What he got, you got too." Adam walked in spiritual death-he was alive physically, but dead in his spirit.

If this is not enough proof, just turn on the news every night. They will tell you how many people were murdered, raped, beaten, and how many embezzled, stole, lied and cheated today. When we listen to the news, we're convinced that Adam was a representative man. He was the world's big daddy. They might as well have said, "Some more descendants of Adam were hard at work today, cheating, lying, raping and murdering people."

We're positive a lot of our politicians are *in Adam*. They remind us that, in Adam, all men died. Many of our news broadcasters remind us that Adam's death still reigns on this earth in the news media. If that were not true, they would speak truth. But they lie and fabricate and distort. It's one thing to say with much sorrow that the world's father is Adam, but what a sad testimony when we can walk up to a Christian and say, "Is your father still Adam?" The way some Christians behave, you have to wonder if they are not still in Adam. Wouldn't you much rather have people walk up to you and say, "Your father is God, isn't He? You act just like Him-you speak just like Him!"

"Yes, how did you know that? What did you see in me?" "Well, because you're healthy like Him; you're not depressed: you're happy; and you're joyful, just like He is. You are prosperous like Him; yes, you even speak like Him. You look like Him. You walk in love like Him. You live like Him. You think like Him. You forgive like Him. I see Jesus in you. Jesus acted like His father and you act like Jesus."

Many Christians don't have this kind of testimony, but we should. We should be giving evidence of our union in Jesus Christ. When people look at us, they should see Jesus. The most the world will ever see of God is you. Let the Lord Jesus rule and reign as Almighty God in and through you everyday!! It's a shame that so many Christians have not grasped that fact. We think that witnessing is only a banner in the end zone in a football game, stating John 3:16.

You're God's Dream

One time as T.L. Osborne was teaching, he asked, "Do you want to see God's dream?" He said, "Look at me. I'm God's dream."

You may think, "Well, that's pretty prideful, isn't it?" No, not at all. He knows who he is in Christ Jesus. He said, "Here I am. I'm God's dream."

Peter told the lame man at the gate Beautiful, "look at us" (Acts 3:4). Do you know that you're God's dream? You're God's dream for the future of the world. And do you know that the world is not going to know Him except through you? When people tell you they want to see God, say, "Just look at me and you'll see God." How many Christians even dare to think that-let alone say it?

And then someone will say, "I can't say that." That's because you don't know who you are in Christ. When someone says, "I wish God would speak to me, say to that person, "Look at me. I'll talk to you." (That will usually get a good conversation going.) We are God's mouth pieces on the earth. We are His hands extended, because we are His Church!

Should we not be so established in the things of God that people will mistake us for God? We think so. Now don't get religious on me and say, "Nobody was ever mistaken for gods." Oh really? Haven't you read Acts 14:11, where Paul and Barnabas were mistaken for gods? God did a miracle through them. And people came running up to them and said, "The gods have come down among us." God used them to heal a man and the whole town went upside down. They gathered animals to sacrifice to them. They said, "The gods have come down among us."

When was the last time people mistook you for God? When was the last time you saw somebody sacrificing some animals for you? You'd have to rush out there and say, "I'm not God. Put out that fire. Put down that knife. Don't kill that animal!" You ought to have a difficult time convincing them that you are not God.

Paul and Barnabas had this happen to them, and it took them quite a while to convince the people that they weren't gods. Barnabas was called Jupiter: Paul was called Mercury. Can you imagine how much God was evidenced in their lives, that people thought they were gods come down from Heaven? Wow! How's your life?

We want our lives to so imitate God-we're talking about the eternal being, the eternal God-in such a manner that it would take us a couple of hours to convince people to the contrary. No, neither of us is Jesus, but we should talk and act just like Him. Don't you want people to mistake you for Jesus so that you would have to convince them you're not Him?

"You're not Jesus? I thought you were. You talk just like Him. You act just like Him. You even think like Him, because the words coming out of your mouth are so holy and full of love." How many Christians have that kind of testimony? How many even come near that? What's your testimony like? Just ask your neighbor he'll tell you.

Do you remember the story of Smith Wigglesworth when he was traveling on a train one time? The train made a stop at the station, and he got out to refresh himself in the bathroom. As he came walking out of the bathroom, all of a sudden a man confronted him, fell to his knees and cried out, "You convict me of my sin." All he did was go into the bathroom to refresh himself. Going to the bathroom isn't an act of spirituality, is it? Yet, when he came out, a man fell to his knees totally convicted of his sins. Jesus must have been exuding from Smith Wigglesworth, even though he never said a word. When was the last time that happened to anyone you know?

Being "In" Christ Means What?

Listen, this doesn't happen just because you try to act like Jesus. We have to understand what it's like to be "in" Jesus. When we are *in* Jesus, we will <u>think</u> like Him, <u>act</u> like Him, <u>talk</u> like Him, <u>live</u> like Him; and it will come naturally to us. We won't have to act. Most of us live out of a spiritual façade. Have you ever noticed that? Our spirit man hasn't even begun to experience the life of Jesus Christ, but we force our outward man to act like Jesus. When we have Jesus established in our lives, we are not going to even have to try to be like Jesus, because everything we say, do and think is going to be just like Him. Paul prayed for Jesus, who lived in the Galatian Christians, to be formed or demonstrated in every area of their lives (Galatians 4:19). To be normal is to be like Jesus. Everything else is abnormal.

If you catch hold of what follows, you are going to be set free. When we were *in Adam*, what belonged to us? <u>Death, sickness, poverty, fear, torment, oppression, lack and defeat,</u> everything the curse offered. Everything the law of sin and death produced; curses (sickness, depression and doom): we were utterly defeated *in Adam*. God saw us as being identical to Adam and considered and treated us the same. In Adam, we were helpless and hopeless.

When you were in Adam did you find it difficult to get worried, sick and oppressed? Did you have to get up each day and say, "I'm going to believe to feel miserable today? I'm believing for a good upset stomach; I'm just believing for a good whopper of a headache today. Body you will be sick today." Did you have to do all that to be sick? No, it just came on you whether you wanted it or not, didn't it? How about being broke? Did you ever have to work at having lack in your life? No, when you were in Adam, all he had was automatically yours. You didn't have to go to a seminar to learn how to be sick.

Who are you in now? You are in Jesus Christ. What is yours, now that you are in Jesus Christ? <u>Life, peace, health, riches, deliverance, success, victory, justification, wisdom, righteousness, prosperity</u>-everything that's under what the Bible calls the Law of the Spirit of Life in Christ Jesus. The <u>Law of the Spirit of Life in Christ Jesus</u> *has* (past tense) made me free from the Law of Sin and Death (Romans 8:1,2). So, if all these things are ours in Christ Jesus, why is it so hard to receive them? Why do we fast, pray and go to seminars hoping God might hear our desperate pleas for these things?

When we were in Adam, they just came along so easily. No sweat, no seminars, no praying or fasting. If healing is ours in Christ, why do we have to work and struggle and just maybe get healed? What Adam offered just showed up, didn't it? With no struggle. But in Christ, we sweat; fuss, cry and maybe once in a blue moon, we get something. Is not the Law of the Spirit of Life in Christ Jesus more powerful than the Law of Sin and Death? In other words, isn't what God did in Jesus more powerful than what satan did in Adam? Emphatically YES!!

The Apostle Peter said, "I have given you all things that pertain unto life and godliness, "Yet, even though it is ours, we still beg, fuss and cry for it. Jesus said, "I have come that you might have life and have it more abundantly." Yet, how many of us are living in abundance? How many have victory over sin and satan?

When we were in Adam, we never had to listen to any tape to get sick.

We didn't have to read any book to get broke. We never had to confess all day to get a headache. And above all, we never had to go to a depression seminar to get depressed. We were just simply "in Adam." What was his was automatically ours. We were simply identified with Him.

Shouldn't it be as easy to receive all that's ours in Christ as it was to receive all that was ours in Adam? Can we not identify as easily with Christ?

"Well, I thought I had to use faith to get it."

Already Yours

No, faith is not required to get something that is already yours. Faith is used to bring those things into manifestation in the natural realm, but they are <u>already yours.</u> Faith is not to get God to give you something that has already been given, paid for and taken care of. <u>Faith is believing that what God has said is true. And as long as you believe His Word and act as if it is true, it will come to pass for you.</u> Faith means you don't accept anything contradictory to what God has said. Faith is really simple when you truly understand it- God made faith simple; after all, we are required to live by it.

You're identified with Christ. What He got when He rose from the dead, you got also. The problem is, we haven't chosen to believe it, or maybe we have never been taught what is ours in Christ. If you haven't been taught, you don't understand that these things are already yours by virtue of the fact that Jesus already paid the price for them, and you are now in Christ.

The devil is going to keep blinders on you. He will try to make you deaf, dumb and blind to what is yours in Christ. He is going to convince you day after day that God's Word doesn't mean what it says; He did it back there in the garden, didn't he? God said to Adam and Eve, "It's all yours" Now was God lying or was God telling the truth? He said, "There's only one thing I don't want you to do. Just don't eat of one tree in the garden. Everything is yours." Then the devil came along and began to use his intelligence against God's Word. He talked Eve right out of what was hers. Go back and read the first couple of chapters of Genesis.

Are you beginning to see how important it is to understand being in Adam and being in Christ? Both are representative men and we can be identified with both. We'd rather identify with Christ.

What is The Problem?

Now that you've made a switch. Now that you're in Christ. We have some questions for you. Why do you sweat? Why do you toil? Why do you struggle and struggle to have what Jesus said is already yours? We didn't operate that way in Adam. Why do we operate that way in Christ? *Because we don't believe what the Bible says.* We can give no other explanation. We don't believe what the Bible says, even though God never lies.

Ephesians 1:3 states, "…Jesus Christ, who <u>hath</u> blessed us with all spiritual blessings in heavenly places <u>in Christ…</u>" Has blessed. He says, "They've already been given to you, every one of them." Past tense. They're yours paid for by the blood of Jesus. Why isn't the body of Christ walking in every spiritual blessing in heavenly places in Christ Jesus, if God says, "I have given them to you'? It is because we don't understand our identification with Jesus, or we don't believe it.

The Scripture says when you understand something the devil can't take it from you. Meditate in the Epistles. Every place you see "with Christ," "in Christ," by Christ," he's talking about you. Christ didn't do anything for

Himself. He did it all for you. You know it must be quite a disappointment to be the One who died such a horrendous death on the cross and paid such a horrendous price and not even one-third of the Body of Christ appropriates what was paid for.

Jesus, sitting on His throne, must be thinking, "Did I die in vain? Don't they understand what I did? Don't they understand what's theirs in Me? Why won't they believe my Word?"

Study Galatians 2:20:"I am crucified with Christ: nevertheless, I live; yet not I, but Christ liveth in me: and the life which I now live in the flesh I live by the faith of the Son of God, who loved me, and gave himself for me."

Make A Firm Commitment

Learn that Jesus Christ became a curse for you (past tense) that the blessing of Abraham might come upon the Gentiles. Study how He bore our sicknesses and carried our diseases and by His stripes we were healed (past tense). There's one thing that we must do in order to have these benefits operating in our lives and that is to make a firm commitment. It's going to have to be an irrevocable commitment.

You commit yourself, in faith, to believe God's Word and trusting Him no matter how the circumstances look. You must constantly put a guard on your lips-you must watch what you say because you can be snared by the words of your mouth, taken captive by the words of your lips. Proverbs 6:2 states:" Thou art snared with the words of thy mouth, thou are taken with the words of thy mouth."

This means that every day, we have to get up and make statements like this: "I am in Christ Jesus. I am no longer in Adam. I have been translated out of the power of darkness, and I am in the kingdom of Light, the kingdom of God's dear Son. Satan, you have no dominion over me anymore. I am seated in heavenly places in Christ. I rule in this life with Jesus Christ. I can do all things through Christ who strengthens me." These are things all of us should say.

Now when you first begin to do this, you will have some opposition from the devil. He is going to try to oppose you and counter everything you declare as the truth of God's Word. So be ready. If you have a symptom in your body or a pain, he's going to try to constantly keep your mind on that pain. He's going to bombard you from morning to night so that your focus is consistently on the pain rather than on what God's Word says. God's Word says He, Himself, bore your pains. So, say what God's Word says and not what your symptoms are screaming out to you.

Speak The Word

Now there can be no identification without substitution. We are going to talk about the substitutionary work of the Lord Jesus Christ. He was your substitute, and therefore He can identify with you. Therefore you can identify with Him. He took your pain that you could have His health. Do you see the exchange?

The devil is going to come along and say, "Well it works for everybody *but you*. You see, you have such pain that even God can't remove it." Jonah called them lying vanities.

But every time the devil brings it up, say, "I cast that thought down as a vain imagination. It is contrary to what the Word of God says, therefore I choose to believe what the Word says." You may not fully believe it yourself but say it anyway. He does not know whether you believe it or not.

Satan is not a mind reader. He cannot read your mind. Only God can do that. Satan is a mastermind of psychology though, so never underestimate him. He watches your reactions and actions. He puts something in front of you to see if you bite for it or if you will stand up and say, "I don't fall for that. I'm not under your dominion anymore. Take your hands off me."

And don't quote scriptures flippantly at the devil. Instead, as you quote them, *think* about what you say. And when you say it out of your mouth, God says, "...that whosoever shall say unto this mountain, be thou removed, and be thou cast into the sea; and shall not doubt in his heart, but shall believe that those things which he saith shall come to pass; he shall have whatsoever he saith," (Mark 11:23). We ought to put that scripture deep into our spirit man.

But you have to keep saying it. You can't say today, "Oh, Jesus bore my sicknesses" and tomorrow, when the pain gets worse say, "Oh, that pain! I guess it didn't work. I guess I'm not healed." You just nullified everything you said the day before. You know why? The devil is right there, and he'll intensify the pain even more. The next day when you get up and the pain is worse, you'll say, "I believe I'm healed, devil. The Word says Jesus bore my sicknesses, bore my distresses, bore my pain. He was my substitute. He identified with my pain, so I can identify with His health. That's what the Bible says, devil." And keep saying it. You need to believe it more than the devil does! He must believe the Word to some degree. Or why would he fight it so much? He doesn't want you to receive what God has promised to you.

The devil comes along and says, "Yeah, but you see your circumstances are getting worse and that pain is going to be there for a long time. You're going to wait too long and it's going to be too late. The doctors are not going to be able to help you."

Are you getting the picture? Immediately you respond: "That's a vain imagination. That's vain reasoning. The Word says that by Jesus' Stripes I am healed!! I will not change my testimony today. It is the same as it was yesterday. It will be the same tomorrow."

Do you think you'll discourage him after a while? You sure will. Don't be moved by what you see or feel. Only be moved by what the Word says. Now we're not going to tell you that this is easy. It can be very difficult, especially if the devil has an all-out attack on you and wants to keep you defeated. He wants to keep you thinking that he has dominion over you. He's going to hit you with every thought, one after the other-bang, bang, bang. You better be ready with what is written. No matter what he says, your reply must be, "It is written." Then quote whatever scripture applies to your particular circumstance.

Be strong. Be consistent. Hold fast to your confidence for He who has promised will fulfill it (Hebrews 10:23). He's faithful. God is not a man that He would lie. The Word of God says, "There is no Word of God without power in it" (Luke 1:37). He has put His power in the Word. Consistently hold fast to it; declare what He says; proclaim it boldly; and say, "This is mine in Christ Jesus. Devil, let go of my body; let go of my finances!" When the devil gets on your case, keep saying, "But I'm influenced only by the Word. I'm looking to Calvary. He who looketh shall live. I keep looking at Calvary. I don't care what you say, devil. You're a liar. You've been a liar from the beginning. You think I'm going to believe you over my God? My God is telling the truth. I'm standing on the truth that's setting me free right now."

We're just telling you what you have to do. We're not saying it's easy. In fact, it's difficult sometimes. You have to confess the Word when you're at the office, at home and even in the shower. Constantly affirm what you believe in the Word to the Lord (Isaiah 43:26). Keep rehearsing it so it keeps going in you. You'll hear it, gain faith, and then act on it. Keep running it through your mind, constantly meditating, saying, God I believe Your Son died for my sin. He took my sin. I don't have it anymore. He took my guilt. I don't want it. I won't have any guilt."

Have you ever noticed when you sin and go to the Lord and confess your sin, how the devil tries to keep guilt on you? Oh, if you could get a hold of the Word. If you could just say "It is written in the Word of God, if I confess my sin…"

Now the devil will tell you, "Yes, but you went over the limit. You did it too many times." He'll lie to you. But the Word of the Lord lets me know that God's forgiveness is unlimited. Get back up and say "I'm sorry." Confess it. It's sin. Repent! Turn around and start walking in fellowship with God. He says, "I'm faithful and just to forgive you your sins and cleanse you from all unrighteousness" (I John 1:9).

"Thank You, Lord." Now go on.

The devil says, "You're going to go to church tonight? Look what you did today."

You reply, "What do you mean, what I did today? What are you talking about? Are you lying to me again? It's already under the blood. It has been forgiven. So shut your mouth, satan. I am not going to be guilty. I don't care what you say. My God forgave me. I'm going on. That's it."

That's what you have to do with everything and then just walk away and forget it. Don't be standing there saying, "Oh, I'm guilty. I did this. God must be mad at me." He's not mad at you. Do you understand? We can't find a place in Scripture where it says God is mad at us. We're in Christ. If He's mad at us, He's mad at Christ. He's considering us the same as Jesus.

Remember to identify means to make identical. Everything God thinks of Jesus, He thinks of you. Everything God has done for Jesus, He's done for you. The reason we don't get this is because we don't believe Him.

Why could T.L. Osborne say, "You want to see God's dream-you're looking at him"? He knew who he was in Christ. When you get a hold of this, you're going to stand up and kick that devil out. Once and for all you're going to have dominion over him and he's going to stop having dominion over you.

CHAPTER

6

THE FIRST ADAM AND THE LAST ADAM

Adam brought the effect of the curse, which brought alienation from God. In other words, the life of God was no longer in Adam. Once he disobeyed God, he experienced condemnation, guilt, disease, sickness and poverty. Adam brought these troubles upon the whole human race simply because he was a representative man. Sickness, disease, etc., are not part of God's Kingdom.

Now Jesus, also a representative man, took us out from underneath the effects of the curse and brought us back into right relationship with His father. He gave us peace with God, right standing, righteousness and all the blessings of the new covenant, and there is no longer condemnation or guilt. Through Jesus, we can enjoy what the Kingdom offers.

So, on one side of the spectrum we have Adam who brought judgment and all the effects of the curse, which leaves the world in its present deplorable state. But Jesus came along and all who will believe on Him will receive peace with God, righteousness from God and will be taken out from the effects of the curse. That, in part, is what salvation is all about.

Now in Christ Jesus through the new birth, we should begin to resemble Jesus, act like Jesus, speak like Jesus, and think like Jesus. We should now be able to give evidence that we are in union with Christ. And God is telling us that since we are in union with Christ, He expects us to bear fruit (John 15:1-8).

Through the new birth, you belong to the Lord Jesus Christ. The Scriptures say you've been bought with a price. Your body belongs to the Lord Jesus Christ. You are no longer in Adam: you are now in Christ. The Bible says that where sin abounded, grace abounded much more! What God did for us in Christ was far greater than what the devil did to us in Adam (Romans 5:15-21)! Please grasp this.

So why do we struggle for the things Jesus Christ bought and paid for at the cross? If they're ours, because we're in Christ, why are we struggling for them? Shouldn't they just be part of our lives?

"Why am I having such a hard time? You know I might pray for two weeks and fast for two weeks and just maybe if I meditate long enough, I might get my healing." Is this the way God wants your life to be lived out?

Why do we have to do this? When we were in Adam, we didn't sweat it. We went through half our lives being sick, poor, broke and depressed and never even thought about it. It was just automatically part of us because we were in Adam.

Why can't we just simply say, "Now I'm in Christ. I'm healthy, wealthy, wise, and I will never have a depressed day again." Doesn't the Word say that God wishes above all things for us to prosper and be in health even as our soul prospers (3 John 2)?

You see, the world flows negatively compared to the Kingdom of God. As Christians, we are living in the world but we are not part of it. Everything is already finished and accomplished for us through Christ at Calvary. But we have an enemy (the devil) who wants to stop us from fulfilling God's calling on our lives and experiencing all of the blessings of the Gospel. We have to step out with our faith in God and resist the devil and expect to walk in the fullness of our completion in Christ! God wants to use us in establishing His perfect will in Heaven on the Earth (Mathew 16:18,19)!!

A Rest In Christ

Hebrews 4:1 says, "Let us therefore fear, lest, a promise being left us of entering his rest, any of you should seem to come short of it." Look at the promises of God-what do they offer us as believers?

Now what he's talking about here is a rest, R-E-S-T, in Christ. Jesus does not want us going through our lives struggling, sweating, toiling, knocking ourselves out all day *for something that is already ours.*

Hebrews 4:2: "For unto us was the gospel preached…"

The Gospel is good news. The Gospel has been preached to us concerning the death, burial and resurrection of the Lord Jesus Christ. It is the crux and foundation of Christianity. When you understand about the cross of Jesus Christ and what took place at the cross, then you can enter into that rest. It goes further.

> *For we which have believed do enter into rest, as he said, As I have sworn in my wrath, if they shall enter into my rest: although the works were finished from the foundation of the world.*
> *For he spake in a certain place of the seventh day on this wise, and God did rest the seventh day from all his works. And in this place again, If thy shall enter into my rest. Seeing therefore it remaineth that some must enter therein, and they to whom it was first preached entered not in Because of <u>unbelief</u>, (Hebrews 4:3-6).*

Now here's where we have to take an account of ourselves. Are we not receiving what God's Son already paid for because of our unbelief? It must be, because God said so. You see, so many are struggling, trying to get something that God has already paid for, and they haven't stepped into the rest and said, "It's mine because God says so." The reason must be <u>unbelief.</u>

Someone may say, "How dare you say that I am in unbelief." We are not saying it. We just read it. God is saying it. We're just the messengers. We have to be honest enough to admit if we don't have enough belief. Faith can be developed. Faith comes or is developed by hearing the Word of God (Romans 10:17).

He's very willing to help us develop our faith and have a better understanding of His Word, if we would just ask. There are times when we must stop our spiritual pretenses. The first step into God's rest is honesty.

Verse 7: "Again, he limiteth a certain day, saying in David, Today, after so long a time; as it is said, today if ye will hear his voice, harden not your hearts."

He's first talking about unbelief and now He says you've hardened your hearts. Don't harden your hearts. Someone else may say, "Well, I don't believe in that faith stuff. I don't believe in healing for today." This person has hardened his heart. How do you expect God to get to you if you have a hard heart? He can't do it.

He's not going to violate your free will, force His way and say, "Well whether you believe it or not, it's true. Here. Here's your healing." No, you're not going to get it that way. He says you must believe Him. He says, "... Today if ye will hear his voice, harden not your hearts."

Verse 8-10: "For if Joshua had given them rest, then would he not afterward have spoken of another day."

"There remaineth therefore a rest to the people of God."

"There is a rest God wants us to have. "For he that is entered into his rest, he also hath ceased from his own works, as God did from his," (Hebrews 4:10)

If you're in God's rest, you won't be saying, "I don't know what to do to be healed. I hope that God will heal me." God says, "I've already done it. Just walk in, sit down and cease from your labors. Start believing what God says." Verses 11-14:

> Let us labour therefore to enter into that rest, lest any man fall
> after the same example of unbelief.
> For the Word of God is quick, and powerful, and sharper than any two-edged
> sword, piercing even to the dividing asunder of the soul and spirit, and of the
> joints and marrow, and is a discerner of thoughts and the intents of the heart.
> Neither is there any creature that is not manifest in his sight: but all things are
> naked and opened unto the eyes of him with whom we have to do.
> Seeing then that we have a great high priest, that is passed into heavens,
> Jesus the Son of God let us hold fast our profession [which is confession].

God is saying, "Just simply take My Word and confess that you believe it. If you believe in your heart what I've said in my Word, then say it." Faith is not complex. You and I decide what we are going to believe, and we believe it (Mark 11:23)

Say, "I believe it: that's what you said. It can't be a lie, God. You said it. I believe it." Say it out of your mouth. "God, I believe it." The Greek word for "profession" which is the same as the word, "confession," is *homologeo*-which simply means, "To say the same as," meaning that you say what God says. The Lord Jesus said that if you will sow or plant your faith like a seed, by saying, then nothing will be impossible to you (Mathew 17:20).

This is a good way to start your day. Wake up and first of all worship and praise the Lord. Then declare some things." I'm the righteousness of God in Christ Jesus and I have no condemnation (Romans 8:1; II Cor. 5:21).

Devil, you are defeated! I believe I have dominion over you because God said so. His Son bought that for me. Your head is crushed under the heals of my feet (Ephesians 1:17-23; 2:4-7)!" God has given me His name. So I use the name of Jesus.

"Father, I submit my will to your will. I'm here to be used as an earthen vessel for the excellence of your power to flow through (II Cor. 4:7). I can do all things through Christ who strengthens me today.

Father, I believe what Your Word says- I'm a new creation in Christ Jesus. I have been redeemed from the curse of the law, Jesus having been made a curse for me. As it is written, 'Cursed is everyone that hangeth on the tree. that the blessing of Abraham might come upon the Gentiles in Jesus Christ.' Therefore, since I'm in Jesus Christ, I have all the blessings of Abraham, Thank You, Lord. I'm filled with the Holy Spirit and I live by faith."

Then you just simply rest. You've made your confession of what you believe in your heart. You rest. Now you don't have to say, "Man, I wonder if it's going to happen today. I think I better confess it about 20 more times and maybe it will happen." No, your confession isn't to *make* it happen. Your confession is in the fact that it has already happened, and you believe it. God said it. You see, you're not in the devil anymore. You're in Christ Jesus. You've transferred kingdoms. You used to be in the kingdom of darkness, the devil's quarter, but now you're in the Kingdom of Light, in Jesus' quarter. You abide in Jesus and His words abide in you (John 15:7).

Jesus said in His Word that He would never leave me nor forsake me. He said, "All that call upon the name of the Lord shall be delivered." Tell the Lord what you believe in your heart, and let the devil hear it too. Say to him, "I'm off limits to you. You know why, devil? I've been bought with a price by the blood of the Lamb. He owns me, not you. You put your hand on me today; you're touching the apple of God's eye. If you touch me, you're going to answer to Him. I belong to Him."

God says, "Whatsoever you say you shall have if you don't doubt in your heart, but believe in your heart those things which you say shall come to pass (Mark 11:23).

Know Where You Are

You are in Christ, if you are a born-again Christian. That's a fact. There's no condemnation on you anymore, no more guilt. You should not be depressed anymore. You should not be sick anymore. We're just stating some of the things that should not operate in our lives, if we understand what it means to be in Christ. Yes, the devil will still come against you with these things, but now you have the right and the power as a child of God to run these things out of your life in Jesus Name!

First Corinthians 15:45: "And so it is written, the first man Adam was made a living soul; the last Adam was made a quickening spirit."

Verse 47: "The first man is of the earth, earthy: the second man is the Lord from heaven."

Most Christians have not seen this in the Word, because it is often misquoted. Notice here that Jesus is referred to as the second Man and the last Adam. But nowhere in the Word of God is Jesus ever called the second Adam. You may have heard preachers say that Jesus is the second Adam. You may have yourself referred to Jesus as the second Adam. But there is no reference to Jesus being the second Adam throughout the pages of the Bible.

The Bible calls Jesus the *last* Adam and the *second* Man. You see, if God called Jesus the second Adam, our minds can conceive of a third Adam, a fourth, a fifth, even a hundredth Adam, etc. What that intimates is that Jesus did not do a complete job; that another Adam must come down the road someday and pick up where Jesus left off. But Jesus is not the second Adam. He's the last Adam. God called Jesus the last Adam, and He had a reason for calling Him this. God is saying that this second Man, this last Adam, is all we will ever need. What Jesus did on the cross was perfect, a completed eternal work of God. No one else and nothing else is ever going to be required, my friends. Nothing. Our redemption is complete in Christ (Hebrews 9:12).

What this personally means to each of us is that through our faith in Jesus Christ, we are eternally redeemed! We will not need anybody else to do anything else. For example, 1,000 years from now, when all of us are in Heaven, we're not going to hear a voice come over a loudspeaker and announce, "One thousand years are up. The blood of Jesus has just lost all its power. You all must go back to earth. I have to try you all over again to see if you're going to be obedient. We're going to release the devil to work on you again to see how you will do this time."

You're not going to hear that. One hundred million years from now the blood of Jesus Christ is going to be just as efficacious as it was 2,000 years ago. It will never lose its power. We're never going to need another Adam. Jesus is the last Adam.

Now verse 47 tells us that Jesus is the second Man. He is the second Man to father a new race. He is the father of a new creation, a creation that never before existed. Now keep in mind our topic: "Identification." We said the two most important men in the Bible were Adam and Jesus. They are representative men. They both represented all of mankind. And so as a representative man, Jesus was used of God to father an entirely new race, a new creation, a race of new creatures, creatures who never existed before.

The first Adam fathered a race of dead people, alienated from the life of God. A doomed race under the effects of the curse and under satanic control. A wanting and unsuccessful race. A defeated race of human beings. That was what we were like in Adam. Oh, but the second Man brought forth a new creation. A race full of life with the potential to obtain the highest success spiritually, soulishly, bodily and financially. A group of new people reconciled to God, redeemed from the effects of the curse, full of God's life, full of faith and hope. A race that could genuinely represent God to a dying world, and give it a hope that it never had.

This is what God sent Jesus to the cross for. So that we could be new creatures in Christ. So each of us could go to the world, that's filled with darkness and say, "Here I am, a representative, a presentation of what God is like. Look at me. Do you want to hear God talk? Listen to what I say. I talk just like Him." We re-present Jesus to the world. Now, don't get religious on us and think that's blasphemy. This is Bible.

Remember in the last chapter we said that Paul and Barnabas were mistaken for Gods? Shouldn't people be beating a path to our doors saying, "I see the light shining right out of your house. You've got to be someone special"?

And we reply, "Come on in. I represent Jesus."

Now you're beginning to see the importance of being in Christ versus being in Adam. Now let us say it this way: Adam was the first to experience the new birth. However, he experienced it in reverse or in the negative, so to speak. He was born again into death. Jesus was the first to be born again into life.

Jesus, Our Substitute

Now you say, "Why did Jesus have to be born again?" If Jesus was our substitute, and indeed He was, He took our place, didn't He? As such, He became what? Sin. "He who knew no sin became sin for us." So when Jesus became sin, He was alienated from the life of God. He bore the entire effects of the curse on Himself for us. When He did that, God identified Jesus with all of us. We became identical, and God considered and treated Jesus the same as He would have treated us in Adam.

Jesus while He was on the cross, asked the Father: "Why have You forsaken Me?"

The Father replied, "Because You are now identified with Adam's race. You are now sin, and I had to turn My back on You. I'm going to walk away from You. You no longer have My life flowing into You and in you."

If Jesus is identical with us, then God, being just, must consider and treat Jesus exactly the same as He would treat us if we were in Adam.

Remember, "To identify" is to make identical, to consider and treat as the same. Now Jesus had to be judged. If sin were on Jesus, He had to be judged. What was the verdict? Guilty, just like God judged us. God said, "Jesus, You're condemned because, you see, I had to treat Adam that way when Adam disobeyed Me. I said, 'Adam, you're condemned.' Now you're taking the place of the human race and so I say you're condemned. You're being judged. You have to go through everything that every human being would have to go through."

Think about it now. When Adam disobeyed God, what did God say to him? "Get out of this garden. I can't look at you anymore. You are sin. You are guilty and condemned. You must go to the place called Hell for what you've just done." And all of us who were in Adam received exactly the same punishment. It was like God saying, "In you, Adam, every man, woman and child who will come on the face of this earth is judged guilty and condemned. Every single one of them deserves Hell."

Jesus then says to God, "Father, I'll be the substitute for the human race. Let me stand in for all mankind."

The Father replies, "Good, this is the only way these people are going to be restored back to Me."

So Jesus had to identify with us in *every single facet* of our lives. Nothing could be left out. Everything God said that was due Adam, was put upon Jesus. God says, "You're alienated from My life, Jesus. You are going to be made poor. And because you have been made sin, you are going to be made sickness, Jesus. Every sickness and disease, all the effects of the curse, I'm placing on You as the substitute for the entire human race. Listen carefully! You can't leave anything out or it won't be a complete redemption."

So Jesus took our place. Jesus took your place. He identified with all of us. And because He was our substitute, we can now identify with Jesus in His resurrection power. A person cannot understand identification with the mind. It is a spiritual subject. We have to get a revelation in our spirits and have our minds renewed in order to understand what our spirits have already received as a revelation.

You see, your mind, apart from a spiritual revelation, is going to say, "This doesn't make sense to me. Are you trying to tell me that we were in a man who lived 6,000 years ago? That doesn't make sense." Again, that's what our minds tell us-but what does God tell us in His Word?

Does it make sense in God's Word where it says He loved you from the foundation of the world? God loved something that didn't even exist. Does that make sense to you? It probably doesn't, but because God said it, it's true. He did love you from the foundation of the world. And when God says you were in Adam, even though you didn't exist, then it must be true even though you can't understand it with your mind. Just believe what God says and not what your mind compiles.

Defining Representation

The Bible was not written to keep you in a quandary all of your life. In the *Living Bible*, Hebrews 7:1 states,

> *This Melchizedek was king of the city of Salem, and also a priest of the Most High God. When Abraham was returning home after winning a great battle against many kings, Melchizedek met him and blessed him; then Abraham took a tenth of all he had won in the battle and gave it to Melchizedek.*
> *Melchizedek's name means **Justice**, so he is the King of Justice; and he is also the King of Peace because of the name of his city Salem, which means **Peace**. Melchizedek had no father or mother and there is no record of any of his ancestors. He was never born and he never died but his life is like that of the son of God—a priest forever.*
> *See then how great this Melchizedek is:*
> *Even Abraham, the first and most honored of all God's chosen people, gave Melchizedek a tenth of the spoils he took from the kings that he had been fighting.*
> *One could understand why Abraham would do this if Melchizedek had been a Jewish priest, for later on, God's people were required by law to give gifts to help their priest because the priests were their relatives. But Melchizedek was not a relative, and yet Abraham paid him.*
> *Melchizedek placed a blessing upon mighty Abraham, and as everyone knows, a person who has the power to bless is always greater than the person he blesses.*

*The Jewish Priests, though mortal, received tithes; but we are
told that Melchizedek lives on.
One might even say that Levi himself (the ancestor of all Jewish
Priests, of all who received tithes) paid tithes to Melchizedek through
Abraham. For although Levi wasn't born yet, the seed from which
he came was in Abraham when Abraham paid the tithe to Melchizedek.*

When Abraham met Melchizedek, the tribe of Levi was not yet born. But when Abraham paid tithes to Melchizedek, in a spiritual sense, God wrote in the record book of the tribe of Levi that they themselves had paid tithes to Melchizedek.

A good question to ask God right here is: "Lord, if there were only two men out there,

Melchizedek and Abraham, how did you figure that when Abraham paid the tithe to him, the tribe of Levi did the same?" Good question to ask the Lord. They didn't even exist then.

How did that happen? What would God's answer be?

"I know you couldn't see the tribe of Levi," He might say, "but they were there in Abraham because they came out of the loins of Abraham. Abraham's actions affected them."

Even though the tribe of Levi was not physically present, God considered them to be so real that it was just as though they walked up to Melchizedek and handed him the tithe.

God saw it that way.

The *English Bible* says, "One could even say that Melchizedek received ten percent from Levi through Abraham because when Melchizedek met Abraham, Levi was still in Abraham's body."

Abraham was, in God's eyes, a representative man when He paid tithes; even though the tribe of Levi was not in existence at that point.

Someone might say, "That doesn't seem real to me." It was real to God. He gave them credit for the tithe. He actually recorded it as a credit. Representation, friends, is real.

We need to accept biblical truths.

When your representative goes to Washington on your behalf and votes, it's like you are there in him, casting a vote for yourself. Let's take this out of the spiritual realm and put it in a natural setting. We'll use your great, great-grandfather. Let's say that he died physically when he was ten years old. Would you be here today? No. Why not? Because you would have died in him. Do you see it! That's reality. If he had died then, even though you were not physically alive, you would have died with him, because you were in your great, great grandfather's loins. You didn't have a choice.

You were in him. You would have never been born.

What if your great, great-grandfather was aborted in his mother's womb in her second trimester. Would you be here today? No. Why not? Because you would have been aborted with him. He was your representative. You participated with him in his death. Both you and he suffered the consequences of his mother's action. As he was murdered in the womb, so were your grandfather, your father and you.

Let's go back further. If your fiftieth great-grandfather took his own life by suicide, would you be here today? No, because you were in him. When he died, you died. It doesn't matter how far we go back in your family tree-to your 100th, 200th great-grandfather. If he died back then, you died in him and wouldn't exist today. When you are dealing with representative people, time and place make no difference.

Do you remember Romans 5? One died-all died. In the great, great-grandfather scenario, when he died would your next-door neighbor have died also? No. Why not? Because your neighbor wasn't in your great, great-grandfather. Only those he represented would have been affected by his actions.

Let's go all the way back to Adam. He lived about 6,000 years ago. What if Adam had physically died the moment after God created him?

Would you be here today? No. Why not? Because you were in Adam. Oh, but your neighbors would be here, right? No, because they would be in Adam. Adam was a representative man. To find out just how many would have died, find out just how many he represented.

If he represented all, as the Scripture says, then all would have died. And if you can understand this concept of a representative man, then Romans 3:23 is easy to understand: "All have sinned and come short of the glory of God." If Adam came short of the glory of God. All sinned when he sinned. Well, how can God put this on all of us because one man fell? Because the one man who fell was our representative man.

Romans 5:12 says, "Wherefore, as by one man sin entered into the world, and death by sin; and so death passed upon all men, for that all have sinned."

Jesus and Adam were the two most important men who ever lived in history. Why? Simply because they're representative men. What happened to Adam happened to you. What happened to Christ can happen to you, if you get in Christ. As your substitute, Christ identified with you.

If you were dead in Adam, then Christ had to take your sin and He became dead in Adam. That means He had to be revived, just like you had to be revived. If Christ were revived, and you're in Christ, then you were revived with Christ, weren't you?

Who are you *in* right now? Christ went upon the cross as your substitute. He identified with you and took the curse on Himself. You are in Christ. You identify with Him. You both were cursed but now He said, "I'm going to take your place. I'm going to remove the curse for you so you could have all the benefits of Calvary. If you're in Christ should there be any sickness in you? Any disease? Any poverty? Why not? Because you're in Christ and He redeemed you from it all. You don't have poverty, sickness, disease, or depression because Jesus was your substitute. He made Himself identical with you, and now you're in Christ.

Christ is seated in heavenly places. He's ruling and has all authority in Heaven and earth and says, "As long as you're in Me, I give this all to you" (Mathew 28:18-20). So, let's quit struggling, and rest in Christ' finished work! It's that simple, isn't it? Why are we trying to complicate it? The reason we struggle with all this is simply because we don't believe it. Some people become indignant when they hear this and say, "Of course we believe that!"

We're not saying you don't believe in the Lord Jesus Christ and are not born again. We didn't say you aren't going to Heaven. We simply said people often do not believe what God says in His Word about them. They behave just like Eve did in the garden. When God says, "These are all your promises, " the devil comes along and says, "Don't believe him." He tries to get us to doubt God's Word. That's why Timothy speaks of the good, "fight of faith." We don't have to battle the devil. Why? Because Jesus already did that for us. He simply said, "Stand and believe."

When you start believing God's Word, you enter into His rest (Hebrews 4:9,10). No more struggles and trying to do things out of your flesh. You cease from your own works as God did from His. You know that this is not about what you (in the flesh) can do anymore, but it's only about how God sees you through Jesus' Blood! When you believe that, you'll be at peace, and like Jesus, you'll be able to take a nap in the middle of a storm!! You are fully persuaded that what God has said, He is able to perform it!! You just enjoy what Jesus finished for you at Calvary! You can get up every morning and say, "Thank You, Lord Jesus." You see you already told the devil he can't touch you. "Thank You, Jesus." You want a slice of your daily bread? Reach up and slice off a piece. It's yours.

God says, "Will you reach up and slice off a piece? It's already yours. You're in Christ."

Now you are translated out of the kingdom of darkness into the kingdom of light. Everything Jesus has, you have, not "will have"-you already have it. If you're in Christ, you have it. You're not in Adam anymore. You have to keep telling the devil what you know, and act like it's true. When you begin to act like it's true, you don't fret, because God says, "Fear not; for I am with you" (Isaiah 41:10; II Timothy 1:7).

We can't walk in fear and say we're in Christ at the same time; to do so nullifies, for you, who the Word of God says you are. If God says, "Fear not; for I am with you, " then stop fearing. Making a decision not to fear and say it out of your mouth, "I will not fear. I don't care what you say, devil. My trust is in the Lord. I lean not to my own understanding. In all my ways I acknowledge Him and He directs my path. I have nothing to fear. I live by faith in God."

But what about when the devil says, "Down around that corner-boy, if you knew what was coming up, you'd really get into a sweat."

You reply, "Devil, I don't care what you say. I don't care when I round that corner what's there. My God said He'll never leave me nor forsake me. He said that He would protect me and that all who call upon the name of the Lord shall be delivered. I have no fear" (Psalm 91).

"Yes, but you see, you remember the last time..."

"Well, the last time, I might have, but I'm stronger in faith now, and I don't swallow your lies anymore, devil."

"Yeah, but you know what? You're going to lose your job next week." "Well, I guess God has something better for me. Praise the Lord." Don't let the devil complicate it for you, and above all don't let other Christians complicate it for you. We're going to talk about the "but" Christians. Do you know what we're talking about? "Oh, I know what the Bible says, *but...*" Whenever you hear: "I know what the Bible says, but I'm smarter than God." Don't listen to it. You are not smarter than God. You're not going to mock Him. He has never been mocked and never will be (Galatians 6:7). If He said it, it's true. Some may try to mock Him, but He'll have the last laugh. He always does. We have to start saying, "If He said it, I believe it!" It's that simple.

CHAPTER

7

SEVEN IDENTIFICATIONS WITH CHRIST

The Apostle Paul received some very important revelations from our Lord Jesus Christ. The other apostles didn't get this kind of revelation. Much was written in the Gospels about Jesus' life, but when we get over into the Epistles, particularly those written by Paul, we begin to see how we can identify with everything the Gospels say about Jesus.

High Treason With Adam

When we use the term, "in Adam," we're using it in reference to the fact that he is a representative man. Whatever Adam did in the Garden of Eden, he did as our representative. So what did he do? He committed high treason. We use the term, "high treason," because Adam received his command about that particular tree being forbidden not from just anybody. He got it from the Supreme Being of all the universe. So to blatantly disobey the Supreme Being would, we think, place Adam's actions in the class of high treason.

So when Adam committed high treason against the Almighty, we were in Adam: and God saw us committing high treason along with Adam. From the *Phillips translation*, look at

Verse 12: "Sin made its entry into the world through one man and through sin, death. And sin and death passed on to the whole human race and no one could break it for no one himself was free from sin."

Our identification is and was with Adam. Whatever Adam received, we received. He was our representative. He stood in our place. When Eve picked that forbidden fruit off the tree and handed it to her husband, it was, in God's eyes, as though all of us were standing right next to Adam. Picture yourself standing there. When Eve took that fruit and said, "Adam". Picture yourself standing there. When Eve took that fruit and said, "Adam, this is really good; look at it, " she was really saying, "Here, Terry, here Bill, here Joyce, eat of it." From God's viewpoint, we all were there. All of us were there *in* Adam.

All of us were there. And when Adam took the fruit, brought it to his mouth and took a big bite out of it, picture yourself biting into that "apple" because you were there in Adam. He was a representative man. This is real to God. It might not be real to you, but to God, you were standing right there taking that forbidden fruit, putting it in your mouth, taking a bite, eating it and swallowing it. That's how real it was to God. He saw you disobey him in Adam even though you weren't born yet.

And our participation with Adam brought spiritual death on every single human being. All were alienated from the life of God instantly, because God saw us there partaking of that forbidden fruit along with Adam. Because all were in sin through Adam, and no one remained who could help man out of his sinful condition. No other human being who was in Adam could come along and help the rest of us out of Adam. Every single human being was in Adam. Therefore, if we all were in Adam and Adam sinned, we all sinned with him. Romans 3:23 says, "All have sinned and come short of the glory of God."

A certain denomination celebrates a feast that they call the Immaculate Conception. Many in that denomination think that this particular feast day is dedicated to the Lord Jesus, and that it pertains to Jesus, who was born through an immaculate conception.

But we want you to know that we don't believe that it pertains to Jesus. We believe their teaching pertains to His mother. This feast for Mary is called the Immaculate Conception, and according to this doctrine, Mary was conceived without sin. Does that line up with what God teaches us in His Word?

Let us ask you a question. Was Mary *in Adam?* Then if Mary was in Adam, then Mary sinned along with the rest of us. Don't take offense here.

We're not doing this to be facetious: we want to show you the error of that denomination. What they teach contradicts God's Word. Whom do you choose to believe? It's very right and correct to honor Mary, but don't deify her. We don't pray to her, or to any other great man or woman in the Bible. In John 16:23,24, the Lord Jesus told us to pray to the Father in Jesus Name. Only Jesus redeemed us! Only He is the Way, the Truth and the Life! No one can come to God except through Him (John 14:6)!

If Mary were in Adam, then she needed a Savior like the rest of us, didn't she? What does the Bible say? If you don't want to believe that Mary was in Adam, then let's set up some scriptures for you. Again, Romans 3:23 says, "*all* have sinned and come short of the glory of God." How many are "all"? Does that eliminate anyone? Does that mean that the Lord Jesus' mother was eliminated from "all"? Does it mean she was born without sin? No – she is included in *all*. She needed a savior just as we all do. It may sound blasphemous to some who want to idolize Mary, but it's God's Word.

If all have sinned and come short of the glory of God, that means "all." Nobody in the human race can say, "I'm free from sin, and I can come and deliver mankind." Not if that individual came through Adam. Mary came through the loins of Adam.

Romans 5:12 says, "That death passed upon <u>all</u> men..." Mary came through the loins of Adam, therefore she was born in sin. She needed a Redeemer just like all of us needed a Redeemer. Mary had to be born again. She was one of those 120 in the Upper Room, waiting her turn to receive the Holy Spirit and be saved. So we don't care how powerful and big denominations are in declaring certain doctrines. We must always take it back to the Word of God. Man-made doctrines mean nothing. They don't hold water. You have to go to the Bible to see what God says. The doctrine that counts is the doctrine He gives. It's called the doctrine of Jesus Christ. God's Word! Eternal Truth (John 17:17)!

Jesus said," All have sinned and come short of the glory of God." So, if all who came into the world were in Adam, that is, we came through Adam's loins, then how can we all get out of Adam? If all of us were born in Adam, we are a pretty hopeless, helpless bunch of people in a hopeless, helpless situation. Not one person is free to help the rest of us out of bondage.

"Well, I don't like the characteristics that I'm stuck with through Adam." It doesn't matter. You are what you are because of Adam. He was your representative man. Whatever he received, you received. You might not like it. We've heard people say, and we've said it ourselves, "Well, we don't like what Adam did to us." That's too bad. He was our representative man.

There's not a thing we can do about it. When God called judgment down on Adam's sin, he called judgement down on our sins. We were all in Adam.

If you don't like what you look like, for example, are you going to be able to say, "Well, I can change my looks. I'm going to shoot my daddy." Will that change your looks? "I'll shoot my granddaddy." Is that going to help you? "I'll shoot my great-granddaddy." Is that going to help you? No. You are what you are. You're not going to change it.

So, how can man get out of Adam? Obviously, the only way out is to die-not physically but spiritually. The spiritually dead nature has to die. The nature of sin and death that connected us with the devil through Adam. "But can we kill ourselves on our behalf? Will that do any good?"

People who want to commit suicide (and we do not, I repeat, do not advocate suicide) have, in a sense, the right idea. But, you see, they kill the wrong person. All of a sudden they realize something isn't going right in their life. Such a person may think, "Every time I look around I'm sick, I'm poor, and I'm down and out. All I seem to do is lean toward nothing but trouble and sickness and poverty. I think I'll kill myself and end this." He has the right idea, but he wants to kill the wrong person. You see, you can't kill the outside man and take care of the inside problem.

So, many kill themselves on the outside (their physical bodies) and think things will be better. Oh no, things will only grow worse if you kill yourself and you are not saved. In that condition (unsaved, that is), your spirit man is spiritually dead. You're going to spend eternity in Hell. Many people say, "I'll kill myself; this life is not worth living." They kill the wrong person when they do that. They needed to kill the inner man-the one who had the nature of Adam. But they can't do that themselves. They can only destroy the outer man. We needed someone to come along and kill the sin nature in our inner man. The inner man has the sin nature, the adamic nature.

That's why God sent Jesus. He wasn't born through Adam. He did not come through the loins of Adam. Jesus came to kill everyone. That my not sound so great to you, but that's really good news! Maybe we said that a little boldly, but in reality, this is the reason Jesus came. He didn't come to kill our physical bodies. He wanted to kill the sin nature in our inner man. The sin nature (spiritual death) had to die! Before Jesus could save us or give us new life, He had to get rid of our old life. We couldn't become a new creation in Christ until the old creation (nature) was eliminated.

Let's wade in a little deeper. Did you ever find yourself getting ready to go into a small pond, river or swimming pool, and you put your little toe in and you go. "Ooh, that's cold! I don't know if I want to go in there." But you kind of ease yourself in, very reluctantly, and after a very few moments you say, "Hey, the water's not bad at all. In fact, it's pretty nice." Well, that's how this material may feel to some.

You may feel reluctant to go down into deeper water or deeper revelation in God's Word. And we're going to tell you why; you're going to have to put your thinking cap on. Many Christians are spiritually lazy. They don't want to work or dig for what they want from God, but the Bible teaches that we should hunger and thirst after God's wisdom and press into the things of the Lord! Proverbs 2:4,5 says, "If thou seekest her (wisdom) as silver, and searchest for her as for hid treasures; Then shalt thou understand the fear of the Lord, and find the knowledge of God."

Identification Comes First

A couple of chapters ago we gave you a definition of the word "identify." We said that you need to put that to memory because everything in this book has to do with identification. So you ought to know what the word "identify" means. What does the word "identify" mean? To make identical; to consider and treat as the same. Now we asked you to memorize that for a reason. Everything to do with identification has to do with that definition.

The reason we said we can identify with Jesus Christ is simply because He identified with us first. In 2 Corinthians 5:21, we read: "He who knew no sin was made to be sin." He identified with our fallen nature or our fallen state as sinners. Then the second half says, "...that we might become the righteousness of God in him," This is identification. Jesus first had to identify with us in our fallen state as we were in Adam. Jesus had to identify with that nature. What was that nature while we were in Adam? A sin nature. So it says God made Jesus to become sin for us. "He made him to be sin who knew no sin."

Notice that expression, "for us." When studying identification, we see Jesus who has either done something with us or for us. And whenever we see those words, we need to understand exactly what Jesus did. Jesus had to first identify with us before we could become what He became once He was resurrected from the dead. There is no substitution without identification.

Jesus became your substitute, but He could not become your substitute until He first identified with you. In Adam, you were a sinner. The Bible says that God made Jesus to be sin for us-He who knew no sin. Jesus was not a sinner. Jesus was the pure Son of the living God. He had no guile. He had

93

no sin. He never committed a sin. He had no sin, but God said, "I'm going to make You sin for them." That's identification-He became what you were.

In other words, He's going to be made identical with us. Then once He becomes identical with us. God can consider Him the same as us and treat us the same as Him. So the second half can only come about after the first half. It says God made Him to be sin for us so that the righteousness of God might become ours. So, He has to identify with us first and then we can identify with Him. Everything that Jesus became, through His death, burial and resurrection, we can become, since He first took on our nature.

In Galatians 3:13, we read that, "Christ hath redeemed us from the curse of the law, being made a curse for us." Jesus was not a curse, but He was being made a curse for us. Why? Because all the effects of the curse that God laid out to Adam and Eve in the Garden of Eden, became ours. Remember? Everything Adam got, we got. We had to suffer the effects of the curse. So God says, "In order for you to have the blessing of Abraham, Jesus first has to be made a curse for you. For it is written 'Cursed is everyone that hangeth on a tree: that the blessing of Abraham might come upon the Gentiles through Jesus Christ.'"

So Jesus had to become sin. Jesus had to become a curse for us. And because He did, we can receive the blessing of Abraham. He had to get the curse out of our lives so that He could bless us. Jesus was our substitute. He was our representative man. Now you're beginning to see why Adam and Jesus were the two most important men in the Bible. First, in the negative sense, there is Adam: everything Adam became, we became. However, on the positive side, there is Jesus: everything He became (when God made Him alive), we've become in Him. We have been identified with Jesus in His death, burial and resurrection. Don't just leave it death and burial; go all the way to His resurrection.

Everything Jesus acquired in His resurrection is yours. God looked at you and identified you with Jesus, saying, "As I see Jesus, I see you" (I John 4:17). So when God sent Jesus to the earth in human form, He meant for Jesus to identify with you in <u>every aspect</u> of your fallen nature. In order for it to be a complete substitutionary work, Jesus had to take on everything you received in Adam. <u>Nothing could be left out.</u>

What did God say to Adam when Adam sinned? He said, "I'm going to banish you from My presence. You cannot stay in the presence of a Holy God. You are now sin." When God told Adam and Eve, "Get out of My sight, "He also told each of us, "Get out of My sight," because we were in Adam-in sin. God said, "You can't stay here." Adam became alienated from the life of God, and so did we at that same moment.

God then pronounced a three –fold curse upon the earth. Sin caused a spiritual alienation from God. We call it spiritual death. Some will say, "Oh, Christ didn't die spiritually," because they're thinking in terms of Christ being God. And they say, "God can't die." Well, Christ didn't die as God, He died as a human being. He first had to become a human being. He had to be exactly like us. He couldn't do it as God. That wouldn't be fair, because God can do anything. He had to do it in such a way as to take your place. You're not God. You're a human being. He had to be exactly like us.

That's why God made Him a body-so He could be tempted in every way just as we are tempted. Yet, He was without sin. But God says, "I'm gong to make you sin (not commit sin), Jesus, because they're sin. I need to identify You with humankind. They are in Adam, and are therefore under the curse which is poverty, sickness, disease and complete eternal alienation from God. Jesus, You're going to have to become that. Nothing can be left out, Jesus, or Your work won't be a complete substitutionary work."

The only thing Jesus didn't have when God sent Him down here was sin. We know that He came as the Spotless Lamb of God, with no sin, through a virgin birth (Isaiah 7:14; John 1:29).

We know what it means to be in Adam. We also now know what it means to be in Jesus Christ.

When Adam sinned, he was immediately alienated from the life of God. Alienated-that is what we call spiritual death. That doesn't mean that you cease to exist, as some people who write these books about spiritual death think. You are a spirit being. You never, ever, ever cease to exist. Once God breathed His life into you, you were destined for an eternity. He can't blow you away and say, "I made a mistake with this guy. Bang, bang, he's gone." No, you're part of eternity. You will never cease to exist.

Every one of you who reads this will be in existence one hundred billion, trillion, zillion years from now. You will never cease to exist, although you may exist in a condition of spiritual death. That is, a person can be alienated from the life of God for eternity, but still exist. It is a state of being dead and yet existing.

Adam was judged and sentenced immediately. When God came in the garden and found out that an offense had been established against God, Adam was immediately alienated from the life of God. Since we were born in Adam, we got what he got. So as Jesus identified Himself with Adam's offspring, God made Him identical with us and considered and treated Him as if He were us. So when Jesus identified with us, we in turn could identify with Him!

God Perspective

And now as Jesus sits exalted on the right hand of God. God makes us identical with Jesus Christ and considers and treats us the same as He treats Jesus-exalted and seated at the right hand of God. Exactly!

As you're reading this, you may be saying, "Oh, wait a minute. I can't believe that. You're telling me that God treats me the same way He treats Jesus?"

Well, what does the Word say? He says you reign in life with Jesus Christ (Romans 5:17). You are seated in heavenly places in Christ (Ephesians 2:5,6). You are an heir of God and a joint heir with Jesus (Romans 8:17). You were once in Adam, but now you are in Christ. You've been given every spiritual blessing in the Heavenly places in Christ (Ephesians 1:3). That's everything God has!! Do you have to sweat, toil and drive yourself crazy to figure out that all of these blessings are yours? NO! The Word simply says, "You are seated in heavenly places with Christ Jesus." God sees you there or He wouldn't have said so in His Word.

Either you believe the Word of God or you don't. "As He is, so are we in this world"(I John 4:17). Now that's real to God. It may not be real to us, because our finite minds can hardly seem to grasp it. But God sees it as real. When He looks at Jesus, He sees you. This is called identification, friends. The Lord Jesus identified with us, so we could identify with Him.

Of course, it goes without saying that we are not God. We are not Jesus. There is only one God and it's not us. We are not saying we're God; but by faith, we have God dwelling in us. And because we were born again by the incorruptible seed which is the Word of God, we now have all of God's characteristics within us with all the potential for thinking, speaking and acting just as God does. We are one with Jesus (I Cor. 6:17). We have His nature in our spirits (II Peter 1:4).

Our Defeated Enemy

What stops many believers from realizing this? They're own crazy thinking. Many listen to what the devil says to them. They listened today. They listened yesterday. They will listen tomorrow. They choose not to believe what God says. So it's not His fault that they haven't found themselves seated in heavenly places, ruling and reigning in life with Christ Jesus, even as the Word says. How can they blame God? They need to blame themselves.

Flip Wilson used to say, "The devil made me do it." The devil can't make you do anything you don't want to do. You have authority over him (I John 4:4). That's what the Word says. He's been stripped clean of all his authority over every believer. Jesus made an open show of him publicly and stripped him (Col. 2:15). All he has now is a growl. He can't hurt you because the Word says he can't (Isa. 54:17). So he can come growling around, but you know the Scripture says to be vigilant and sober for your adversary comes around "like" a roaring lion. He didn't say he was a roaring lion. Satan tries to roar like a lion to make you think he is a lion. He wants to intimidate you and back you away from God's Word.

You know what you must do with the devil when he comes around with that growl? Say, "You can't hurt me. I destroyed your power over me through Jesus' precious Blood at Calvary!" Did a growl ever hurt anybody? Well, he can growl all he wants; but if you know who you are in Christ and your identification with Christ, all you have to do is speak the Word to him. Command him to leave in Jesus Name and he will flee from you (James 4:7)!

The Gospels tell of the death, burial and resurrection of Jesus. They spell out what Jesus went through. The Epistles, as noted earlier, spell out in detail what God saw every believer go through in His death, burial and resurrection. Paul says, "We were crucified with Christ." Now crucifixion doesn't mean death. A lot of people say, "I was crucified with Christ. That means I died with Him." No, no. Crucifixion means you <u>suffered</u> with Christ. That's important to know.

Crucifixion means suffering. You suffered with Jesus. He suffered with you. God saw you suffer all of the curse of the law when Jesus suffered it for you. Jesus suffered all of the curse for us. We were suppose to suffer all of the curse for the rest of our lives, but when we were crucified with Christ, he took that off of us and bore it in Himself and suffered it for us. Therefore, we never ever have to suffer any of the curse again! The suffering that the Bible says we will suffer is persecution. When God saw Jesus on the cross. He saw you nailed up there with Him. It's real to God. He saw you up there. You were in Christ on the cross (Colossians 2:14). Again, it's very real to God. It should be very real to you.

So, the Word says, "I am crucified with Christ: nevertheless I live." What was crucified with Christ? The old nature. We have to die before we can live. Second Corinthians 5:14, states, "We died with Jesus." In Romans 6:4, we read, "We were buried with Jesus." So, we were <u>crucified</u>; we <u>died</u>; we were <u>buried</u>; we were <u>raised up</u> with Jesus Christ; and we were <u>made alive</u> with

Him. Ephesians 2:3-5 confirms this. And when Jesus was resurrected, <u>we were resurrected</u> with Him, because Colossians 3:1 says so.

Become Established

We tend to doubt these things because our minds cannot comprehend them. But you see, if Jesus says so, if the Word says so, we have to be established in that. One thing the devil does not want is for you to be established in the fact that you were crucified; you died; and you were buried, made alive, resurrected and raised up with Jesus Christ.

For every scripture in the Gospels which describes what happened to Jesus, there is a parallel scripture in the Epistles that describes what happened to the believer. When you see in the Gospels what happened to Jesus, you can go over to the Epistles and see a parallel scripture that says, "You did it with Jesus." Paul got that revelation. We can read in the Epistles that God treats us identically with Jesus Christ.

The words "in Christ," and "with Christ," become very important to us. God's plan of redemption included mankind's identification with Jesus Christ.

Once you receive information from God, you're going to be held responsible for it. Once the light has been poured out upon you concerning the Scriptures, God says, "I'm holding you responsible." That's why we must take the Word seriously and become established and stabilized in it. There are going to be false teachers, false prophets, and all kinds of false things going on in the last days. Even the devil himself is going to be transformed into an angel of light, and he's going to be able to dupe Christians who are not established in God's Word. Even the elect may be pulled away at the end. Don't be deceived.

We've already begun to see the pulling away of the elect. Do you know why? They are not willing to spend any time at Calvary. They want a direct flight, but there are no direct flights in the kingdom of God, especially for lazy Christians. We all have to layover at Calvary. The reason most people don't like to layover at Calvary is because they have to pay attention, study, and meditate upon it. Most Christians do not want to do that.

Some pastors and church counselors say that when little bits of homework are given to those being counseled, they can't even do the simplest assignment.

"Well," the excuse begins, "I was going to, but I sat down and just happened to turn the TV on. Before I knew it, it was midnight and time to go to bed."

Do these people use pastors and teachers as sounding boards with no intention of doing what they are counseled to do? We all need to layover at Calvary.

Someone may say, "I need to be delivered from something."

Well then, go to Calvary! If you don't understand what took place at Calvary and you make a direct flight to healing, you may not keep it. The devil may talk you out of it tomorrow.

Too often when people come to healing lines and God shows His miraculous, merciful power and heals them, they're back in line again two days later. Why? Because they didn't bother to get established in what took place at Calvary. They didn't bother to say to God, "That was wonderful. I better study about that. I better get established in that." They think their whole life is going to be one miracle after another. God did it once, and He'll do it again and again.

No, He won't! He did it for you because you were a baby Christian. He said, "You needed something from Me, so My mercy, My grace is yours. You've got it now, but tomorrow you had better get in the Word and start studying it for yourself."

That's why we keep saying, "Get stabilized," because things are coming that are not going to be pleasant. Become established; stabilize yourself in the Word.

People can keep running to all the healing places they want and going to all the deliverance centers they want. But the only way they're going to keep what God has in His Word for them is to become established in it. They have to know what Jesus did in His crucifixion, death and burial. What does it mean to be quickened? What does it mean to conquer with Jesus? What does resurrection mean? What does being seated mean? If you don't know these things, the devil will unseat you tomorrow.

We are not in Adam anymore; we are in Jesus. The devil will say, "Well, this doesn't really pertain to you. You're really a sinner. You're still in Adam. You're still condemned. You're going to go to Hell." Jesus is saying, "If you're in Me, you're not going to Hell."

What does the Word say? "There is therefore now no condemnation to them that are in Christ Jesus, who walk not after the flesh, but after the spirit" (Rom. 8:1).

Are you allowing the Holy Spirit to direct your path? Are you walking with the direction of the Holy Spirit in your life or are you in the flesh? Everybody who's in the flesh always feels condemned.

Don't feel condemned when you sin. When you sin, the devil will come along and say, "You sinned!"

You should say, "That's right, but I have an advocate, Jesus Christ, the righteous. I'm in Him, therefore all I have to do is <u>confess my sin</u>, <u>repent of my sin</u> (turn back on that sin) and keep walking. You can't condemn me, devil, because God doesn't. I'm in Christ and I'm cleansed by His Blood (I John 1:9).

Remember your identification with Christ. God sees the two of you as being identical, and so He considers and treats you the same as He does Jesus. But not everyone will do that when satan comes around because they're not established in the Word. We're not saying you should go out every day and sin just because you know you're not condemned.

No, we don't have a license to sin. But when we get off track and sin we still know that we have Jesus Christ, the Righteous, and we are in Him. He is our lawyer. We have His redeeming Blood! He is seated next to the Father saying, "Father he's going to confess, and he's going to repent. He knows what the Word says. Look, he's going to 1 John. He's reading it. Yes, he found the right place."

And the devil is standing over there accusing you. "You're a sinner. You're a sinner."

"Shut up, devil. I'm in Christ. I'm not a sinner anymore. I'm a new creation! It is written that man does not live by bread alone, but by every word that proceeds out of the mouth of God. I'm going to speak back to God what His Word says."

Seven areas of study are ahead of us in this book. **Number One,** you're going to be learning about <u>crucifixion.</u> That means suffering. **Number Two,** you're going to learn about <u>death.</u> **Number Three,** <u>burial.</u> The Scripture says you were buried with Christ. **Number Four,** <u>quickened.</u> Have you had much teaching on God's quickening power? We're going to find out what that word "quickening" means. What does the believer have to know about that word "quickening"? **Number Five,** <u>conquered.</u> We're going to identify with Jesus in all these areas. Conquering means triumphing. He triumphed over satan and made an open show of him, stripped him. That's being a conqueror. **Number Six,** <u>resurrection.</u> There is a resurrection greater than that from physical death. And last, **Number Seven,** we're going to talk about being <u>seated.</u> All these areas pertain to your identification with Jesus; and if you're not established in them, the devil's going to come along and do a number on you.

So you say, "Well, where do we begin?" We begin at Calvary. We always go back to Calvary. We can't leave Calvary until we're established in Calvary.

Someone will say, "Yes, I know all about Calvary. I picture Jesus up there on the cross, and I feel sorry for Him. He died for my sins." That's true, but you know something? All the disciples were probably down there below the cross looking up and pretty much thinking the same thing you were thinking. "Poor Jesus. He said He was going to die and He did. He really suffered. Thank you, Jesus for dying for my sins."

The Apostle Paul comes along, and it's as if Jesus said to him, "Come up hither, I've got some revelation to talk to you about (Gal. 1:11,12). Come on up here, Paul. I want to talk to you about something. (2 Cor. 12:2-4). You see, my other disciples, couldn't grasp this. They didn't know what was going on. Oh, their hearts were hurting; because they saw their Lord and Savior die up there. But they didn't know what else took place on Calvary's cross. They didn't know what took place behind the scenes in the spirit. Come up hither, Paul. I'm going to tell you what took place, and then I want you to go and write it to the church. Put it in your Epistles and go around teaching it to everybody until they're established in it (I Cor. 4:17).

Yet today, 2,000 years later, throughout a lot of churches, do you ever hear people talking about their identification with Christ? Many would say that we need to teach more on loving one another, and that is very important. But to be firmly grounded in the love of God, one must be established in his identification with Christ. Identification is the epitome of love. When you grasp this, you're going to understand God's love for you. You're going to understand what Jesus accomplished for you. And if you're in Christ, you get it all free of charge. The things that surround Calvary tell about real love. They reveal to us that God loves us as much as He loves Jesus (John 17:23)!!

Just ask someone how their day went today, then, listen. You'll find out if they're in the Word or not. They talk about everything but God's Word. They don't talk about what they meditated on and how God revealed things to them. They don't talk about that. In fact, some Christians today are busy writing books against the gifts of the spirit, against tongues, against healing. They spend all their time doing that, but they never know about their identification with Jesus Christ. Isn't that a pity?

Books are being printed and published by the thousands by people who are very well known. They say that speaking in tongues is not for today, and healing is not for today. This is the kind of stuff that's being printed today, and taught in a lot of churches across the United States. Yet you'll never hear one of them talk about our identification with Christ. Do you know why? Because they don't know it. They are to busy telling us what isn't for today. Tell us what is for today!

Tell us that Jesus went on the cross and became a curse for you so the blessing of Abraham might come upon you. When someone comes along and says, "Healing is not for today," say, "Wait a minute. Isn't sickness under the curse? My Bible tells me that Jesus became a curse for me so that the blessing of Abraham might come upon the Gentiles (Deuteronomy 28:1-14; Galatians 3:13,14). Did you ever find out what the blessings of Abraham were?"

You'll stop them right in their tracks. Why don't you just take out your Bible and say to them, "Show me where it says that healing has ceased. Show me where it says tongues ceased. Show me all this in the Bible. **Show** it to me in the Bible." They can't do it, because it is not in there. What is in there is the death, burial and resurrection of the Lord Jesus Christ; and it says He did it all for you-that the blessing of Abraham might come upon you. Notice the word, "might"? It's all up to you.

8

SOME IMPORTANT FACTS ABOUT
YOUR REDEMPTION

The knowledge of who we are in Christ will make a major difference in our approach to every single thing in our lives. We are going to find a new inner peace. Turmoil is going to leave us. Fret and worry will be part of the past. And we'll be able to experience victory, not as a once-in-a-while experience, but as an everyday occurrence. If you need a higher standard of living, you need a higher standard of learning.

Many churches today are languishing because they have never been taught who they are in Christ. This is one area in which the devil is going to try to keep blinders on people so they won't see nor hear the glorious Gospel of the Lord Jesus Christ. We can't get any closer to the heart of the Lord Jesus than to study our identification with Him.

In a later chapter, we will discuss, in greater detail, spiritual death and will look at the question, "Did Jesus die spiritually?" To many, that is a very controversial subject, but to God it is not controversial at all (I Timothy 3:16). So, what is spiritual death?

Adam was alienated from the life of God because he was spiritually dead. He had a nature that was contrary to the nature of God. He was a sinner. And so God comes along and says, "I've got to do something about that old nature." And so He took His sinless Son and said, "Go down to earth and take care of that situation of hopelessness." When you are spiritual dead, you are in the most despicable, deplorable, hopeless situation possible. There is no hope in that situation unless Jesus Christ comes and does something with the inner man. Our old nature needed to die. God knew that. We needed to be given a new nature.

Look at 2 Corinthians 5:14: "For the love of Christ constraineth us; because we thus judge, that if one died for all, then we're all dead." The old nature in our inner man needed to die and as you can see from this scripture, it really is saying that in Christ all died. One died for all. In one, all died.

Under the Old Testament, with its Old Covenant rules and laws, Jesus Christ had not yet come as Redeemer. For a moment, let's assume you lived in Old Testament times, one individual in a big nation of hopelessness. You were one who came out of Adam's loins. You realized that Adam was a representative man and that when Adam sinned against Almighty God, spiritual death came upon him. He was alienated from the life of God. You're in a state of hopelessness and despair, and God appears to you and says, "Listen, my son, my daughter, I'm going to grant you whatever you desire the most, so think real hard. Whatever that desire is, I'm going to fulfill it for you. Think carefully because I'm not going to give you two shots at this. Whatever you want, whatever you desire, I am going to give it to you." So, what do you desire?

What would you say? What would you want most from God? Hopefully, the answer would be, "Get me out of this mess, Lord. I realize that I'm in Adam. That I am trapped without hope. That I'm sick, poor and above all, I have no relationship with You. I'm spiritually dead. I live perpetually in darkness. I'm under a curse and everything that I touch turns negative. I realize that Adam represented me and got me into this hopeless situation, and I need deliverance. Lord, this is what I want from You: I want You to get me out of spiritual death, and get this spiritual death out of me."

God would respond, "I have some good news for you then. I'm going to grant your request. I'm going to remove the nature of sin and death out of your life, and here is how I'm going to do it. I'm going to kill you! You may not understand it now, but later you'll know that I gave you good news!"

You see, when you're talking about the mess you're in spiritually, you're talking about the condition of your inner man. And God is saying, "I've got to destroy the nature of sin and death in man's spirit. I've got to kill the spiritual death in man's inner man. It must die before his spirit man can be reborn. I'm going to send My Son, Jesus Christ, and when I crucify Him on the cross, I'm going to put you on that cross with Him. So when He is crucified and dies, you will be crucified and die with Him. Jesus' death will be the death of your sin nature. But when I make Him alive, you are going to be made alive with Him and that's why it's good news. I'm going to give you a new nature." The old nature will no longer exist (II Cor. 5:17,18).

That's exactly what Paul is saying. We all died in this one man, Jesus. If one died for all, then all died. II Cor. 5:14 did not say, "If one died for all, then all live". In better understanding what Jesus did for us at Calvary, we must understand that Jesus died for us so that we could die; that is, so our old nature could die. Many times in preaching, we've declared that Jesus died for us so that we could live, and when you look at the end result of Calvary, He did. But in studying every aspect of our redemption you'll see that Jesus died to provide us with death for our old nature, and He was quickened or made alive so that we could be made alive or live unto God. Let me give you an example. If I was crossing the highway and you saw that a car was about to hit me and you pushed me out of the way, and the car killed you, how would people describe that event? They would probably say that you died for me. You saved me from dying. You gave your life for me. But, if all that Jesus did for us when He died was to just push the old man, the old nature (so to speak) out of the road; then we would still have that old sin nature. Do you see that? So Jesus' death for us wasn't to preserve the old man. He wasn't trying to save his life. He was identifying with my old self so that He could take me out into the spiritual highway with Him, so His death would be my death. God had to destroy the old creation or our sin nature, before He could make us into a new creation. You don't resurrect something that's not dead. Now God couldn't just crucify us, without Christ. Christ was our representative man. And since we were in Jesus, we all were crucified and died in Him.

If this sounds repetitive, we're doing it for a reason. You must understand that when you accept Jesus Christ, you accept all the benefits God provided through Jesus. So when Jesus died, it was as real to God as anything you can imagine. God saw you on that cross nailed with Jesus. So when you read in the New Testament about Jesus' crucifixion and death, you are really reading about your own crucifixion and death. Every time you read about Jesus Christ being crucified, dying, being buried, raised from the dead and seated next to the Father, then you should always, every single time, picture yourself going through every phase Jesus went through, because you were in Him.

See yourself on that cross-tortured. See yourself nailed up there with Jesus, because that's the way God wants you to see this. See yourself in torment-the nails being driven into your hands. See yourself dying on the cross with the Lord Jesus. See yourself being taken down from that cross and being buried. See yourself being resurrected from the dead. See yourself being seated at the right hand of the Father. Can you do that? It's important that you do because that's exactly how God sees you. The story of Jesus dying on the cross is a story about you and your old nature dying with Jesus. The nature of sin died. Praise God! The sin nature is gone out of your spirit, but not out of this world. Jesus did not get rid of the devil, but He did defeat him for us. You are a new creature in Christ. Now, you're living in this world, but not part of it. You are born again!

One Nature in Christ

Some people, and we're going to be talking about this in one of our future lessons, are going around saying that we have two natures in our reborn spirits. Baloney. We don't have two natures. God's nature and the devil's nature do not exist in us simultaneously.

Now, we still have our flesh to deal with. Jesus' death and resurrection did not eliminate our flesh or it's nature. We have to take control of our bodies and make them line up with the Word of God. (I Cor. 9:27) But, when we are reborn, God gives us the power by the Holy Spirit to live a holy life (Romans 8:13). Someone may say, "Well, I get up some days and I have a mean streak coming out of me a mile long. That's just my old nature." No, that is not your old nature. That is a memory that the devil is bringing up in you about your old nature, hoping that you'll act on it. Again, II Corinthians 5:17 says that if anyone is in Christ, he is a new creation; old things have passed away; behold, all things have become new. So, what part of us has become new? We didn't get a new body when we got saved. We didn't get a new mind either. Our mind still has to be renewed to the Word of God (Romans 12:2). It was our spirit that was totally recreated, made brand new. Therefore, since all of the old things passed away, removed right out of our spirits, then everything in our reborn spirits is brand new! Did you get that? Since all things have become new in your spirit, that means that all of the old things are gone. All things on the inside of you are of God. It didn't say, "Some things still belong to the Adamic nature. The devil still has part of your spirit and God's got the other part." That's foolish thinking, and it's not Biblical.

In Christ, a person does not have two natures. We have been changed totally by the incorruptible seed that was placed in our spirit. We are now totally in Christ. There's nothing of the devil left in you-you're a new creature.

Are you in Christ? Then why do you still act as if you are still in Adam? You are a new creation in Christ Jesus, so act like you are. You see, the reason why you don't act like you're a new creature in Christ is because you still don't get the fact that Christ took you out of Adam. We haven't been taught about that enough. We still hear teachings and read books that say we have two natures in us. Friends, we do not have two natures in us. You have one nature in you. It's the nature of God. The nature of Deity. (II Pet. 1:4) He has placed His seed in you. Jesus Christ is in you. You are in Jesus Christ. The devil has no part of you. You were bought with a price. We want you to get that. If you are in Christ Jesus you are a new creation. A new creature. Old things have passed away. All things have become new. All things are of God (II Cor. 5:18).

We're talking about the spirit now. Concerning the spirit, you are a new creature. You are no loner in Adam, you are now in Christ. When we reckon this to be true (Rom. 6:11), scripturally true, then we are going to start changing the way we talk, the way we think and the way we act. No longer are we going to let the memories of our past haunt us. We're not going to let the devil bully us. Just because we're babes in Christ doesn't mean that we can't catch onto something very fast, stand on it and say to the devil, "Stop bullying me. I may be a baby, but I know I'm in Christ. And if I'm in Christ, I'm not in Adam. I am now out of Adam. I'm a new creation. I'm something that never before existed. God lives in me, and you do not have any power over me!"

Again let us say that being *in Jesus* simply means you have accepted Jesus Christ as your personal Savior. His blood has washed you clean of your sins. You recognize that when you accepted Christ, it was as if you were nailed to the cross with Jesus. At that point all your sins were put on Jesus. You came out of Adam and transferred into the kingdom of light. You have no part of the devil anymore. No part of Adam's nature anymore. You are a new creature, if you're in Christ.

Why are we still gossiping, lying, cheating and causing strife, if we're in Christ? Now we're not going to get rough with you. We're simply going to ask, "Why is any Christian still doing these things?" You see, if you're gossiping, you haven't realized the fact that you're no longer in Adam. You still think you have an old nature, and you give all kinds of excuses. "Well, the reason I do that is because I have a second nature."

No you don't! The reason you do that is because you don't recognize you are in Christ. In Christ, you don't gossip. In Adam, you gossip. In Adam, you slander. In Adam, you do all those things that sinners do; but in Christ, you don't do any of those things. And if you're still doing those things, you haven't reckoned with the fact that you've been crucified with Christ. The old man is dead. You are a new creation in Christ Jesus. It's simple, isn't it? Don't complicate it with your theology-just accept what the Bible says.

If you gossip about somebody, then you have listened to the memories of the old man. You're just simply saying, "Yes, okay, devil, you still have a part of me." What you should say is, "No, you don't! You can entice me. You can tempt me. You can do anything you want. You can try to lure me, but I know without a doubt in my heart that I have been crucified with Christ. Old things are passed away, behold ALL things have become new and all things are of God."

Make A Choice

You can simply act as if all things are of God. You make a choice. "I don't hear what you're saying, devil. You're talking to a dead man. He doesn't exist anymore. I'm a new creature in Christ. I'm alive unto Christ. You're talking to the old guy. He's dead. He's buried. "Devil, you're talking to a dead man. I used to listen to you when I was in Adam, when I was in spiritual death; but that man is dead now. You can't succeed in tempting him anymore. I'm a new creation. You're talking to the wrong guy. I'm in Christ. I don't gossip anymore. I walk in love and forgiveness." You see, you make a choice right here. Are you in Christ or are you still thinking you're in Adam? Is the devil convincing you that you're still in Adam? No, he's not going to convince you of that anymore. You must know for a fact that you're in Christ.

Unfortunately, too many in the body of Christ haven't caught on yet. That's why there's so much gossiping going on, so much slandering, so much sin in the body of Christ; because you see, the devil has convinced half of the body of Christ, if not more, that they are still in Adam. The devil says, "Just imitate your father, Adam." And we listen to his lie and do it.

The Holy Spirit says, "You're not in Adam anymore. Your old man is dead."

You're in Christ now so think on things above. (Col. 3:1) Think on things that are pure, just and holy. (Philippians 4:8) Start thinking that you can do all things through Christ who strengthens you. You don't have to gossip anymore. You don't have to slander anymore. You don't have to get nasty with people anymore. You don't have to let your temper flare up anymore. You're in Christ now. You have peace within. You've been reconciled to God. You're an ambassador for Christ., and you have to start acting like an ambassador. Be a reconciler for Christ, treat people like Christ treats them, bring them to Christ and pull them *out of Adam* (II Cor. 5:20).

> In John 15:1-4 Jesus says,
> *I am the true vine, and my Father is the husbandman.*
> *every branch in me that beareth not fruit he taketh away:*
> *And every branch that beareth fruit, he purgeth it, that is*
> *may bring forth more fruit.*
> *Now ye are clean through the word, which I have spoken*
> *unto you.*
> *Abide in me, and I in you. As the branch cannot bear fruit of*
> *itself, except it abide in the vine; no more can ye, except ye*
> *abide in me.*

Abide In Him

Heed what Jesus is saying here. He's saying that you have to learn to abide in Him. The word "abide" means to live constantly in the presence of the Lord Jesus. That means you get up every day and consciously walk out your day realizing that you are a new creation; that you are in Christ Jesus, that every thought, every action, every word is geared to the fact that you've been grafted to the vine. What flows through the vine, flows through you.

Look at verse 4 again: "Abide in me." In other words, live in Me. Not just for a moment, but every day, moment to moment, day by day. Literally, you are attached to the Lord Jesus, because you know that without being attached to the vine, there is nothing being fed into you. So you have to keep yourself hooked into the vine. Keep His life, Divine life, moving through you.

Verse 5 says that if we abide in Him, He'll abide in us. Then we'll bear much fruit and glorify God in our lives. The preposition "in" shows relationship: abide "in" Him. It tells you how one thing is related to another. Being in Christ shows relationship. As we said before, when we're in Christ, we share the life that is in Christ. He is the vine. We are the branches. What flows through Him goes into all of us who are in Christ.

You have to abide. You can't let yourself get detached. You can't allow yourself to get cut off because of your unbelief. You have to keep believing that He's the vine and He feeds you. Stay hooked to Him. Keep getting fed (John 6:54-57). Then you can say, "I can do all things through Christ who strengthens me." The strength is coming through the vine into the branch. Whatever is in the vine goes into the branch.

You see, when One died, all died. Again, Jesus is your representative man, so when He died as your representative, you died with Him. We need to stop saying that Jesus died for us 2,000 years ago and let it go at that. We need to add that when Jesus died, we died with Him. We need to meditate upon that. It must be driven into our spirit man. Jesus did not die alone. We died with Him. You died with Him. When we died with Him, the old man, the old nature died as well. We are no longer in Adam; we do not possess the Adamic nature. It is dead, and each of us is now a new creation in Christ, and His life is now flowing through us! Look again at 2 Corinthians 5:14: "For the love of Christ constraineth us; because we thus judge, that if one died for all, then were all dead."

Paul is not using the word "if" in the sense of doubting what the facts are in this verse. He's not doubting them at all. But the love of Christ controls us, so we make a judgment. After looking at the facts, we declare that Jesus Christ is the one who died for all. You look at it, and you make a judgment. It says it, therefore, you believe it. You say, "That's true." If it says Christ died for all, that includes me, that includes every body.

You see, most Christians have not made that judgment. That's why their lives are so defeated. They have not judged it to be true or factual. They do not include themselves when they read it.

See Yourself Crucified-Paul Says You and I Were

Your assessment of what took place on Calvary must be as real to you as it was to Paul. Paul saw himself crucified with Christ; he said it. He saw the old man annihilated. He saw himself cut right off Adam's family tree and grafted into the vine as a brand-new branch. That's how you have to see yourself. In visualizing this, see yourself cut off from Adam. See Jesus take you and just graft you into Him. He said, "Here, you're now grafted. Stay there because everything that's in Me is going to come into you."

When we make this judgment as Paul did, and start acting like it's true, all that Jesus purchased for us at the cross will become a reality in our lives.

In John 12:23-32, we read:
And Jesus answered them, saying, The hour is come, that the Son of man should be glorified.
Verily, verily, I say unto you, Except a corn of wheat fall into the ground and die, it abideth alone: but if it die, it bringeth forth much fruit.

He that loveth his life shall lose it; and he that hateth his life
in this world shall keep it unto life eternal.
If any man serve me, let him follow me; and where I am,
there shall also my servant be: if any man serve me, him will
My Father honor.
Now is my soul troubled; and what shall I say? Father, save
Me from this hour: but for this cause came I unto this hour.
Father, glorify thy name. Then came there a voice from
heaven, saying, I have both glorified it, and will glorify it
again.
The people therefore, that stood by, and heard it, said that it
thundered: others said, 'An angel spake to him.'
Jesus answered and said, "This voice came not because of
Me, but for your sakes.
Now is the judgment of this world: now shall the prince of
this world be cast out.
And I, if I be lifted up from the earth, will draw all men
unto me.

We sing that song in our churches, "If I Be Lifted Up, I Will Draw All Men Unto Me." We sing about it, but most Christians do not understand what that means. They have no idea what it's all about. If you asked them the meaning, they would answer, "Well, of course we're talking about Jesus Christ up on the cross. If we lift Jesus up and tell people about the cross, they're going to be saved." Well, friends, that statement is true, but that's not all of it.

Verse 32 states: "And I, if I be lifted up from the earth, will draw all men unto me." There wasn't a Jew in Israel at that time who did not understand that statement. They all knew exactly what it meant. The phrase, "If I be lifted up"- meant crucifixion.

When Jesus said, "If I be lifted up," He was talking about the manner of death He was about to experience.

Verse 33 says, "This he said, signifying what death he should die." Jesus was stating by the remark in verse 32 that His death would be by crucifixion. Tie this together with what 2 Corinthians 5:14 said, "If one died for all, then all died in that one." In John 12:32, Jesus was saying that when you crucify Me, you crucify yourselves, because you will be drawn into my death. "When I die, you are all going to die in Me." Jesus is saying, "I'm not an ordinary man. I'm your representative man. When they drive those nails into My hands, they are driving those nails into your hands. You will be drawn into it. You can't stop it."

It would be like a very powerful magnet pulling all human beings right to the cross, with all being nailed up there, dying with our Lord Jesus Christ. He said, "If I be lifted up, you're going to be drawn into it, *because when one dies all die with Me.*"

Here are five important facts, which will help you in gaining a fuller understanding of your identification with Jesus Christ. You need to meditate upon these. They are crucial to your understanding of who you are in Christ.

Jesus was our substitute.

The dictionary says that a substitute is one who takes the place of another, or to put or use a person in the place of another. The word in the Bible that is used mostly in reference to substitution is the word" propitiation." In Greek, it means "mercy seat, expiation and atonement." These last two words can parallel each other. Jesus was an expiation and an atonement for us.

Philippians 2:6-8 states: "Who, being in the form of God [Who are we speaking about? Jesus.], thought it not robbery to be equal with God:

> *But made himself of no reputation, and took upon him the form of a servant, and was made in the likeness of men: And being found in fashion as a man, he humbled himself, and became obedient unto death, even the death of the cross.*

This is simply telling us that Jesus was the substitute for all mankind. God so loved the world that He provided for us a mercy seat, a propitiation and atonement. Jesus was more than willing. He made Himself of no reputation, taking on the form of a servant. In this context, the word for "servant" in the Greek is *doulos*-a love slave.

Look at Romans 5:8: "But God commendeth his love toward us, in that, while we were yet sinners, Christ died for us."

In the *Twentieth Century* translation it says, "God put his love for us beyond all doubt by the fact that Christ died on our behalf while we were still sinners." Jesus, it says here, died on our behalf. That's a substitute. The term "for us," or "on our behalf," is more than just a nice thought. We are to see substitution here-someone taking another's place, as the definition goes, by accepting full responsibility for the position assumed.

Jesus was more than willing. He said, "Father, I'll assume full responsibility for mankind. I will die for them." Jesus literally became us in substitution. Before He died on the cross. He suffered in my place taking all the effects of the curse on Him, for me. God put sickness, disease, pain, sorrow, rejection, and all that the curse offered on His Son, Jesus. He said, "That's for you, mankind. Jesus is your substitute." That was all meant for us. That was all meant for you. It was our pain. It was our sickness. It was our sorrow. It was our rejection. It was our poverty.

Jesus was saying in His atonement, " I'll substitute for you. I'll take all that on Myself for you." While you were at home, sick, He was on Calvary's cross taking your place-you thought. But wait a minute. Remember, He said, "If I be lifted up (a large magnet) I will draw you right up on the cross with Me." You thought you were home, and Jesus was taking care of it for you; but oh, no, the Word says you were on the cross with Him.

Paul said, "I am crucified with Christ." When Jesus went on that cross, you went up there with Him. He was your substitute. He took your place. Everything that was due you, He took. But God saw you as being up there with Him. You weren't at the mall shopping while Jesus died and arose from the dead. You were right there in Him through every event. What those events did for Jesus, they did for you. Glory to God!

There can be no identification without substitution.

This is very important. Galatians 2:20 says,

I am crucified with Christ: nevertheless I live; yet not I, but Christ liveth in me: and the life that I now live in the flesh I live by the faith of the Son of God, who loved me, and gave himself for me. Substitution and identification are in this verse of Scripture. He identified with us upon becoming our substitute. There can be no identification if He did not substitute for us. He became a curse for us. That's substitution. Then we can identify with Him in His glorious resurrection. The English Bible says, "The law put us under condemnation, but Christ took that condemnation away." Galatians 3:14 says that Christ did this so that God's promised blessing could be given to all His people. In either translation, we see substitution in Galatians 2:20 and identification in Galatians 3:14.

Romans 3:25-26, states:
Whom God hath set forth to be a <u>propitiation</u> through faith

113

in his blood, to declare his righteousness for the remission of
sins that are past, through the forbearance of God. To declare,
I say, at this time his righteousness: that he might be just, and
the justifier of him, which believeth in Jesus.

Here again, we see substitution in verse 25. Do you see the word "propitiation" (sacrifice, expiation, atonement, substitution)? In verse 26, we can now identify with Him in His righteousness through faith in His blood. In this same verse, we see the words, "To declare..." To declare what? That God gave Jesus to be our righteousness. "...that he might be just and the justifier of him that believeth in Jesus." You see, you can substitute the word "righteous" for the word "just." It's the very same word. The just shall live by faith; the righteous shall live by faith. Verse 26: "...that he might be righteous and the righteousness of him that believeth in Jesus." This verse tells us that we are now identified with Him in His righteousness. You see, He was our substitute. He bore our sins, our unrighteousness, and now that He is in right standing with God, God has declared His righteousness and the righteousness of those who believe in Jesus.

We are now in right standing with Almighty God. This idea of substitution and identification can be seen clearly in the Old Testament. The book of Leviticus will tell you all about substitution. When Israel sinned and wanted to get right with God, what did God tell them to do? God always told them, "Get yourself a substitute animal-a goat, a bull, a heifer-and sacrifice it." Why? Why didn't God, in all His power and all His almightiness, turn to the people and say, "I'm going to speak the command of faith and you will all be clean." Why didn't God do it that way?

Doesn't God's Word tell us that He has all power in Heaven and earth? Can't he just stand up there and tell them, "Be clean?" Can't God do everything? No, God can't do everything. He can't lie, can He? He can't do bad things and evil things. He can't tempt you with evil. He can't fail. He can't change nor can He break His Word. So don't try to tell us that God can do everything. He can't, He is sovereign within the boundaries of His Word. God will never ever break His Word (John 10:35b).

A principle in God's Word is that there can be no identification without substitution. And all those types of atonement in the Old Testament simply pointed to the final atonement, the Lord Jesus Christ, the Lamb of God on the cross. All the types in the Old Testament required a substitute-then there could be identification. Why do you suppose we can enjoy health today in our bodies? Because Jesus first became our substitute. The Scripture says

He bore our sicknesses in His body, and that was substitution. So now we can enjoy His resurrection life, His health in our bodies. We are identified with Him now in His health.

First Peter 2:24, is one of the greatest substitutionary verses in the Bible: "Who his own self bare our sins in his own body on the tree, that we, being dead to sins, should live unto righteousness: by whose stripes ye were healed." Can you see substitution?

Let's go one step further. Why is it possible for us to enjoy financial prosperity in our lives right now? Because Jesus, as our substitute, bore our poverty (II Cor. 8:9). Now we can identify with His resurrection riches.

> Look at 2 Peter 1:4-9
>
> *Whereby are given unto us exceeding great and precious promises:*
> *that by these [exceeding great and precious promises] ye might be*
> *partakers of the divine nature, having escaped the corruption that*
> *is in the world through lust. And besides this, giving all diligence, add*
> *to your faith virtue; and to virtue knowledge;*
> *And to knowledge temperance; and to temperance patience;*
> *And to patience godliness;*
> *And to godliness brotherly kindness; and to brotherly kindness charity.*
> *For if these things be in you, and abound, they make you that ye shall*
> *Neither be barren nor unfruitful in the knowledge of our*
> *Lord Jesus Christ. But he that lacketh these things is blind, and*
> *cannot see afar off, and hath forgotten that he was purged from*
> *his old sins.*

We must not forget what Christ did for us on the cross. He was our substitute; He took our place. There could be no identification without a substitutionary sacrifice. An offering had to be made before we could enjoy all the blessings of this new life in Jesus Christ. Jesus bore our sin. Jesus was our propitiation. He was our mercy seat. He was our sacrifice. He was our expiation. He was the Redeemer who took your sin and mine on Himself.

Isaiah 53:6 says, "All we like sheep have gone astray... " How many? "And the Lord hath laid on him the iniquity of us all." Who is "Him"? Now look back at verse 3: "He is despised..." Why is He despised? Because God made Him to be sin who knew no sin. "He is despised and rejected of men; a man of sorrows..." That word "sorrows: is *makob* in the Hebrew language. It means pains, physical pains. "...and acquainted with grief..." The word grief is the Hebrew word *choli*. It means sicknesses, physical sicknesses. "And we hid as it were our faces from him; he was despised, and we esteemed him not. Surely he hath borne..." the word for "borne" is *nasa*. Our space program is named after that word. It means to lift off, to take something from this place and carry it away to another place.

"He has borne our griefs and carried our sorrows: yet we did esteem him stricken, smitten of God, and afflicted. But he was wounded for our transgressions, he was bruised for our iniquities: the chastisement of our peace was upon him; and with his stripes you were healed."

"Someone may say, "Wait a minute, that's all of a spiritual nature." No it isn't. If you know anything about the New Testament, you know Matthew 8:16, states that when evening was come, Jesus went about healing all that were sick so it might be fulfilled what the prophet Isaiah said in Isaiah 53:3, that He bore our sicknesses and carried our diseases. Substitution and then identification. Jesus became like us. He became our sin so that we could become His righteousness. He took our sicknesses so we could take His health. He took everything that was under the curse. Paul said, "Cursed is everyone that hangeth on the tree that the blessing of Abraham might come upon the Gentiles through Jesus Christ." Substitution=Identification. He took our sickness, our pains, our sins, our sorrows, our rejection-everything under the curse, our poverty, our eternal death. These He took on Himself and became our substitute. Now each of us can say, "I'm no longer in Adam. I'm now in Christ, so the blessing of Abraham is mine!"

CHAPTER

9

MORE IMPORTANT FACTS ABOUT
YOUR REDEMPTION

We now understand that we have an inheritance already bought and paid for and the reason we study the Word of God is to discover for ourselves what is in that inheritance by way of studying the Cross. It's amazing that so many church-going people do not understand what our identification with Christ is all about. That's a sad commentary on churches. Few churches are teaching their people who they are in Christ, what Christ has done for them on Calvary's cross, and what benefits belong to them as a result of what Christ did on the cross through His death, burial and resurrection.

We have been looking at this very carefully, building on it chapter by chapter. In the previous chapter, we began to look at five important facts regarding our identification with the Lord Jesus Christ.

In Romans 3, we're going to look at what God says about our identification. It is important to be a doer of the Word, not just a hearer. Do it. Meditate on it. Try to comprehend what you read. It's not difficult if you apply yourself and trust the Holy Spirit to teach you.

Remember what we said earlier about those who want to bypass Calvary? You can't bypass Calvary. We used the example of how if you're flying down south, everything seems to go through Atlanta. In Christianity, everything goes through Calvary. Calvary is the crux of Christianity. If we become established in what took place at Calvary, we can go on to the other things.

117

We'll have a foundation when we understand Calvary and what became ours as a result of what Jesus did there. You can't ignore the work of the cross.

We've been looking at the position of Jesus as a substitute for us at Calvary's cross. We're belaboring that point because it is so important that you understand it. We are not going to rush through it. Your life will become much easier-much more victorious when you fully grasp this truth. In fact, if you want a quality life, you'll spend time at Calvary.

We continue to study this ourselves, and each of us keeps asking the question: "How does this apply to me?" Every time you read the Scriptures ask the Holy Spirit, "How does this particular truth apply to me? Where can I make application to this in my own personal life?"

When He shows you, walk out in it, take a hold of it and do it. And the next time, just add a little bit more. And you know what? You'll become more and more like Christ all the time. Your life will become victorious and much easier. You will learn to REST in the finished work of Christ (Hebrews 4:9,10)! You will live in the Peace of God, no matter what is happening in this world! Learn all you can about identification-it will affect every area of your life.

So, let's quickly review the previous chapter.

1. **Jesus was our substitute, our sacrifice.**

   Jesus was our propitiation, our mercy-seat. In other words, Jesus took our place. A substitute, we found out, is one who stands in for another, who takes another's place.

2. **There can be no identification without substitution.**

   So we must understand the fact that Jesus was our substitute before we can identify with Him.

   The scriptures have to become real to all of us. We can't just *hear* the Word of God and not *see* it in terms of ourselves being at Calvary with Jesus. Brace yourselves with us for this, because if we don't get a personal view of being on Calvary's cross with Jesus-being there with Him as the Father sees us there-we won't understand this subject. It must be real to us. That's what meditation in God's Word is all about. It's like getting out one of your old high school class pictures and trying to find yourself in it. You know you're in there, but sometimes you have to look very closely and intently to see yourself. Just like Jesus found Himself in the Word (Luke 4:17-21).

It must be real to us. When each of us says, as Paul says, "I have been crucified with Christ," that has to be so real to us that we can actually see the nails driven through Jesus' hands right into our own hands and see ourselves on the cross with Him. We have been crucified with Christ, we have a special unity with Christ, but more importantly, we have to know and understand why we have been crucified with Christ. Why was it necessary for us to be crucified with Christ? Why was it necessary for Jesus to be crucified at all?

Romans 3:25-26 says,
Whom God hath set forth to be a propitiation through faith in His blood, to declare His righteousness for the remission of sins that are past, through the forbearance of God; to declare, I say, at this time his righteousness: that he might be just, and the justifier of him that believeth in Jesus.

What Can We Declare?

Now the question is: What have we, at this point in our understanding of identification with Jesus, to declare? What do we have to say about this subject? Have we learned anything so far? If Jesus appeared in front of us right now and said, "Look, it is very important that you know this. What have you to declare about what you've learned so far?" What would we say?

There is a reality in life. What is reality in your life? Someone may say, "I get up, eat, work, pay bills, that's reality. I'm married and I have children for whom I'm responsible, that's reality.

And we know that's real. We're not denying that those things exist. We all have issues that we are dealing with, but God expects us to think deeper than that. Those things should <u>not</u> be the number 1 reality in our lives (Mathew 6:33)! What is the main reality in your life today? You see, the reality in your own mind and heart is what you'll declare out of your mouth. <u>Our reality is that Jesus is Lord.</u> Bottom line. What else do we have to say once we declare that Jesus Christ is our Lord? Declare what He's done for you on Calvary's cross. Be totally convinced in your heart of what He's done, and say it out of your mouth, "It is so." That's reality in your life. That's what you live by. That's what we teach: the reality of Jesus Christ as Lord in our lives, and His finished work on the Cross. I like to think of it like this: the spiritual atmosphere that we breathe and live in on this earth is the death and resurrection of our Lord Jesus Christ (Colossians 2:6-10).

We said that in order for us to enjoy the blessings of God today, Jesus had to be our propitiation, our sacrificial substitute on Calvary's cross. We also said it is a principle in God's Word that there must be a substitutionary sacrifice. And why did we say that? Because it's a principle out lined in the Old Testament. When we look at the animal sacrifices of the Old Testament, we see that there had to be some kind of blood covering, something that God could put over the sins of mankind. Animals had to die and blood had to be spilled. That's what God both ordained and accepted.

Romans 3:25 tells us why we can enjoy righteousness in our spirits today. Notice what we just said. Righteousness manifests itself, not in our little finger, but in our spirit man. This is important. Righteousness is neither in our bodies nor in our minds. We enjoy righteousness in our spirits. Now, God's righteousness in our spirits is manifested as holiness in the rest of our lives. That's why God could command us to be holy as He is holy (I Peter 1:13-16). It's not because we are God, but because we have His nature in our spirits.

Why is it possible to enjoy righteousness, as noted in these verses, in our spirits? Because Jesus was our substitute and bore our unrighteousness or our sin in His spirit-not in His mind or body, but in His spirit. Sin is spiritual. Now, that's another fact we can't forget-sin is spiritual, and resides in our spirits. So where did Jesus bear our sins? In His mind? In His finger? No, in His own body where His Spirit is. Our sin was placed in His Spirit. Also, please understand, the affect or result of sin in a person's spirit can be sickness in his body (John 5:14), or the suffering of any part of the curse.

If you commit adultery or rob a bank, that sin does not reside in your feet does it? Sin is spiritual. It abides or stays in your spirit, even though it can produce bad affects in other areas of your life. Your spirit man bears the sin not your foot, not your ear, not your hand. Your spirit man is darkened because of sin. We're just going to wet your appetite a little bit in the area of Jesus dying spiritually. We will study it further down the road. The only method of getting this sin out of our spirit was to have a substitute take our place —remove the sin from our spirits and put it in the substitute's spirit. Not in His finger. Not in His mind, but in that substitute's spirit. In other words, what's in my spirit (sin) must be transferred to someone else's spirit in order for me to be rid of it. Are you following this?

It goes from your spirit into your substitute's spirit because, again, sin is spiritual. Jesus became our substitute. He took our place. While sin was in our spirits or while we were still Adam, what was the status of our spirits?

Now think scripturally. The Scripture says in Ephesians 2:1, "You were dead in your sins and trespasses." If you were in Adam, and sin was in your spirit, you were dead in your sins and trespasses.

So, you could be walking around breathing, eating, doing sports, sleeping and working, and still be dead. What part of you was dead? Your spirit man was dead, not your body. It was still breathing and functioning. Then the sin that made you dead had to be in your spirit. And therefore, it was your spirit man that was dead, not your body. You were walking around before you met Christ. You were eating, breathing, sleeping, playing, and working. Yet the Bible says you were dead in your sins and trespasses. Sin is spiritual. Therefore, if you're still walking around when the Bible says you're dead, then your death has to be in your spirit. Jesus became your substitute. He became your substitute and as such, He must identify with you in every aspect. The definition of the word identify is <u>to make identical, to consider and treat the same.</u>

He was made to be sin for you-He who knew no sin (II Cor. 5:21). When was Jesus made to be sin for you? Was it not while He was still on the cross? Was He still physically alive when He was made to be sin for you? Then where was the sin placed on Jesus? In His spirit. Look at 1 Peter 2:24. (Pay close attention to words; don't go rapidly past words no matter how small they are. Because if you read them and your mind is set on something else when you read, you'll read it incorrectly and place a thought in your heart that will be very difficult for you to remove even though it may be incorrect.)

Understanding Spiritual Death

First Peter 2:24, states: "Who his own self [Jesus] bare our sins..." [Now notice this next word. Does it say *on* His body? It says <u>in</u> His body. In His spirit man.] "Who his own self bare our sins in his body..."[In other words, where is the spirit man residing? On the inside of the shell of the man.]

We are three-part individuals; we are spirit, soul (mind, will and emotions) and body. This could be rephrased more correctly by saying that each of us is a spirit, each of us has a mind and each of us lives in a body. We're three parts. Why are we three parts? Because we're made after the image and likeness of God. If you were dead in your sins and trespasses and the sins were transferred from your spirit into Jesus' spirit, then He totally identified with you. Let's repeat that. If you were dead in your sins and trespasses, and those sins were transferred from your spirit man-sin is spiritual-into Jesus' spirit man, then He must have totally identified with you in order for your redemption to be complete.

Can He leave any part of the redemption process out? If He did, something would be dreadfully wrong. He has to identify with mankind totally. Then, since that is the case, what happened to Jesus when sin was placed in His spirit man? He died. But what part of Him died? He was still physically alive on the cross when this happened to Him. Therefore, His spirit man must have died or experienced separation from the Life of God.

Now we have to understand what spiritual death is before we can complete our thinking on this. To many, this is a controversial subject. There are people who say, "Jesus never died spiritually, because God can't die." That's a ridiculous statement. Everybody knows God can't die. If He dies, we're gone. The Lord Jesus wasn't just God walking the earth. He was the incarnate One. God manifested in the flesh. Everything that He did on this earth wasn't because He was God, but because He was a sinless man anointed with the Holy Spirit. That's how He could identify with us, because He became a man. He just did not commit any sin. Jesus was a sinless man when He became sin for us. God laid our sin upon Him, and He identified with us by bearing our spiritual death, therefore, He had to be separated from the Father. When Jesus died on the cross, we died; but we got life put back into us. If Jesus died spiritually, couldn't we call that spiritual death? It was for us, it had to be for Him also. Don't you agree that's spiritual death? Yes, death was in His spirit.

What immediately took place in our spirits when sin entered, God who is a Holy God, could not possibly stay where sin was residing. He must withdraw Himself.

What did Jesus say with a loud voice on the cross when my sin and yours was transferred to His spirit? "My God, my God, why hast Thou forsaken Me?" What does the word "forsake" mean? The Greek word is *egkataleipo*. That means to desert, to abandon. When God leaves you and abandons you, His life goes out of you. God is light. Your spirit became darkened immediately. You were alienated from the life of God. Your spirit then was doomed. Why? Because you did not have the life of God. You had the life of satan or the absence of God's life. You were physically alive but you had the nature of satan (sin and death) in your spirit.

So we see Jesus bearing our spiritual death. Where? In His spirit, so we could be made alive by identification in His quickening, resurrection power. Jesus had to be our substitute. There is no identification without substitution. Therefore, if He cannot identify with you in your sins and trespasses, you cannot relate or identify with Him in His resurrection power and life. There must be a substitution first, followed by identification.

Look at Ephesians 2:5: "Even when we were dead in sins..." [Notice when? When did God quicken us?] "...hath God quickened us..." [Look at the next word.] "...together with Christ, [By grace ye are saved;] and hath..." [What tense is that word?]

"...and hath raised us up together, and made us sit together in heavenly places in Christ Jesus."

These are foundations that will last a lifetime in Christianity. Ephesians 2:5, says we were quickened together. God quickened us together with Christ. What does the word "together" mean? The Greek word is *suzugos*. It means to be co-yoked. If you were dead in your sins, that means your spirit was alienated from God's life. Correct? And if you are co-yoked with Jesus in this condition, then that means He was also in the same condition you were in. Why is that? Because, as your substitute, He took your place, and your sins were put into His spirit. Together, both of you were dead in sins, and both of you needed to have God's life put in you.

It was as if Jesus said, "I've got to get you back in right standing with God so I'm going to be your substitute. Transfer that sin, Father, from them into Me. We will become co-yoked."

On the cross, Jesus said, "My God, my God, why have You forsaken Me?" Why? He who knew no sin became sin that we might become the righteousness of God in Christ Jesus. Because of Jesus' identification with us, He became sin. He took our sin and transferred it from our spirit into His spirit, and the life of God went out of His spirit. His spirit was dead. Spiritually dead.

We should understand what that means now. When a spirit is dead, it is alienated or *separated* from the life of God. When God quickened Jesus, we were quickened with Him. It says so in the Scripture. We were made alive with Him.

What's Real?

Do you see how important it is to have substitution and identification? As Paul put it, we, with Christ, were quickened and have been put in heavenly places, seated at the right hand of God. God says, "That' real to Me. When I raised up Jesus from the dead, I raised you up with Him." That's a reality in God's mind. He sees you raised up. How do you see yourself? Or, let's put it this way-how *should* you see yourself? Raised up. What else? Seated. Where and how? Together with Christ in heavenly places. Any biblical position that the Bible says we have is because we are *in Christ.*

I could not be raised up to sit with Christ until Jesus was raised, and that meant that Gods life had to be put back into Jesus. Jesus had to be made alive again from spiritual death. When He was made alive, so were we. So were you.

Now remember, we're studying spiritual death, not mental or physical death. Death was in our spirits, and our spirits were made alive again. There can be no identification without substitution. Now look at fact **Number Three.**

Jesus became in His spirit all that we were.

Notice the word, "all". If He did not become all that we were, <u>it would not have been a complete redemption.</u> Jesus had to become all that we were-100 percent of what we were, not 50 percent, not 75 percent, but 100 percent of what we were. All that we were, He had to become. That's complete substitution.

Look at 2 Corinthians 5:21 (Many of the scriptures we're going to use will explain several of the things in identification. If you think we're overlapping, we are. You'll see this clearly as you begin to study the "in Him" or "by Him" and 'through Him" scriptures. They all overlap, but you can use them in many different explanations.)

"For he hath made him to be sin for us, who knew no sin; that we might be made the righteousness of God in him."

This verse makes substitution and identification very, very clear. Can you see both sides in the scripture? God made Jesus sin for us-substitution. Why? That we might be made the righteousness of God in Him- Identification. Jesus became exactly what we were so we could become exactly what He is now.

If you get a hold of this, the devil won't be able to take advantage of you anymore. We're talking about realities in a Christian's life. These are realities, whether they are real to us at this moment or not. To God this is real; to the devil this is real (yes, unfortunately, the devil understands this more than most Christians).

As God viewed Jesus when He became sin for us and looked into Jesus' spirit, God literally saw what was in *our* spirit. In God's eyes, Jesus was identical to us. He considered and treated Jesus exactly the same as He would treat us. He has to because Jesus had to become all that we were. When Jesus became all that we were, God had to shift over and say, "If I abandon these people because of sin in their spirits and because their spirits were dead, then Jesus' spirit has to become dead and I have to abandon Him." To be identical means what? <u>To treat the same way or to make identical.</u>

God views Jesus on the cross with our sins in Him. God was actually looking at all of us on that cross. Jesus became all of humanity on that cross because all that we were, Jesus became. The *Translator's New Testament* reads, "God made him to be sin itself on our behalf." The *Good News Bible* says, "God made him share our sin." The *Jerusalem Bible I says* "Four our sakes God made the sinless one into sin." The *New English Bible* says, "God made him one with the sinfulness of men." *Knox's Bible* says, "God made him into sin for us." The *Living Bible* says, "For God took the sinless Christ and poured into him our sins." It's pretty clear, isn't it? And when Jesus became sin for us-listen-He became identified with us; He was spiritually dead.

Jesus Christ could free us only by becoming all that we were. If He did not become all that we were, then we couldn't be just like He is right now, because you see, if only 50 percent of what was wrong with us was changed, how could we be like He is now? Does that make sense? When the Bible speaks literally, then read it literally-it's not difficult.

Remember, to identify means to make identical, to consider and treat as the same. In order for us to become new creations, Jesus had to get rid of 100 percent of the old creation. If that were not done, we would be part of the old creation and part of the new creation. We would have two natures. But the Scripture says, "Old things have passed away. All things are become new." That's talking about our spirit man. Not 50 percent, not 75 percent, but all things have become new. 100 percent!! The Greek word for "new" is kainos, it means unused, fresh and novel. As Christians, we're not like a used car that's been cleaned up real well, but is still used. That's the image that many Christians have of themselves. One translation says that we are new species that never before existed. When God says you are new, you are brand new!

Remember, Jesus was the second man. Adam was the first man to father a race of people who were spiritually dead, separated from God. But, the Lord Jesus fathered a new race of spiritually alive people. Sons and daughters of God!

A dead Man Can't Be Tempted

We are talking about man's spirit. We are not talking about a repaired old spirit. We have had the old man, the old nature, annihilated, wiped out.

125

As one minister says, "Graveyard dead." That old man is dead and buried-destroyed, killed. That old man, that Adamic nature is gone. We now have one new nature.

Don't let anybody tell you that you have two natures in your spirit. You do not have two natures in you. All things have become new. Old things have passed away. The Adamic nature does not reside in you anymore. The memory is there, and the devil knows what's in your memory. That's what he keeps coming after. What was in your memory? Satan will say, "Do you remember the way you used to be? You really haven't changed. Come on. Go back and do the same old thing."

But you see, you can simply say, "That old man of mine is graveyard dead. If a man is dead how are you going to tempt a dead man?"

God credited our account with all that Jesus did for us in His death, burial and resurrection.

God has given credit to us in our account for all that Jesus did for us in His death, burial and resurrection (I John 4:17b). In other words, Jesus did it, but you get the grade. It's like somebody taking a test for you. He gets an "A" pulls out the folder and says, "I'll mark and "A" in your folder." In this case, Jesus got it for you. He was your substitute-He took the test for you. He got an "A"; you got and "A". God identifies all of us with Jesus.

Whatever Jesus did in His death, burial and resurrection, God pulled out your folder in Heaven and marked a big fat A in it and says, "You've passed the course. You've graduated out of death into life. You have complete credit for it even though you didn't have anything to do with it." Jesus did all the work of redemption; and because there was a substitution and identification, God viewed us as being on the cross and credited our account for everything Jesus did. We graduated from spiritual death unto the God-kind of life.

Jesus said, "Father, forgive them for they know not what they do. I'm up here on their account, on their behalf. Please give them full credit. Give them an A for what I'm doing up here." Don't you like that? Jesus passed all of God's requirements-and we got the credit.

Now keep this in mind-because you were credited with all that took place on Calvary, you can now operate with all the authority and power that was released on Calvary's cross. You are in Jesus Christ. Do you remember when God quickened Him and raised Him from the dead? What kind of power do you think was released then? A man is dead, graveyard dead, physically and spiritually. What kind of power did God have to release, to bring that man's spirit back into life with Him and get Him out of that grave-physically dead and back into life again? Friends, that's some kind of power! That's the awesome power that quickened your Redeemer.

Remember now, you were in Christ. You were crucified with Him, buried with Him, raised up and seated in heavenly places with Him. When Jesus got that power and it hit Him, it hit you too. You now have and can operate in all the authority and power that was released at Calvary in Jesus, because God saw you in Jesus on Calvary's cross. The mind has a hard time grasping this, but this is Biblical. This is eternal truth (John 17:17).

Satan was there and saw Jesus do it. It's real to him. He knows exactly what happened. Jesus did it. Satan has no argument with that at all. He knows what happened. We were there in Christ. It *should* be real to us. Meditate on this until it becomes real to you. Let this transform your mind (Rom. 12:2).

What did God say about that? Are you going to call God a liar? He said you were there. Paul said, "I was crucified with Christ." How real do you think that was to Paul, the Apostle? It was so real that he lived out his life in that power. Everywhere he went, miracles took place. Devils were cast out of people. It was pretty real to him. "I was crucified with Christ, nevertheless, I live." How did Paul live after that? Not by his own power or his own ways. He says, "I live by the faith of the Son of God who loved me and gave Himself for me." Paul understood substitution and his identification with Christ, and so can we, if we study it. It's not difficult to understand.

Unmerited Favor of God

Everything He did for you has been credited to *your* account. You graduated with an "A". The devil knows that you passed the course. Everybody seems to know what's going on except we Christians. We just said the devil knows; it's certainly real to him. The Father knows; it's certainly real to Him. The Holy Ghost knows; it was His power that accomplished this, so it's real to Him. The angels know. But we seem to be the only ones who don't know it. If we received that resurrection power released to us on Calvary's cross when Jesus died, why do we still let the devil push us around? The old man is dead and the new man is full of power and authority. So if we would reckon it so and start meditating on these scriptures-on who we are in Christ-and start confessing out of our mouths that it is so, the devil will back off, and our lives would become what God wants them to be-totally victorious, fulfilled, abundant, cooperating with God's plan for our lives (Romans 6:11).

Satan knows it's true. The Bible says Jesus made an open show of him. In other words, He annihilated satan. Jesus made satan powerless over us (Heb.2:14,15). All the devil can do now is go around and growl. Can growling hurt you? He has no real legal power. The devil seeks those he may devour. He does it by <u>deception.</u> He comes along and tells you, "You're nobody. You're just a worm in the kingdom of God." You've probably heard some of those ridiculous teachings from the pit of Hell telling you that you're just a worm. You ought to be happy that you're going to make it to Heaven. You're not worth two cents. Just be thankful that you are going to Heaven. Yes, be thankful, be humble; but know your authority as a believer.

Isn't that what God told us to do? He's telling you who you are in Christ. He said, "You're seated with My Son in heavenly places. That's real to us. Why don't you take that authority Jesus gave you?" If Jesus is seated at God's right hand, that is a position of authority. Aren't you seated there with Christ? Jesus said, "I have all authority in Heaven and earth and I give it to you (Mathew 28: 18-20). In no manner shall the devil harm you or hurt you. You have all power over all scorpions and serpents, and over all the power of the enemy." Jesus understands that you were identified with him. To identify means, once again, to make identical and to treat the same. God gave Jesus all authority: God gave you the same authority. Luke 10:19 tells us this. When will we start believing God's Word? Aren't we called "believers"?

We sit back and say, "Oh God, please get the devil off my case." God says, "He already is. Just reckon it so."

Isn't that the truth? Reckon it so. When you submit to the truth of Calvary and resist the devil in your spiritual authority in Jesus' name, the devil is going to flee. Remember, God put the full credit to your account. He credited your account with what Jesus did in His death, burial and resurrection.

John 1:17, states, "Truth and grace came by Jesus Christ"? God says in His Word that we move on from glory to glory. He says when you behold the truth, He wants you to become that truth. When you behold it, you must become it. God says, "I'm going to give you a truth, a principle in My Word. I am not going to just simply give you truths so that your minds can get puffed up with knowledge. I want you to literally *become* that truth. I want it to be so real to you that you think in terms of 'That's right. I am this. This is real to me. I'm walking in the authority. I'm walking in the power of the Son of God. I see myself seated right next to Jesus on the throne. It's so real to me.'"

See the truth revealed to you and become that truth (II Cor.3:18). Now you say, "Wait a minute. It's one thing to talk about these things and another to become it." Well, that's true. But when you see a truth being revealed to you, and circumstances all around make you want to say, "I can't do it. No way." Jesus is saying, "I also brought grace." What is grace? God's ability to do what you can't do through your own ability. It's favor from God, isn't it? You're seeing the truth in the Word of God; we're telling you to become the truth; and you say, "My circumstances are overwhelming. How in the world am I ever going…" Jesus said, "My grace provides." To Paul He said His grace was sufficient.

What does grace provide? Whatever it is you need to live out the truth. Didn't He say, "Come boldly to the throne <u>of grace</u> to obtain mercy, to find help in time of need" (Heb. 4:16)? How do you see yourself?

Look at fact **Number Five.**

"As He is, so are we."

This statement comes from 1 John 4:17. Now to us that's a gigantic statement. When we look at it-"As He is, so are we,"-we say, "God, that's truly awsome!" If that is true (and it has to be because He said it) that's spectacular!"

"As He…" Who's he? Jesus. "As He is, "God says, "So are we". Don't you see why we're saying that's spectacular? As Jesus is, as God sees Jesus, God sees us. Why? Because God identifies us with Jesus.

Let's look at this. As He is, as Jesus is right now? When you answer that, you're really saying that whatever He is right now, we are also. Not as He was before Calvary. So let's look at it. This statement could only be made, of course, on the finished work of Calvary. Where is Jesus right now? Is Jesus worried about anything? Is Jesus sitting up there wringing His hands in fear of the devil? Is Jesus concerned about anything? Is He wondering how He is going to get rid of a headache? Is Jesus depressed? No, no, no! God forbid!

How Are You Today, Jesus?

As He is, so are we. If we're going around worried and fretting and somebody out in the world hears that scripture, he's going to say, "I thought as He is, so are you supposed to be. So, is our impression of Jesus supposed to be that He's a worry wart? Is Jesus nervous? Is He depressed? Is the devil defeating Him?" No, that's not so! As He is, so are we!!

Look at Ephesians 2:4-6:

But God, who is rich in mercy for his great love wherewith he loved us,
Even when we were dead in sins, hath quickened us together
With Christ, (by grace you are saved ;)
And hath raised us up together, and made us sit together in
Heavenly places in Christ Jesus…

Where are you seated in God's eyes? With Christ Jesus in heavenly places. Is that a position of authority at the Father's right hand? Sure it is. You can't get any more authority than sitting at the Father's right hand, because that's where Jesus is seated and, "He has all authority in Heaven and earth." So when you get up each day and wonder how your day will go, just ask Jesus how it's going for Him. Your existence depends on how it's going for Him; because it says, "As He is, so are we in this world." Are you getting this? We're trying hard to make this clear for you. Your life depends on it.

Do you know how Jesus is? Let me tell you. He's peaceful. He's calm. He's full of authority. He's guiltless. He's happy. He's loving. He's victorious. He's healthy, He's righteous and, my friends, He's not at all depressed. He has no fears. He's full of joy, and He's not broke. You see you're in Christ so you're going to be this way today also. You're going to act just like who you are in Him, and enjoy the abundant life He's given you! If the old man is dead, the old nature's gone. The devil cannot overcome you with temptation. Yes, he can shoot darts at you, but you will quench them all with your shield of faith (Ephesians 6:16). You're a new creature in Christ.

Jesus said, "I have given you total authority, total victory, total joy, total peace, total guiltlessness." Walk around with *those* things in your mind. Why should you have to go absolutely crazy about what the devil is doing in this world when you know that Jesus defeated and utterly annihilated him? Why should you have to worry about that since Jesus took care of him? Too often we have all our attention on the devil when it should be on Jesus (Col. 3:1,2). We should be asking, "How are You today, Jesus?"

"Everything's fine with Me."

"Then it's going to be fine with me also."

That old man had some terrible, sinful habits. There was a nature in that old man that was the same as Adam. But the good news is that the old Adamic nature, your old man, is dead. He was crucified with Christ. And if he is dead, how can a dead man serve sin? Huh? Stay with us now. Look at Romans 6:6-10. Chapter 6 is one that you should try to read everyday. It will set you free.

*Knowing this, that our old man is crucifed with him, that
the body of sin might be destroyed, that henceforth
we should not serve sin.*
For he that is dead is freed from sin.
*Now if we be dead with Christ, we believe that we shall also
live with him:*
*Knowing that Christ being raised from the dead dieth no
more; death hath no more dominion over him.*
*For in that he died, he died unto sin once: but in that he
liveth, he liveth unto God.*

Jesus is living unto God. In the same manner follow after Jesus' example. Verse 11: "Likewise reckon ye also yourselves to be dead indeed unto sin, But alive unto God through Jesus Christ our Lord."

In other words, he says, "Reckon it." The Greek word for "reckon" is *logizomai*, meaning to take an inventory or to consider. He says, knowing this, how much more do you know now than when you began? In other words, knowing this, you have an understanding now. Knowing this, reckon it so. Now you know it. We've taught you a truth; now become that truth. God doesn't reveal something to you just so your head can be puffed up with knowledge. He reveals it to you, saying, "Behold it; become it." Become all that God says you are in Christ. Be totally conformed to His image (Rom. 8:29)!

Now that we know the old man is dead let's not serve sin anymore. Reckon it so. Know this-the old man is dead. The old man doesn't have to serve sin anymore. Now you're going to live unto God. Jesus lives unto God.

Look at Romans 6:11-14:
*Likewise [as Jesus did] reckon ye also yourselves to be dead
indeed unto sin, but alive unto God through Jesus Christ
our Lord.*
*Let not sin therefore reign in your mortal body, that ye should
obey it in the lusts thereof.*
*Neither yield ye your members as instruments of
unrighteousness unto sin: but [because you're a new man;
you're a new creature in Christ] yield yourselves unto God,
as those that are alive from the dead, and your members as
instruments of righteousness unto God.*
*For sin shall not have dominion over you: for ye are not
under the law, but under grace.*

131

Are you getting the whole picture, the full scope? Take an inventory of all you've read so far on identification with Christ and then agree with it. We've shown it to you scripturally. Say to yourself, "Just as Jesus is, I am." That will make all the difference in you life.

Jesus is seated at the Father's side in full authority. Say, "I'm seated with Him. I have the same authority He has. The devil has been defeated by Jesus. All he can possibly do is lie to me and try to deceive me. But you see, I understand this now. So devil, when you come along and try to tempt me, that old man is dead. It doesn't work anymore. The old man is dead. He's graveyard dead. <u>I'm a new creature now.</u> As He (Jesus) is, so am I in this world." We have to make this a reality in our lives. And when we do, we will utterly defeat the devil. We will no longer believe his lies because we now know the truth-and listen-the truth that we know will keep us free.

10

THE OLD MAN IS DEAD

Our prayer should be, as we begin each chapter, "Father, I'm reading this because I really want to understand who I am in Jesus Christ. I really want to grasp the truth, the principles underlying this whole study." Any time you are listening to or reading the Word, you should be asking the Father to speak to you directly and quicken everything to your spirit man. Pray that it becomes a rhema word in your life so you can live and walk in it.

In the last two chapters, we talked about five important facts. Let's quickly review them.

1. Jesus was our substitute, our sacrifice, our propitiation. He took our place. A substitute is one who stands in for another. Jesus was ordained by Almighty God to be our substitute in redemption. Jesus was God's plan for our <u>complete</u> salvation.
2. There can be no identification without substitution.
3. Jesus became, in His spirit, all that we were while we were in Adam. Notice the word
    All. When the Adamic nature was in us, Jesus had to become all of that when He took our place.
4. God credited our account with all that Jesus did for us in His death, burial and

Resurrection. We said in the last chapter that God pulled out each one of our "folders" in heaven, looked at our name and gave us an A-plus. He said,

"Whatever Jesus accomplished, and because He did such a fine job, I give everyone of you an A plus. You all passed the course. You all have graduated." Remember, God treats us the same as Jesus; He identifies us with Jesus.

5. As He is, so are we. Now that's a very small verse from the Scripture, but that's a very important one.

The Way God Sees Us

Every morning when you get up, when you know who you are in Christ, you simply say, "As He is, so am I." That's what the Word says. We also said that as God looked at Jesus on the cross of Calvary and saw the nails driven into Jesus' hands and feet, the crown on His head, the spear hole in His side, and His back torn literally apart by the cat-o'-nine tails with which He was whipped, God saw you on that cross too. He saw the holes in your hands, the holes in your feet, the crown of thorns on your head, the spear in your side, and your back ripped wide open. This may sound redundant, but again, remember this *is* identification.

That's the way God sees us. And here's some good advice-get a picture of this in your own mind, because with God, it's a reality. He sees you on the cross with Jesus, and until you get a hold of this and understand that you were on that cross too, you will never fully realize who you are in Christ. It must become a reality to you. It was real to God; He saw you on the cross. It's certainly real to the devil. It ought to be real to you.

All that you were-the old self, the old man-was crucified. Paul wrote about this in the Epistles and made it clear to us. You see, all the old vices, all the old habits, and all the old bondages were nailed to the cross with Jesus Christ. The old man is dead. The old nature is dead. The old self is dead. You do not have two natures in you. You are a brand new creature-one who never before existed. The Bible says, "Old things have passed away and all things have become new."

We're not saying that these old habits, old vices and old bondages are not lingering in your mind. There are many memories of them. As a Christian, you can still act like the old man if you want to, but you don't have to, because he's dead. The nature of your old self still exists in this world, but you don't have to let it exist in your life any more! If you start acting like the old man, it doesn't mean you have two natures. It means you need to learn to put on the New man (Col. 3: 8-12). You are a new man on the inside, in your spirit, but you have to put on the new man on the outside. When this becomes real to you, the devil will never be able to put you on a guilt trip again. That's why we have to renew our minds through the Word of God. We must transform our minds. We must put God's Word in our minds so that those old memories are obliterated. We take out everything that is old and put everything new in from God's Word.

Sometimes those old memories want to act like a bully. Ever notice how they bully you around? Why do they do that? Because you're a baby and babies are easily bullied. That's why we want to grow up fast. We want to grow in the things of God so the bully, the old man, the old nature will not have any sway over us anymore. We'll be mature enough to say, "Bully, your days are over. I'm taking the ascendancy."

As we renew our minds, the old memories will begin to fade in time, because the mind is now being transformed and renewed by God's Word. The new nature is a baby. It needs to grow up in the righteousness of God. It needs to be fed the proper things so that when God's Word goes in, it replaces those old memories and eventually they are just simply pushed out of the way. When those old memories begin to come on up again, just say, "These thoughts which are from the old man will not take hold of me anymore. I don't wear the garments of the old man. I'm a new creation in Jesus Christ." You see, we were crucified with Christ. Our old man is dead.

> Romans 6:1-7 says,
> *What shall we say then? Shall we continue in sin, that grace*
> *may abound?*
> *God forbid. How shall we, that are dead to sin, live any longer*
> *therein? (We were dead to sin because our substitute took it*
> *into his spirit for us.)*
> *Know ye not, that so many of us as were baptized into Jesus*
> *Christ were baptized into his death?*
> *Therefore we are buried with Him by baptism into death:*
> *That like as Christ was raised up from the dead by the glory*
> *of the Father, even so we also should walk in newness of life.*
> *For if we had been planted together in the likeness of his death,*
> *We shall be also in the likeness of his resurrection.*

Don't let these words just slip by you, Meditate on these words. Think about what's being said here.

Then verse 6 says, "Knowing this, that our old man is crucified with him, that the body

Of sin might be destroyed, that henceforth we should not serve sin.

"For he that is dead is freed from sin." (verse 7)

Behind the Scenes at Calvary

Wow! Paul got a hold of something, didn't he? There's a revelation here from God. We are learning who we are in Christ. We're learning about our redemption. It's not enough for us to simply say, "Oh yes, Jesus died for me on the cross. Isn't that wonderful? He bore my sins." It is wonderful, but it doesn't stop there. It goes much deeper than that. We have to go behind the scenes. We must ask for a personal rhema (for God to speak His Word as spirit and life into our spirits, like a light turning on in our hearts) of the revelation so we can make it reality in our lives.

We don't want to be like the apostles down beneath the cross, looking up at Jesus and seeing a bloodied body. Their hearts were broken. Their friend, their master, their teacher for three and a half years was hanging there dying. They looked up and only saw one man dying. Not one understood what was taking place on that cross. They simply saw a man dying, a friend dying. They were heartbroken. It wasn't until Paul, the Apostle, came along some years later that God said, "I'm going to give you the revelation of what took place behind the scenes on the cross." Paul wrote about it throughout his Epistles. But there's something we need to look at and discuss very carefully about our redemption.

We want to talk to you about the Blood of Jesus. We can never talk enough about the Blood of the Lamb of God, especially in connection with the propitiation and sacrifice Jesus made for us-the expiatory work of Jesus on the cross. For the Scripture says in Hebrews 9:22:"…without the shedding of blood is no remission."

Blood must be shed before sins can be washed away. However, in itself, the shedding of Blood (without Jesus' death) is not sufficient. We're not heretics; just read on. The Blood in itself is not sufficient, that is, sufficient to redeem us. Jesus had to do more than just shed His Blood. If all it took was the shedding of Blood, then all that torture, torment, and agony our Lord went through on the cross was an injustice to the Son of God. All Jesus would have had to do was cut His finger and shed some Blood, if that alone was enough. Isn't that right?

When a man shaves and cuts himself, he sheds blood. Did anyone say you have to be nailed to a cross to shed blood? When you ladies are cooking a meal and open a can and cut yourself on the lid, don't you shed blood? If all that Jesus had to do was shed some Blood, what a shame that He was nailed to a cross and suffered the way He did. What a waist. Why couldn't Jesus just take something sharp, cut His hand and drip some Blood on the ground? Isn't that shedding of Blood? Couldn't Jesus have gathered a huge crowd about Him? How many times did Jesus have four, five, ten, fifteen thousand people, preaching to them? Why couldn't He have said to His apostles, "Gather me 10,000, get 20,000, get a half a million people out here because I'm going to redeem them." So He gets them all together, stands on a high place and takes out a sharp knife. He then cuts Himself, drops the Blood on the ground and says, "Ok, you're redeemed." Why wasn't that kind of blood-shedding sufficient? There must be a reason. Even the animals sacrificed in the old covenant were Killed for their blood. They did not take a lamb, cut it's leg, get some blood, put a bandage on it and give it back to the owner.

Blood Shed Unto Death

Think about this. It is true that there is no remission without the shedding of blood, but we must understand this: Could Jesus shed His Blood the way we described without the cross? Why did Jesus have to go to the cross and shed His Blood? <u>Because He had to shed His Blood unto death.</u> If we asked you, "Could Jesus redeem us without going to the cross?" Most everybody would say, "No. He had to go to the cross." But the next question is, "Why?" Your answer would be, "he had to die." And we would say, "That's correct." But the question remains, "Why did Jesus have to die?" Don't lose us now.

From the first chapter, we said that just having knowledge, or information is not good enough. We must have understanding to grow spiritually and to walk in the fullness of who we are in Christ. We want to know why Jesus had to go to the cross, shed His Blood and say, "You're redeemed."

We're trying to challenge your faith. We're trying to challenge you to think. We want to know *why* you believe what you believe. Someone might say, "My great-grandmother believed a certain way."

Well, good for her; but what if your great-grandmother believed wrong? Are you going to believe wrong also? You tell us that Jesus had to die on the cross by shedding His Blood. Tell us why.

You may be thinking, "My goodness, I wonder what the answer is. Why couldn't He just cut His finger and shed Blood?" Some cuts can shed an awful lot of blood you know. Why did He have to die shedding His Blood? If Jesus had not died when He shed His Blood, we wouldn't have any remission of sin. If it would have worked by cutting the finger, don't you think God the Father would have chosen that, instead of the cross?

Let us give you two reasons why Jesus had to die. Number one: Jesus had to shed His Blood unto death or through death because the Bible teaches that the soul that sins must die (Ezekiel 18:4-20). This is a law of God, a principle of God, a precept of God, and whatever you want to call it, it will be fulfilled. God spoke it. It has to be fulfilled. "The soul that sins shall die." God is just and will fulfill His Word. Adam sinned. Correct? We were in Adam. Correct? Therefore, we have sinned. Remember, he was our representative.

A debt We Cannot Pay

We must also remember that the definition of identify is to make identical: to consider and treat as the same. Adam sinned therefore, we sinned. "The soul that sinneth must die." We owed God a debt. Our punishment was death. If we were in Adam and Adam sinned, we sinned; therefore, we must die to carry out God's justice. But thank God we have a substitute. Jesus came as our substitute. He stood in for all of us. He now can identify with our sin and your sin when God is considering the whole matter. He then makes Jesus and each of us identical, treating us the same.

The sin in our spirit is place in His spirit, and the sin now in Him has a debt. As our substitute, He must die. At His death, our debt to God is completely paid in full, and God's justice has been served. Obviously, if Jesus just cut His wrist, the debt could not be paid.

Reason Number Two: We saw in the last chapter that Jesus had to die to get us out of Adam. There was no other way out of Adam except that Jesus would come as our substitute and identify with us. In other words, the sin was transferred from our spirit into His spirit: He died and got us out of Adam.

Can a Dead Man Be Crucified?

Many Christians, through the years, have read about and heard people making this statement: "You have to crucify self." Have you heard that? People come along, and as soon as they begin to talk to you about your new walk with Jesus, they'll start telling you, "Just remember, you have to crucify self." But when they are asked who this self is, they don't seem to know. The reason for that is, in part, because they do not have a grasp of the composition of a human being. They just really don't understand it. God has created human beings as triune beings-spirit, soul and body.

Let's examine this statement on crucifying self in the light of Scripture. Your Bible tells you that the real you is the spirit man contained within your body. The real you possesses a soul, and the real you lives in a body. Paul calls this body the tabernacle of the flesh. The real you inside the body is born again of incorruptible seed by the Word of God. Your spirit, the real you, has been washed in the Blood of the Lamb. Your foot was not washed in the Blood of the Lamb, was it? We're not trying to be facetious, but we have to understand this. No, your inside man, your spirit man, was washed by the Blood of the Lamb.

These people we hear talking about crucifixion and all these books we've read and you've read which say we must crucify self-do they mean the inner man? "No," someone will say," I don't want you to crucify the new man. It's the old man who needs to be crucified."

But the old man has already been crucified.

"Well," another may argue, "you must crucify him every day."

Let's try to follow their logic: would you go down to the graveyard, dig somebody up, look at him and say, "I'm going to crucify you?" You wouldn't do that, would you? Why not? He's already dead. That would be stupid, then why would you want to crucify the old man? The old man is already dead. You don't have to crucify him daily. He's already dead. One crucifixion is enough. I like to say it this way, "of all of us who died with Christ, there were no survivors."

When people say that you need to crucify self, tell them, "you're too late. He's already dead. You see, I was on that cross with Jesus. God saw Jesus and me die. I'm a new me now and the new me, the new self, doesn't need to be killed. The new me needs to live a resurrection life."

Live a Resurrected Life!

The Bible teaches that we are to take up our cross and follow Jesus. That means we are to take up His cause. We are here to serve the Lord, not our selfish desires. Always remember, <u>the essence of sin is my claim to my right to myself.</u> God wants us to put Him first in our lives, to submit our wills to His will everyday (John 6:38). We need to crucify the works of the flesh, and we need to live in the power of our new resurrected life.

When people die, we say they have "passed away". Well, the old nature *has* passed away. The old man *is* dead. Let's just keep him in the grave.

The New Nature

As we look at Galatians 2:20, don't think that Paul is confused. He's not confused at all. When we begin to read this, you'll understand. Paul says, "I'm crucified with Christ: nevertheless I live; yet not I, but Christ liveth in me; and the life which I now live in the flesh I live by the faith of the Son of God, who loved me, and gave himself for me."

The first time you read that you might say, "Paul seems to be mixed up in his thinking. He doesn't seem to know what he's talking about here." The original Greek says, "I have been crucified with Christ." The old man, the old nature, the Adamic nature has been crucified with our Lord Jesus Christ. Then he says, "Nevertheless, I live." This is a different "I" than the "I" that was crucified with Christ in the old nature. But now the second "I", he says, is living. That's the new nature, the new self.

"Yet," he says, "Not I…" (Is he still confused?)"…but Christ liveth in me." Even the new "I", the new nature now knows that it must give way to the Lord Jesus Christ to lead it, guide it and give the grace to live in the face of the Son of God.

The One who gave the old nature its death-dealing blow and put the nature of Deity within this fleshly body was Jesus Christ. Paul is not confused at all. He knows exactly what has happened to him. The old man, the Adamic nature is dead. Now, the Holy Spirit is leading us through our recreated spirits. Deity is leading us, and our faith is in Him. In other words, since the old man died, Jesus is now living His life through us. And as He is, so are we in this world (I John 4:17b). We are now channels for the life of God to be seen through us.

Galatians 2:20 in the *Distilled* version of the Bible says, "<u>I consider myself as having died and now enjoying a second existence which is simply Jesus using my body</u>."

Don't you like that? Again, we're just channels for God's life to flow through. Therefore, a good definition of the new "I", is Christ liveth in me! If you think of it like this, it will strengthen you. For example, if your pastor ask you to give your testimony at church, and you say to him, "I can't do that". Just substitute the definition for the new "I" and say, "Christ liveth in me can't do that". It doesn't feel right, does it? Because you know it's not true. Substituting the definition for "I" will always help you to stay in faith, and stay free from fear. Philippians 4:13 tells us that we can do all things through Christ who strengthens us! Christ liveth in me can do anything! Paul put it this way in Philippians 1:21: "For me to live is Christ," Paul was absorbed in Jesus Christ. He was totally immersed in Christ. You see, he knew the old man was dead and gone. In Acts 20:26, he said that he was pure from the blood of all men. How could he say that, when his very testimony was that he attacked and persecuted the Church? He had a revelation (rhema) from God that the man who did those things is now dead and gone. Paul understood that clearly. He knew that the old man was even buried and now the life that he lived, he lived by the faith of the Son of God who loved him and gave Himself for him. We are to display this new nature to the world.

Now, we've given you two reasons why Jesus had to shed His blood unto death. Number one, to satisfy God's laws of justice. "The soul that sinneth must die." And Number two, to get us out of Adam. Both required death.

Let's look at Romans 6:6: "knowing this,…" In other words, it's assumed that you already know this.) "…that our old man is crucified with him, that the body of sin might be destroyed, that henceforth we should not serve sin."

The *Living* Bible says it this way: "Your old evil desires were nailed to the cross with him; that part of you that loves to sin was crushed and fatally wounded, so that your sin-loving body is no longer under sin's control, no longer needs to be a slave to sin; for when you are deadened to sin, you are freed from all its allure and its power over you."

That statement is fairly clear. Jesus not only washed away your sin, He killed the man that was satan's slave to do those acts of unrighteousness. But now we have a new Master through the new birth and He directs all our actions in righteousness. Jesus didn't just make us a little less sinful, my friends, He killed the old man. Jesus didn't just make us a shade less sinful. The old man is dead. <u>I am crucified with Christ.</u>

Romans 6:8 states: "Now if we be dead with Christ, we believe that we shall also live with him." Do you see the identification here? If we're dead with Him and we're identified with Him, then we died with Him. But He was raised to newness of life, so we were raised with Him to newness of life. If you're dead with Him, you're also alive with Him. You live with Him. As He is, so are you. Whatever He does, you do. Whatever He is through His nature, you are. Because you have His nature in you.

> Continuing in Romans 6, verses 9-11:
> *Knowing that Christ being raised from the dead dieth no*
> *more; death hath no more dominion over him.*
> *For in that he died, he died unto sin once: but in that he*
> *liveth, he liveth unto God.*
> *Likewise reckon ye also yourselves to be dead indeed*
> *unto sin, but alive unto God through Jesus Christ our Lord.*

You have to reckon it so. That's why it says, "Knowing this…" You can't reckon it so unless you know it. The old man is dead. D-E-A-D. Know that; it's a reality. In God's eyes, it's a reality.

> Verse 12:
> *Let not sin therefore reign in your mortal body, that ye should*
> *obey it in the lusts thereof.*
> *Neither yield ye your members as instruments of*
> *unrighteousness unto sin: but yield yourselves unto God, as*
> *those that are alive from the dead, and your members as*
> *instruments of righteousness unto God.*
> *For sin shall not have dominion over you: for ye are not*
> *under the law, but under grace.*
> *What then? Shall we sin, because we are not under the law,*
> *but under grace? God forbid.*
> *Know ye not, that to whom ye yield yourselves servants to*
> *obey, his servants ye are to whom ye obey; whether of sin*
> *unto death, or of obedience unto righteousness?*
> *But God be thanked, that ye were the servants of sin, but ye*
> *have obeyed from the heart that form of doctrine which was*
> *delivered you.*
> *Being then made free from sin, ye became the servants of*
> *righteousness.*

You see, what you've been reading is scriptural Truth. That's all we brought to you, one scriptural Truth after another. If God wrote it, it's true. If He said the old man is dead once you've been washed in the blood of the Lamb, then it is a fact. If your old man is dead, the old Adamic nature is dead. If the old sinful nature is dead and buried, then why continue living in sin? And why continue living in the results of sin (sickness and poverty)?

It's the old nature that's dead. I'm a new man in Christ. As a new man, I am now dead to what the old man (old nature) was alive to! So, when the devil comes to tempt me. He is tempting the new me, the new "I", Christ liveth in me; and the devil has no authority or power over the new me. The Bible doesn't say that I won't be tempted, but it does say that by the power of the Holy Spirit through my new man, I can overcome and quench every dart of temptation that comes my way (Rom. 8:13; Eph. 6:16). The man that satan could succeed in tempting is dead! And you can not tempt a dead man.

Take a man who drank his whole life, a drunk. He has the bottle of booze and has been drinking for three days. He takes his last swig, has a heart attack and dies right there with the booze all over him. They bury the man and put him in the graveyard. You're an old friend of his, so you think you'll go visit him down at the graveyard. So you take four or five bottles with you because you want to revive the old memory. You go down with your bottles, tap on the grave and say, "Hey Bill, I brought the booze.

Stop Wishing, Use Faith

What do you think he's going to do? Nothing. Why not? Because he's dead. You can't tempt a dead man. He's dead. Again, the man that I am now in Christ is free from what the old man had been bound by. Therefore, as a new man, I am dead to the power of all of the devil's temptations. I can resist them all! I don't have to yield to them! As far as the devil is concerned, I'm dead to him, and as Romans 6:7 says, "for he that is dead is freed from sin." Since we are free from sin, we are also free from all of the consequences of sin; which is poverty, sickness and death! Now, you have to reckon or consider it so (Rom. 6:11). Too often the problem is that Christians go around wishing that it would work for them. "Oh, I wish this would work for me. Oh, I wish I could get healed. Oh, I wish I could get delivered…" God is saying, "Stop wishing and use your faith. If what I said is true, then reckon it so." This is what the Bible calls <u>entering into God's rest (Heb. 4:9-11).</u>

Just act like what God says is true. *That's* faith.

This is the thing that the devil has tried to hide from the Body of Christ for years-our identification. It's not taught in many churches because the devil has told people, "All you need to know is that Jesus died on the cross and shed His blood for you." That's not all you need. It's all that a lost person needs to know to be born-again, but it's not all that a believer needs to know to grow spiritually. We have seen that there is so much more to learn.

We have more wonderful things to tell you that are going to set you free. And when we begin to reckon what God says as truth, scriptural truth, we will begin to say, "Yes, Lord, I believe it. My old man is dead. I'm not going to let that old man be a slave to sin any more. He's dead. Now I'm living unto righteousness. My eyes are forever on the Lord Jesus Christ. I have been crucified with Christ: nevertheless I live; yet not I but Christ lives in me, and as He is, so am I in this world." (Some of you have just had a light go on, and that's good. You are finally catching on to a very important, God-given principle.)

We have been crucified with Christ. Is that a fact or not? Paul understood it as fact. He wrote it in his Epistle: "I am crucified with Christ: nevertheless I live." You're crucified, but you live. Who was crucified? The old man. You have a new life, a new you. You're living but it's not just 'you' anymore because now Christ is living in you. You're living by the faith of the Son of God who loved you and gave Himself for you and as He is, so are you in this world. Now you can let the righteous light that you've become be seen by others (Eph. 5:8). Can we say it another way? Perhaps we've hit it from every angle. We want you to reckon it so. Don't be a slave to sin anymore. Say, "The old man, the old Adamic nature, is buried." When the devil comes to you and starts saying, "Let me just tempt you…" you reply, "No, you're talking to the wrong guy. You see, I'm a new me now. I'm not the old me anymore. If you want to talk to the old me go down to the graveyard. He's buried." Do you get that? You're not only crucified with Christ, you're buried with Christ. The new you is not under satan's control any longer! You have the nature of Deity in you now; you live by faith in God.

Legally, all we've said became ours when Jesus' blood redeemed us. Experientially, it becomes ours as we not only reckon it so, but begin to confess and live it, as it is truth for our lives (Philemon 6).

11

DID JESUS DIE SPIRITUALLY?
(PART 1)

In this chapter, we will look at a controversial subject in this study of our identification with Christ. Many pastors and teachers have created numerous pamphlets, books and teachings on this subject entitled, "Did Jesus Die Spiritually?" This particular topic is crucial to an overall understanding of who you are in Christ and all that we've studied up to this point.

We want to ask you a question, and we're going to ask it two different ways. Read it carefully. <u>Do you read what you believe in the Bible, or do you believe what you read in the Bible?</u> Now think about that. Look at it again because this is very important: <u>Do you read what you believe, or believe what you read?</u> If you're only reading what you believe, that simply means you're reading the Bible to hunt out confirmations of what you already think you know as doctrines. But if you believe everything you read, you'll learn new doctrines and get new revelation from the Lord.</u> We must learn to rightly divide the Word of God (II Timothy 2:15).

You see, we cannot hold ourselves in our little Charismatic circle and say: "We've got it all as Charismatic's," or if we're Pentecostals, "we've got it all; we're Pentecostals;" or if we're Baptists, etc. Why? Because all we'll do is continue to read the Bible and find the things we believe. "Oh yes, that confirms that." "Yes, I believe in water baptism." "Oh, I believe that. You see, I believe in the gifts of the Holy Spirit."

But if we continue to believe what we read, then God is able to open up all new avenues for us, all new scriptures and give us all kinds of new light concerning His Word. So, we just want to encourage you to believe everything that you read in the Bible and ask God to open it up for you. Also know that everything is truthfully stated in the Bible, but it's not all Truth. For example, what satan told Eve in the garden was not all true, but it is truly stated in the Bible. II Timothy 3:16 says that all Scripture is <u>given</u> by inspiration of God. God inspired His men to write down everything that we read in the Bible, but not every word is what God said. Does that make sense? We have the story of Peter denying Jesus. God did not inspire Peter to lie about knowing Jesus, but He did inspire John to write it down. Let's learn to rightly divide God's Word.

Let's first of all go to Romans 5:17. We're going in a little deeper. Now let's just add, if we're teaching something that perhaps might be new to you, or doesn't quite hit you right, don't allow the devil to hold you focused on that. You might say, "Well I don't agree with that," and spend your time thinking about that and miss everything else. Then you're really going to lose a lot. If you don't agree with something, that's fine; just jot it down, get right off it and focus again. Because if you miss something in this particular part of the study, you're going to be lost.

This is a very important subject, "Did Jesus Die Spiritually?" You have to know whether He did or didn't. And we're going to look at the Scriptures, because this will really shake your thinking about a lot of things.

And so, in Romans 5:17, read carefully what it says: "For if by one man's offense, death reigned by one; much more they which receive abundance of grace and of the gift of righteousness shall reign in life by one, Jesus Christ."

The first part of that sentence says, "For if by one man's offense, death reigned by one..." Now look at Romans 6:23: "For the wages of sin is death; but the gift of God is eternal life through Jesus Christ our Lord."

In both of these scriptures we see the word "death." In Romans 5:17, it says, "For if by one man's offence, death reigned by one..." In Romans 6:23 it says, "For the wages of sin is death..." Focus for a moment on this. We have been studying how death has reigned. Adam was our substitute, our representative man. We said very early on in our study that Adam and the Lord Jesus Christ were the two most important people in the Bible.

Put your "thinking caps" on and try to jog your memory about why we said that Jesus and Adam were the two most important men in the Bible. Think about it now. Was not the answer because they were both representative men? Do you remember that? They were both representative men.

Now we also said that, if Adam represented all the human race, whatever he got, we got. Do you remember that? Whatever Adam got, we got, because he represents us. You see, you can't say, "Well I was born 6,000 years later. He didn't represent me." Oh yes, he did. He represented every human being that would come on the face of the earth. He was your representative and he was our representative. So whatever he did, whatever he was paid, however he got paid for whatever he did, we got it too. The wages of sin is death. Sin pays wages, and the Bible calls those wages paid, death.

Romans 5:14 says, "Nevertheless death reigned from Adam to Moses, even over them that had not sinned after the similitude of Adam's transgression, who is the figure of him that was to come." By one man's offense, death reigned and it affects us all.

What kind of death are we speaking about when we refer to death in these scriptural references? We are talking about spiritual death. Now look at Genesis 2:17. This is God speaking to Adam. When God speaks, we should listen: "But of the tree of the knowledge of good and evil, thou shalt not eat of it: for in the day that thou eatest thereof thou shalt surely die."

"Thou shalt surely die." Again, what kind of death are we speaking of here? We're not speaking of physical death, although physical death is involved. Why? Physical death is the by-product of spiritual death. Sickness, poverty and disease are by-products of spiritual death and sin. Let's repeat that. Sickness, disease, and poverty are by-products of spiritual death and sin. When Adam sinned, spiritual death entered his spirit, and along with it came all the by-products. Every single by-product just automatically attached itself as an addendum and followed along; sickness, disease, poverty and physical death.

Adam brought us all into the whole package of the law of sin and death as it is explained to us in Romans 8:2, where it talks about the law of sin and death. So when we read that the wages of sin is death, we are speaking mainly of spiritual death. We have to understand this if we are going to determine whether or not Jesus died spiritually.

It wouldn't hurt to interject right here a definition that we have asked you to remember and memorize concerning the word "identify." Now just think for a moment. We told you to memorize a definition for the word "identify." We said this is important, because we have been seeing it, if you recall, all the way through every chapter. To identify means to make identical, to consider and treat as the same. The reason we told you to memorize this is because we are talking about the subject of identification.

Now, we understand that Adam, as our representative man, stood in our place. He was our substitute. A substitute is one who takes the place of another. So he stood in our place and when he sinned, he sinned for every single one of us. Therefore, when spiritual death entered his spirit, it also entered the spirit of every human being that would come on the face of the earth, because he represented all of us. Over and over we have said-what he got, we got.

So, if spiritual death is what we got, then spiritual death is what we needed to get rid of. Are you with us? If spiritual death is what we got-and let's ad this, that through spiritual death, we were separated from God-then we needed to get rid of spiritual death in order to unite ourselves with God again. Because if God is going to give us spiritual life, He can't pour spiritual life into us, until He has taken away our spiritual death. So in our relationship with Adam, when we were in Adam, we were made spiritually dead. Some kind of relationship must be developed with someone else who can remove us from spiritual death. The word "spiritual" here is our focus. Write down the word "spiritual." It will help you to remember.

Spiritual death does not refer to your mind. It does not refer to your elbow. It does not refer to any part of your body. Spiritual death refers to your spirit. Your body wasn't spiritually dead, your spirit was. Man did not need spiritual life in his body, but in his spirit. The real 'you' is the part we call your spirit man.

Paul calls him the 'inner man.' You've probably read that in several places in Paul's Epistles. He calls your spirit man your inner man. That's where death dwelled while you were in Adam. Death dwelled in your inner man not in any part of your physical body. When you were in Adam, and you got everything Adam got, you got it the same place Adam got it, in his spirit man not in his physical body parts. The spirit of man is where spiritual death dwells; in your inner man, in your spirit. That should be very clear.

Dying Twice

So let's go to Genesis 2:17 again. God is speaking to Adam: "But of the tree of the knowledge of good and evil, thou shalt not eat of it: for in the day that thou eatest therof thou shalt surely die."

It is the tree of the knowledge of good and evil. If that tree is eaten of, God said, "It will cause you to die, Adam." Adam was clearly told by God what would happen to him. God made it perfectly clear. God said, "Adam, in the day that you eat of that tree, you will surely die."

In the *King James* Version you may see a footnote that is a reference. Find it from that Scripture I just read. You will find somewhere in your margin the words, "In dying thou shalt die." That's taken from the Hebrew.

What does that mean to you- "In dying thou shalt die"? To us, it means you're going to die twice. Did you understand what we just said? In other words, in dying, you're dying once, and in dying, you're going to die again. So what is God saying here? God said this: "That when you eat of that tree, Adam, you will surely die." When did God say that he would die? "The day that thou shall eat thereof you will surely die." In other words, "Adam, in dying, if you eat of that tree, you're gong to die. You are going to die spiritually as soon as you eat of that tree, then years later will die physically. Now don't let this confuse you; just stay with us. This is important. In dying, you shall surely die.

Adam didn't physically die that day after he ate of the tree, did he? But he surely died. How do we know that? Because God said that he would. He said, "If you eat of that tree today, you'll die today." And he said, "In dying today, you shall surely die." In Adam's case, 900 years from when God spoke, He died a second death. He died physically, did he not? Well what are we talking about here-he died twice? Follow along.

God said that he would die that day, didn't He? If God said he was going to die the day he partook of that tree, then you can put the money in the bank and say that Adam died that day. But yet, we know that Adam lived to be over 900 years old. How did Adam die? His inner man died, his spirit man-the real man. And then he lived physically for over 900 more years. Remember now, God said that in dying Adam experienced spiritual death on that day, as soon as he ate of that tree. He experienced spiritual death in his spirit. In dying spiritually, God says, you're going to die physically. In dying one type of death, He said, you will also die another type of death. Adam first died spiritually. We'll tell you what that is shortly. And then over 900 years later, he died physically.

Dead Man Walking

Now you say, "Wow, how, if his spirit man died and he was alienated from God in spiritual death, did he manage to live for 900 more years?" Think about it now. Adam wasn't just any man. He walked with God; he talked with God. We don't know how long he spent with God. He was a very intelligent being. He had supernatural power from God to name every animal on the face of the earth. He just wasn't an ordinary man. Why? Because he had such light from God inside him that it took about 900 years before that light burned out.

Can you imagine what kind of a relationship he had with Almighty God, that even though inside he was dead spiritually, he didn't die for 900 more years physically? He had some light in him, didn't he? Now some will say that he really did die physically on that day, and here's their foolish reasoning. "Because," they'll say, "a thousand years to the Lord , is like one day." Do you really believe that? Well, we believe it in terms of what it is to God, but not to you. And if you believe that, and God came to you tonight and said, "Get your house in order, you're going to die in one day," are you going to laugh at Him and say, "I've got 999 more years." You better get with it, because as far as you're concerned, one day is one day. Only to God a thousand years is as one day.

So then, if Adam went through two deaths as our representative man did, our destiny was to go through two deaths also. Rmember, he identifies with us as our representative man. What he got, we get. Are you with us so far? Now if Jesus was our substitute and took our place as our representative man, then He must get all that was due us. Isn't that correct? If He didn't' get everything that was due us, then our redemption is incomplete. Understand that and know that God doesn't do anything and leave it incomplete.

In other words, again, the two most important men who ever walked the face of this earth are Adam and Jesus. Why? <u>Because they are both representative men.</u> Let's say it this way: Adam represented us in a way that was to our detriment. He brought us into spiritual death. But Jesus represented us in a positive sense. He brough us into eternal life with God, if we receive Him as Savior. He justified us to God. In other words, Adam brought us into something bad, but Jesus took us out and brought us into something good. Both represented us, but in different ways.. Nonetheless, they both represented us. Agree?

Let's look at the pattern between the first Adam and Jesus, the last Adam. Adam died twice. Jesus died twice. Adam was tempted in the garden: spirit, soul and body. Jesus was tempted in the desert: spirit, soul and body. The Bible says that because we are in Adam, we all were made sinners. We saw that in Romans 5:12-19. Let's read it again.

Romans 5:12-19
*Wherefore, as by one man sin entered into the word, and
death by sin; and so death passed upon all men, for that all*

have sinned:
(For until the law sin was in the world: but sin is not
imputed when there is no law.
Nevertheless death reigned from Adam to Moses, <u>even over</u>
<u>them that had not sinned after the similitude of Adam's</u>
<u>transgression, who is the figure of him that was to come.</u>
But not as the offence, so also is the free gift. For if through
the offence of one many be dead, much more the grace of
God, and the gift by grace, which is by one man, Jesus Christ,
hath abounded unto many.
And not as it was by one that sinned, so is the gift: for the
judgment was by one to condemnation, but the free gift is of
many offenses unto justification.
For if by one man's offence death reigned by one; much more
they which receive abundance of grace and of the gift of
righteousness shall reign in life by one, Jesus Christ.)
<u>Therefore as by the offence of one judgment came upon all</u>
<u>men to condemnation</u>; even so <u>by the righteousness of one</u>
<u>the free gift came upon all men unto justification of life</u>.
For as by <u>one man's disobedience</u> many were made sinners,
so by <u>the obedience of one</u> shall many be made righteous.
For by one man's disobedience many were made sinners…-
That's verse 19.

Verse 17 says, "For by one man's offense death reined by one…"

Verse 12 says, "Wherefore, as by one man sin entered into the world, and death by sin; and so death passed upon all men for that all have sinned."

Taking Another's Place

Now, if Jesus is going to be your substitute, what is a substitute? *One who takes another's place.* If Jesus is going to be your substitute, if He is going to take your place then He has to take all-ALL-that was meant for you. Isn't that correct? If He's going to substitute for you, take your place, and He says, "Step out of the way, I'm going in there for you," that means everything that was due you, He is going to take it in your place. A-L-L, all, everything that was meant for you, that is, spiritual death and all the effects of it. That is, sin, poverty, sickness, disease, and then He is going to transfer it from you to Him. He says, "All of that is yours, and you're doomed if I don't take it from you. You're dead. You will stay dead for all eternity. But I am going to take everything that's in you, in your spirit man, and I'm going to take the full curse of the broken law-poverty, sickness, disease, spiritual death and sin; I'm taking it from you, and I'm putting it in Me," Jesus said. "I've got it all now. I am your substitute." If Jesus did not take all of it from us, it would not be a complete redemption.

But if some insist that Jesus did not bear spiritual death in His spirit, then note that the pattern is broken. Adam sinned. He had to die spiritually. Then his sin was passed on to us. If Jesus, as our substitute, didn't take the sin for us and experience spiritual death for us, the pattern is broken. More importantly, we are still dead in our sins and trespasses, and Jesus died in vain. Now follow this.

In order to free us from spiritual death, Jesus had to become exactly what we were, nothing left out. And if He didn't, He misrepresented us, and all this talk about substitutionary work on the cross is just misleading people. So why keep referring to this as a substitutionary sacrifice? Can you see that? Well, whom did He substitute for? And what was this substitutionary work all about? If He didn't take our sins into His spirit, how did He bear our sins? After all, in 1 Peter 2:24, it says, "Who his own self bare our sins in his own body on the tree that we, being dead to sins, should live unto righteousness: by whose stripes ye were healed."

We said several times that there can be no identification without substitution. This scripture is talking about substitution. It's also talking about identification. You can live unto righteousness simply because you are now no longer in Adam. You see, Jesus took your sin. You ask, "Well where did my sin go when it left me?" It went into Jesus' spirit.

In Jesus' body means inside Him, that's where His spirit man is. Sin is not physical. It cannot be put on body parts, can it? It cannot be put on our legs, arms, backs, or chests. Sin cannot be put on our bodies. Can you see that? Our sins were placed in Jesus' spirit, not anywhere on His physical body.

Sin Is Spiritual

This may be entirely new to some of you reading this. Sin is not physical. Sin is spiritual. So Jesus, when He said, "Father, You're going to make Me their sin; You're going to make Me sin with their sin," the Father didn't say, "Here Jesus put it on Your back." He didn't say, "Put it on your chest, Jesus."

He didn't say, "Put it on your leg or arm, Jesus." Why not? Because sin is not physical. The Father looked at Jesus and said, "Put it in your spirit, Jesus."

Isaiah 53:6 says, "The Lord hath laid on him the iniquity of us all." Laid on whom? Jesus. What was laid on Jesus? Sins, *our* sins, were place in Jesus' spirit. He did not commit sin. Jesus was the sinless Lamb of God. He did not commit sin. But Jesus had our sin laid on Him as our substitute. "God made Him to be sin Who knew no sin that we could become the righteousness of God in Christ Jesus." As our substitute, He took our sin on Him. As our substitute, He was made to be sin with our sin. He never committed sin. He was the sinless One, but He took our sin. He had to take our sin because if He was our representative man, He had to identify with us totally. We were dead in our sins and trespasses. We had sickness, disease, poverty and everything of the broken law put on us. Jesus took it all on Him. He identified with all of us so we can now identify with Him in His resurrection life-in totality.

We hope you will closely study this material. We're simply stating some scriptural facts and allowing you to draw your own conclusions. We're not here to tell you that we know all the answers to everything. We're simply going to present some scriptural facts. You're going to see them in the Scriptures, and then draw your own conclusions. Did Jesus die spiritually? You will answer that. We're not going to tell you whether He did or didn't at this moment. We're simply stressing some points scripturally for you. You will not be given opinions. We're going to back everything we say with the Scripture so you won't have any doubt concerning this. You will draw your own conclusion. We're just expounding the principles of identification that God had Paul write about in his Epistles. Paul understood this. Why can't we?

What Happened to the Sin?

Let's go a little deeper. It is hard to see how Christians can believe in redemption without understanding what happened to sin, which was charged to their account while they were in Adam. While we were in Adam, we were in sin. Spiritual death was dwelling in our spirit man. Again, if Jesus said, "I will be your substitute," where did the sin go when it left us? Where did that sin go that was in us? We were in spiritual death, and now we are the righteousness of God in Christ Jesus. God said He laid on Jesus the iniquity of us all. Iniquity is another word for sin. Doesn't that mean that Jesus took our spiritual death?

153

Now we are made up of three parts: we are a spirit; we possess a soul; and we live in a body (I Thessalonians 5:23; Hebrews 4:12). Does not Scripture tell us that? The real you, then, is a spirit. We were spiritually dead, which meant we had death in our spirits, and that spiritual death separated us from God. Jesus came to earth as our substiutionary sacrifice to give Himself up for us, to bring us back into a relationship with God.

So let's try to see this from Jesus' perspective. Let's pretend this is before the crucifixion, and Jesus is in Heaven. Jesus looks down from Heaven, and He probably said something like, "All these people for who I will sacrifice Myself are made in My image and likeness." He's looking down on us. He knows that. Why? Because He created us. He knows everything about us. So He must be thinking about our physical and spiritual makeup. He's looking down and says, "They are spirits who possess a soul and live in a body."

Now here's Jesus first question as He is perhaps talking to the Father, perhaps talking to the Holy Spirit: "What do they need to be free from?"

The answer to that is simply (you know this now) spiritual death. Where does that spiritual death reside? Now you know the answer to that-in the spirit man. Well if they have spiritual death in their spirits and need a sacrifice to be offered to free them from their spiritual death, then obviously, a spiritual sacrifice is required. That is why animals could not redeem man. They don't have a spirit. They were not created in God's image.

If man was merely a body, then a physical sacrifice would do. But you see, man is a spirit and to keep some sort of correlation here, a spiritual sacrifice is needed. If man were simply a soul, then to keep this in harmony only an emotional or an intellectual sacrifice would do. Are you following this? But since man is a spirit, a spiritual sacrifice is demanded.

Understanding Life and Death

Somehow, we need to get across just two words to everyone who wants to understand redemption. The two words are simply "life and death." If you want to understand redemption completely, then you need to understand, "life and death." This life we're talking about is the very life of God. So that life must be spiritual, because God is a spirit. And also understand that the term "eternal life" doesn't mean necessarily that you'll go to Heaven and live forever in Heaven. Sinners don't have eternal life, yet they're going to live forever, separated from their creator. That is they don't have eternal life as most people understand it. So without confusing you, let's say that every spirit being will live forever. Every single spirit being will live forever, no exceptions. So living forever is eternal life, but you can live forever and yet be spiritually dead, separated from God.

In W.E. Vine's *Dictionary of Greek New Testament Words*, he gives a definition of spiritual death, which will help you. Vine says, "Spiritual death is the opposite of spiritual life. It never, never denotes non-existence.. Spiritual life is conscious existence and communion with God." Let's repeat that. Spiritual life is conscious existence and communion with God.

On the other hand, spiritual death is conscious existence and separation from God.

Simply put, because man is a spirit, he will live forever, either with a conscious existence with God or a conscious existence with the devil, eternally apart from God. So, when we talk about eternal life, let's go beyond the statement that we will live forever. Everyone will live forever. Let's say that we will live forever in the presence of God, because we have been washed in the blood of the Lamb. We no longer have spiritual death in us, but rather have spiritual life. We will live in an existence called eternal life in the presence of God in full communion with Him, in total bliss and joy!

So when people make such statements as, "Jesus could not have died spiritually, because He wouldn't have existed; then we know the one making that statement has much lacking in their understanding about eternal life. They don't know what they're talking about. They need to get an understanding of what life and death in the spirit of man is all about?

Look at Matthew 25:41. Jesus is speaking here. We will just read part of this: "then shall he say also unto them on the left hand, Depart from me ye cursed…"

Living Forever-But Where?

Now stop right there. Jesus said to those on His left hand, "Depart from me, ye cursed." Spiritual death does not mean ceasing to exist. We have said that already. Sinners will live forever, and they are filled with spiritual death. When Jesus tells a sinner at the judgment, "Depart from Me, ye cursed," do they stop existing? No. Because in their state of spiritual death, they cannot spend eternity in God's presence. So Jesus goes on a little further, in that same verse 41: "Then shall he say also unto them on the left hand, Depart from me, ye cursed, into everlasting fire, prepared for the devil and his angels…" Notice the word "everlasting." The Greek word *aionios*, means eternal, perpetual, forever.

So those who die in the state of spiritual death will live in a conscious existence forever, eternally, in everlasting fires. That's what Jesus said. They have eternal life, yet they are spiritually dead. That is, they do not have the life of God in them, which is spiritual life. They will exist forever in a state of spiritual death.

Have you followed this? It is important that you get this, because when we go on further about our sin being in Jesus, you have to understand all that we're giving you as a preliminary to what we're going to say in the next chapter.

Eternal life. Very often, a person will say, "I have eternal life." Or if you ask, "What is eternal life?" many will answer," Well, that means you go to Heaven and live forever." Not necessarily. Everyone is a spirit being, including angels, the devil, the Holy Spirit, God, the Lord Jesus Christ. We are going to live forever, but *where* we live forever is determined by our relationship with Almighty God at the time of death. Only Jesus, our Redeemer, can bring us into a right relationship with God.

If you die without having asked Jesus to be your Lord and your Savior, you still have spiritual death abiding in your spirit. You will live forever in a consciousness, an awareness of everything about you, including the everlasting fires, but you will never be allowed to be in the presence of God for all eternity. You will live forever, but spiritual death resides in you. Therefore, you cannot be in the presence of that Holy God.

But if you are now in Adam, and sin abides in you, and somebody comes along and asks, "Do you want to come out of that spiritual death?" All you need to do is confess Jesus as your Lord and Savior (Rom. 10:9). Get washed in His blood. Believe that He'll take away your sin, and give you His own righteousness. Then, your eternal life will be spent with Almighty God in a conscious existence of communion with Him. Away from the devil and his angels. Away from the everlasting fires. You'll spend eternity in Heaven with the Lord. That is spiritual <u>life</u> eternally.

Remember, when you talk about eternal life, don't just say, eternal life? "Oh I know what eternal life is-it's spending eternity in Heaven with God." No! Not necessarily. It depends what state you're in when you die. If you're still in Adam, if you still have sin when you die, you are going to go to those everlasting fires. And the last words you'll hear will be from Jesus: "Depart from Me you cursed into those everlasting fires." But if you die *in Jesus*, you're no longer in Adam, and your sin has been transferred to Jesus' Spirit. He took your sin as your substitute; and when you die, you have eternal life. But you will have a consciousness about you and communion with Almighty God, the Lord Jesus Christ, and the Holy Spirit for all eternity.

Are you still part of Adam's race but not taken out of his lineage through the Lord Jesus Christ? Are you still abiding in spiritual death? Is death still in your spirit man? If it is, you need to come to Jesus, because Jesus will give you God's righteousness. If you've never asked Jesus Christ to be your Lord and Savior, then humble yourself before the Living God and say, "Please God, have mercy upon me; I am a sinner." The Lord will say, "Receive My Son, Jesus, and He'll give you My righteousness. He'll take away your sin. He'll wash away everything you've ever done, and then you can have eternal life with a conscious existence and communion with Me forever."

12

DID JESUS DIE SPIRITUALLY?
(PART 2)

As we look at Part Two of this particular phase of our study to unravel *the mystery* of our identification with Christ, we've been trying to answer the question "Did Jesus Die Spiritually?" As noted earlier, this is a controversial subject to man, but as we progress, we will see that it is not controversial to God. Not at all. He said this is without controversy. And we're going to see that from the Scripture. In other words, you should have a full handle on this. You should understand it. It's not hard to understand, if you'll study the Scriptures. If you'll begin to dig in the Word of God, you will very soon find the answer to the question, "Did Jesus die spiritually?" This is not some new doctrine. God established it through Paul the Apostle. We've studied it, we have somewhat of an understanding, and we are bringing these Biblical facts to you.

Sin-More Than a Bad Shot

Look at Romans 6:23: "For the wages of sin is death; but the gift of God is eternal life through Jesus Christ our Lord." Did you notice the word in there-sin? The wages of sin is death. You know some of the Greek scholars have dug down deep, and they've found several Greek words for that word "sin." And one of the meanings they came up with simply means "to miss the mark." It was a term used in archery. But we think, as you begin to study God's Word (in particular what Jesus Himself had to say about sin), you'll find out that sin is more than making a bad shot. You'll find out that Jesus said in Luke 13:3, "If you don't repent you will likewise perish." He's speaking about sin. We have to repent of our sins. Repentance is important.

You see, repentance is not a one-time thing. In other words, you don't go before God and say, "I repent of this sin," and then just go out and take the chance of committing that same sin over and over again. But that's usually what happens if you don't truly have godly repentance. And if you really want to know about godly repentance, you can find it in 2 Corinthians 7:8-15. Repentance is something you continually do, especially in regard to one particular sin, until that sin has dissipated or been removed from your life, and is replaced with righteousness. It's not a one-time thing-"O God, I repent," –and then you go on your merry way and commit the sin again. You must think of that sin as being serious, because He says that the wages of sin is death. How much more serious are we going to get here? The payment for sin is death. That's pretty serious, isn't it?

When we begin to repent and bring about righteousness, then and only then can God release His power, through us. God will not release His power to anyone who is not walking righteously. And so we have to be very, very careful, that we understand what true Biblical repentance is all about. There's a whole lot more to it than just saying that I repent. We must believe that when we ask God to forgive us, He does (I John 1:9). It has to do with our thinking. We must think differently. We must pursue holiness! Godly sorrow and zeal must accompany repentance. We must not make excuses for our sin, or try to justify it. Do you ever try to justify going into sin? We try to give all kinds of reasons to justify our sin. Paul says we have to get rid of that. Justification is a form of compromise.

We must have vengeance against sin, according to Paul. When we begin to cast down vain imaginations and every high thing that exalts itself above the knowledge of God, we just have a readiness, so that when we disobey, we have a vengeance to take on that sin and command it out of our lives. For some reason, the Holy Spirit focused on this right in the beginning of this chapter. We have to understand this. We take sin too lightly in the Body of Christ. Now God says, "I want you to repent with godly sorrow." **Godly sorrow brings godly repentance. Repentance brings righteousness. Righteousness releases the power of God.** We all need to understand the fear of the Lord more than we do.

If there's no power in the body of Christ, it's because we're walking in sin and not truly repenting of our sins. Again, Jesus said, "Unless you repent, you will likewise perish." So it's not a matter of just missing the mark. It's not a matter of just making a poor shot at something. Jesus didn't look at it as a poor shot. Just missing the bull's eye somewhere. And if you want to look at it that way when you miss the mark, you might miss the kingdom and all it offers the believer. So, if you sin, repent and turn from it. Ask the Lord to forgive you and to wash you clean in His Blood. Believe that He does! Then obey His Word and walk in His righteousness (II Cor. 5:21). You have been made God's righteousness in Christ!

Eternal Life-God's Gift

So as we begin to discuss whether Jesus died spiritually, let's look at that verse of Scripture-"For the wages of sin is death..." Death! Death! The wages of sin is death! That's what it says right here-death. "...But the gift of God is eternal life through our Lord Jesus Christ" (Rom. 6:23). Now notice how eternal life comes-through Jesus Christ. Eternal life comes through Jesus Christ.

Now we have been talking about eternal life. Be sure that the definition of eternal life, coming from one who has been washed in the blood of the Lamb, is going to be quite different from one who has not been washed in the blood of the Lamb. For example, let us give you a hypothetical case. If you went down to Yankee Stadium tonight-let's say there's a ball game there-and walked in to see 60,000 people, would you agree with the statement "Every one of these people will live forever, spiritually?" If you said yes, then you are absolutely correct.

You see, there is a big difference between the person who's washed in the blood of the Lamb, and one who isn't. Every spirit being is going to live forever eternally. But if you don't have Jesus Christ, you're going to live forever alienated from the life of God-no communication with or from God-never having any communion with God. But if you die and have been washed in the blood of the Lamb, then you will have a conscious existence eternally in God's presence, accompanied by communion and communication with God forever.

So we have to learn to expand when people say, "Do you have eternal life?" Or if they say to you, "What is eternal life to you?" A lot of people don't understand this, and it is extremely important when we're talking about our identification with Jesus Christ. We don't mean to belabor the point with you, but you cannot go on to step Number 2 until you fully understand step Number 1. That's the way it is with everything.

In answering the question, "Does everybody have eternal life?" some people will say, "No,"; some, "Yes,"; and some will say, "Well, what is the answer?" You must know what the answer is: "Yes, every human being, every spirit being, angels, devils, every created spirit being, every being, (which would include God who is not a created being but is, nevertheless, a being), lives forever, eternally. But if you're not in Jesus Christ, your eternal existence will be shrouded by spiritual death. You will be alienated from any communion and communication with and from God who is life.

Let's go a little bit further. We're talking here about a subject that should be absolutely one of the most important subjects to you. Your life depends on knowing what we're teaching here and what we've been teaching for several chapters now. We've been talking about spiritual death. In particular, we're trying to answer the question: Did Jesus die spiritually? As we said, we're not trying to establish a doctrine. It's already a doctrine of Christianity. So we're not establishing anything. We're simply going to take you through the Scriptures and show you what they say. And then you're going to form your own opinion whether or not Jesus died spiritually, based on Biblical facts.

What does the term to identify," mean? To make identical, to consider and treat as the same. And just as Adam was our representative man, so Jesus is our representative man. Everything Adam got, we got. Everything Jesus got, we got. We also said there is no identification without first having a substiutionary work. No identification without substitution. When people make such statements as, "Jesus couldn't have died spiritually because He then wouldn't have existed," we now know that the one making those kinds of statements is lacking much understanding concerning eternal life. They actually have no understanding of what eternal life is.

What they need is an understanding of just two words: life and death.

Most Christians don't have that understanding. When we're talking about life and death, we're talking about life and death in the spirit of man. Spiritual death, as you now understand it, is not cessation of life, it is not a state of non existence. This is one of the most important teachings you could ever be subjected to in the Body of Christ-your identification with Jesus Christ. The devil does not want this being taught anywhere. He will try to stop this kind of teaching by bringing opposition to discourage the one who's teaching it. He'll bring people to argue and be argumentative about it. We don't need to argue. So, please, open up your spiritual eyes and ears. Don't let the devil cause your mind to drift off.

Did Jesus die spiritually? Or, did Jesus bear spiritual death in His spirit? We are going to show you what the Lord did for every person from the Word of God. At the end we believe you are going to see and agree with what the Word says, and you will understand the love of God for humanity with much greater magnitude!

Living-Though Dead

Sinners will live forever, but they're going to live in the state of spiritual death. Death in their spirits. Again, let us ask you this question: At the judgment, when Jesus says to the sinner, "Depart from Me ye cursed," do they stop existing? No, and Jesus goes on and says a little bit more so that you know that can't be true. He says in Matthew 25:41: "Depart from Me, ye cursed, into everlasting fire, prepared for the devil and his angels." Now notice the word Jesus chose to use in there-"everlasting." In Greek, the word "everlasting" is *aionios*, meaning forever, eternal, perpetual, a non-ending time continuum.

So those who die in a state of spiritual death will live in a conscious existence, eternally in an everlasting fire apart from and having no communion with Almighty God. They have eternal life while they remain in spiritual death. Spiritual death separates them from God who is spiritual life. Spiritual death separates one from the life of God. You can be alive physically, but be spiritually dead.

They have eternal life while their spirit exists in spiritual death. When we say they have eternal life we don't mean they have the life of God, but simply that they are going to live forever in torment with the devil and his angels. Again let's look at W.E. *Vine's* definition of spiritual death, as noted in the previous chapter. He says spiritual death is the opposite of spiritual life. It never denotes non-existence. Spiritual life is conscious existence and communion with God. Spiritual death is conscious existence and separation from God. That's why Jesus said to the ones who were cursed, "Depart from Me into those everlasting fires." Just because they're cursed and living in the state of spiritual death does not mean that they're going to cease to exist. They're going to exist for all eternity, but their existence is apart from Almighty God, because they have sin in their spirit and cannot come into the presence of a Holy God.

So God says, "Depart from Me, because there's death in your spirit; but you'll live forever in those everlasting fires that I prepared for the devil and his angels." Did you notice that those everlasting fires were never prepared for humankind? God never intended humankind to go to Hell. Isn't that interesting? Hell was prepared for the devil and his angels. So man, as a spirit, will live for all eternity either with the devil or with God.

Again, when someone says, "Jesus couldn't have died spiritually, because if He had, God couldn't have existed," that statement reveals much ignorance. Spiritual death does not mean a ceasing to exist. Spiritual death simply means, again separation from God. No communication and no communion, while consciously existing. Please, get a hold of this.

So with that in mind, look at Ephesians 2:1: "And you hath he quickened, who were dead in trespasses and sins." Read it again: "And you hath he quickened, who were dead in trespasses and sins." Before you got saved, your spirit was full of spiritual death. Your sins made you that way. Every time sin comes into your spirit man, death arrives there, prior to your knowing Jesus Christ. You were alienated or separated from God. Did you exist during that time? Of course you did. Yet, God says you were dead. We're not tying to confuse you, but when you had spiritual death in you, you existed. You walked, talked, smiled, ate, slept, worked, and played, and yet God says you were dead. You were a dead man walking. What part of you was dead? Your spirit man. Your spirit was dead or separated from God. So when God quickened you, or made you alive, what part of you was made alive? Your spirit. Did it affect your body? God was dealing with your spirit, not your body.

Tasting Death For Every Man

Hebrews 2:9 says, "But we see Jesus." Thank God that we can see Jesus. We see Him with our spiritual eyes. "But we see Jesus, who was made a little lower than the angels for the suffering of death, crowned with glory and honor; that he by the grace of God should taste death for every man," Let's read that again so you can get the full impact of it:

> But we see Jesus, who was made a little lower than the angels
> for the suffering of death, crowned with glory and honor
> that he by the grace of God should taste death for every
> man.

It says here that Jesus should taste death for every man by the grace of Almighty God. Notice the word "taste." The Greek word is *geuomai*, and the word, taste; *geuomai* means to eat, or to experience. To eat or to experience. Jesus experienced or ate death for every single person on the face of the earth, whoever has lived and or ever will live.

Now remember those five important facts we gave you a few chapters ago? We'll give you fact Number two again-no identification without substitution. We said to you that those five facts were very important. We said that the reason we could enjoy physical health in our bodies is because Jesus bore our sicknesses in His body and bore our pain. That's substitution-one that takes another person's place. And Hebrews 2 says that He tasted, ate of, death for every man. That is substitution.

If He does something for you, He's taking your place. He tasted death for every man. Does that include you? That means that Jesus ate of, experienced death for every single person. That means He took your place. Therefore, Jesus was your substitute. Is that correct? He was a representative man. Is that correct? He and Adam were the two most important men who ever lived on the face of the earth. Why? Because they're representative men. Adam represented you and brought you down to the negative, into sin. Jesus Christ represented you to the positive, brought you out of sin into righteousness. The two very most important men that ever walked on the face of the earth.

Jesus tasted death. It was not a figment of His imagination. It wasn't just a thought that He had about death. It says Jesus *tasted* or experienced death for every person. He experienced it, ate of it, and partook of it for every single person. Tasting death for every person was as real an experience as His tasting sickness and disease on His body. Isaiah chapter 53 said that Jesus bore our sickness and our diseases and by His stripes, we were healed. We have been looking at God's pattern, the way He does things, in His Word. God doesn't change. It says that in the Scripture, does it not? "I, the Lord, change not" (Malachi 3:6; Heb. 13:8). So if anything is being changed, it's not God's fault, it's our fault.

We shift and change, because we don't take time to understand the things of the Bible. And so if we don't understand something, we simply say, "Well, it can't be true." That's false reasoning. If God says something is true, friends, it doesn't matter if you don't understand it, it doesn't matter whether you like it or not-it's true.. Isaiah says He bore our sicknesses. Those who don't understand will say, "No, He didn't " Isaiah says, "Yes, He did." And the people who don't want to take time to understand it, keep saying, "No, He didn't." But we're here to tell you that what Isaiah said was inspired by the

Holy Spirit. Who inspires what you say? Are you inspired by your intellect? Are you inspired by the devil? We'll just choose to trust the Holy Spirit, how about you? In the beginning of Isaiah 53, it says, "Who shall believe our report?" We do!

The Need For Redemption

The redemption we needed from Adam was not a physical redemption. You must understand this. It was not physical redemption that we needed. It was a spiritual redemption. Sin and spiritual death were not in my body, nor in your body. Spiritual death was in our spirits. If it were a physical death spoken of here, then after dying physically, we could look forward to a physical resurrection. But that would be sad, because our spirits would still be dead. Jesus experienced spiritual death in His Spirit. Spiritual death had to be transferred from my dead spirit into His spirit. Spiritual death, which was in your spirit before you came to Christ, had to be transferred from your spirit into Jesus' spirit. He had to take it as your substitute.

If Jesus were our substitute, we call it a substitutionary sacrifice, don't we? What did He substitute for? Now remember, a substitute is someone who takes another's place. So He took our place. Nobody argues with that; we've been saying that for centuries. But did He take our place? Shouldn't' we know why we call Jesus our substitutionary sacrifice? Why state something like this if we have no understanding of it?

He was to get us back in right standing with Almighty God. So, at this point, are you still following this? Don't let go now, just hold on. If we are to get God's righteousness into us, then someone had to first take our sin and spiritual death out of us. The two can't coexist. Someone had to somehow get us out of Adam. If we were in Adam, everything Adam got, we got. Adam's spiritual death was passed on to the whole human race. Everything he got, we got. Hebrews 2:9 says Jesus tasted-experienced-death for all men. Now let's ask this question, "How did He do that?"

Second Corinthians 5:21 says, "For He hath made him to be sin for us who knew no sin." Understand, we're not calling Jesus a sinner. He's the spotless Lamb of God. But the Word says, "For he hath made him to be sin, for us who knew no sin that we might be made the righteousness of God in Him." Fact Number 2: there can be no identification without substitution. We keep bringing you back to that. Since Jesus was my substitute, He can now identify with us.

Concerning Hebrews 2:9, *Knox's* translation says, "Jesus was to taste death, and taste it on behalf of all." The *New English Bible* says, "In tasting death, He should stand for all of us." Now, in order for us to be freed in our spirits of spiritual death, Jesus had to taste or experience this death in His own spirit. Sin is spiritual. He couldn't experience it in His big toe, nor in His mind or in His character, could He? Because sin is spiritual, we can't take our sin from our spirit and put it on Jesus' body. Can we? But He can take it into His spirit. Spiritual death is in your spirit, and that's where Jesus had to taste it. In His spirit. He had to experience it in His Spirit. See, He's taking our place. If He's our substitute, we have to transfer what's in us into Him. He has to identify with us. In order to free us, He has to become what we were, in order for us to become what He is in His death, burial and resurrection.

Even though God says there is no controversy over this subject, men want to make it controversial. We're going to tell you some of their arguments as we go along, but you're going to see how foolish they are. Actually, we might say they're pretty ridiculous. When you get a hold of this, you're going to understand what we're talking about. It's going to be so clear in your own heart when we get done, that you're going to say, "Why doesn't everybody see it?"

This teaching is a matter of life and death for you. The day will come when the devil will talk to you about some things, and if you're not prepared, he's going to whammy you. He's going to pulverize you. But if you know what the Word says, you can simply stand up to him and say, "Devil, you're a liar. I don't believe what you're trying to sell me."

In Isaiah 53:9, we see a prophesy about Jesus Christ. It says there, "And he made his grave with the wicked and with the rich in his death; because he had done no violence, neither was any deceit in his mouth." Notice now, that Jesus was the one who made His grave with the wicked. Jesus made His own grave with the wicked. How did Jesus make His grave with the wicked? Don't answer; just think. Put your thinking cap on. How did Jesus make His grave with the wicked? "Oh, that's just saying that Jesus was buried with the wicked." Are you sure that that's what it means? Let's jog your memory. The bible told us and we're sure yours does too, that Joseph of Arimathea came to Pilot after Jesus died, and asked for Jesus' body, that he might bury Jesus in Joseph's tomb. Is that Biblically correct? Then how did Jesus make His grave with the wicked? I thought He was buried <u>alone</u> in Joseph's tomb? Then what in the world is Isaiah saying?

Wherever the wicked had their grave, that's where Jesus made His grave, because Isaiah said so, and he was inspired by God. So the grave Isaiah is

167

speaking about cannot be a physical grave, because we know where Jesus' solitary physical grave was. Joseph of Arimathea got Him that grave. Yet, the grave spoken of by Isaiah was with the wicked. Wicked? Could that mean more than one person? It could and it does. So this must not be a physical grave, because Jesus' physical body was buried alone. Solitarily. Could this then refer to a spiritual grave? This is important. Where do the wicked make their grave, according to the Word of God? In the center of the earth (Mathew 12:40).

Ephesians 4 says that Jesus descended first into the lower <u>parts</u> of the earth. That's the pit of Hell, the place of torments where the wicked go when they die. The unrepentant, the fornicators, the liars, the disobedient go there. And Jesus chose to make His grave with the wicked. He, who knew no sin, was made to be sin for us. Thus, it was His spiritual grave, because He experienced spiritual death in His spirit. God (because Jesus was our substitute) took our spiritual death in our spirit and placed it in Jesus. He identified with us. He cannot choose to identify with us in part. He must identify with us in totality. This is God's pattern, not mine. And so if Jesus is my substitute, and there is no identification without substitution, He said, "I'll take your place. Let me pull that sin out of your spirit, and put it in Mine."

He's now totally identifying with me. He took my sin. What I had, He now has. He's my representative man. In other words, my substitute identified with my sin, took my spiritual death from me upon His own spirit, and then further identified with the punishment that was due me, which was to be with the wicked or those who died in spiritual alienation from Almighty God. Those who died in spiritual death were to remain in Hell, the grave of the wicked.

When Jesus made His grave with the wicked, where was His body? In Joseph's tomb. So to what grave did He go where the wicked were? Is that not the punishment of the wicked? When God judged Jesus, He judged Him on the basis that He had your sin and my sin. It was where? In Jesus. What would you call Jesus' spirit if the Father judged Him and said, "You must go to Hell?" Wasn't His Spirit alienated from God? Isn't the place designated for the wicked called Hell?

Jesus Died Twice

Look at the rest of Isaiah 53:9:"...and with the rich in his death." If you have a *King James Bible*, you will see a footnote, it's number nine in the Bible we're using, and it says, "the Hebrew word for death is actually plural, deaths." The word used in Hebrew here is not a singular word, it is a plural word. It is saying simply that Jesus made His grave with the wicked and the rich in His deaths. It says that Jesus died twice.

Now in the Book of Romans, we're told that Jesus died *once* for all men. When it says He died once in that context in Romans, it's simply saying that He'll never have to die again. Once sacrifice is sufficient. He died once for sin. That's good forever. It was an eternal sacrifice. And over here in Isaiah 53:9, the word "deaths" was not used to emphasize the importance of it. It literally means that Jesus actually died twice. Jesus died spiritually, and Jesus died physically; and He arose spiritually and arose physically. Jesus had a two fold resurrection.

If Jesus only died physically, it seems that He didn't have as much courage as the first martyr, Stephen, had according to the Book of Acts. This first martyr stood up boldly, like a man, and let them stone him to death. So his death was just physical, wasn't it? Now follow this. But Jesus, in the garden, tried to get out of His death, didn't He? "Father, if this cup can be removed from Me. Father, if there's some other way, take this cup from Me." Stephen never said anything like that, did he? Are we saying that Stephen was a braver man than Jesus?

If Jesus only died physically, His faith didn't seem as strong as Stephen's. Stephen just went up there and said, "Father, I commend my spirit to you. Forgive these men for stoning me." He never said to the Father, "Oh, Father, don't let it happen to me." But Jesus, when He was in the garden, said, "Father, if there's any other way, if there's any other way, please remove this cup from me!" But He finished with, "Not My will, but Thy will be done."

This is an important point. Jesus knew it wasn't just physical death that He wanted to get out of. "Father , if there's another way...", was the cry of One who was going to experience separation from His God. He had never known what that was like, and it tormented Him. What do we call that kind of death? Spiritual death. What is spiritual death? Did Jesus cease to exist? You know what was torturing Jesus? The thought of having to be separated from His Father, not the thought of physical death. Jesus was concerned about being made to be sin. He was sweating, as it were, drops of blood.

Did you ever see any other man at any time, even under conviction and judgment, even a man going to the electric chair, shed drops of blood? Never! They might sweat; they might be nervous; they might be tortured mentally as they're on their way to that chair, but we are not aware of anyone who has ever sweated blood-except Jesus.

We ought to begin to see how serious sin is. Jesus was tormented. When our sin was put on Him, He knew what was about to happen. He was going to experience total separation from His Father. That is called spiritual death. He agonized over spiritual death, not over physical death. He wasn't asking the Father to remove the cup of physical death. It was the cup of spiritual death He was concerned with. The sins of the whole world were going to be placed on Him and in His spirit as our substitute. The idea of separation made Jesus sweat blood. And if we understood spiritual death, it ought to make us avoid sin to the point of even sweating blood. Who in their right mind would want to be separated from God?

Isaiah said, "Your sins will separate you from Your God." He was going to be made to be sin for us- the Sinless One. And God was gong to treat Jesus the same as He would treat each of us as condemned sinners. It's so important for you to understand that a substitute is one who takes another's place. When He took our place, then God said, "You're fully identified with the Human race. Therefore, Jesus, by justice, I must condemn you to the punishment that I've condemned the world to." Jesus had to go to Hell, the place of unrepentant sinners.

Now we're not using profanity here when we say, Jesus went to Hell. The Father said to Jesus, "You have to go to Hell." The word "Hell" is a noun, it's a place. And that doesn't give glory to the devil, as some argue. That shows the tremendous love God has for us. That He'd send His own Son to Hell in our place. Are you following this? Jesus was our sacrifice, our substitutionary sacrifice.

Are you beginning to see how serious sin is in the eyes of the Almighty God? He loved Jesus, but the Scripture said He turned His back on Jesus. That's why Jesus cried out, "My God, My God, why hast Thou forsaken Me?" Jesus —trying to figure this out, a man on the cross. He never committed any sin, but He was made to be sin. Why? Because He was our substitute. Once a person becomes a substitute, then He can fully identify with the other person. He became our representative man. In order to get us out of Adam, and into the righteousness of God, this had to take place.

CHAPTER

13

DID JESUS DIE SPIRITUALLY?
(PART 3)

In this chapter, we are continuing to answer the question: Did Jesus die spiritually? Our overall subject matter is entitled "The Mystery", which is our identification with Christ.

We're taking our time because those who don't understand this topic find it controversial. But God says it's not controversial (I Tim. 3:16). He says you can learn and understand it. If you'll apply yourself, it's not difficult.

So look at Hebrews 2:9: "But we see Jesus, who was made a little lower than the angels for the suffering of death, crowned with glory and honor; that he, by the grace of God should taste death for every man."

In this last chapter, we were talking about the fact that Jesus was crying out to the Father. The scene we depicted for you was the scene in the Garden of Gethsemane where Jesus was crying. Really try to picture Jesus in the garden. Blood is coming out of His pores. He's in agony. He's crying to the Father. He's screaming to the Father. "If there's some other way," He said. "If there would be another avenue...another possibility, Father, would You please remove this cup from Me?" You all know this scene very well.

As noted before, Jesus was not crying in agony or in despair over what most people think. Most think He was crying to get out of physical death. But Jesus was not in torment because He was about to go through a physical death. If that were the case, then our first martyr, Stephen, was more courageous than Jesus in facing death. Because when Stephen stood before those who were about to stone him, he didn't call out to God, "Remove this cup from me, if there's another way." He never said anything. He stood there, boldly and courageously, and was stoned to death.

Picture Jesus in the Garden

So, from this viewpoint, we can certainly see that Jesus wasn't crying to the Father to deliver Him from physical death. So what was Jesus going through? What was His torment, this thing that was just enveloping His mind to the point that He was screaming to the Father? What was Jesus going through right then? What was he thinking? His thoughts were all focused on the fact that very soon He was going to have every sin of the entire world dropped into His spirit. What He was tormented about was the fact that He was going to be separated from the Father. Sin separates you from your God. He was no longer going to have communion with the Father. There would be no more relationship for Him. He was going to be alienated, as it were, from the very life of God.

Now, once again, picture this: Jesus' sweat, as it says in the Scripture, was as drops of blood at the prospect of losing His communion with the Father. He who knew no sin, was about to be made sin, that you and I could receive the righteousness of God through Jesus Christ our Lord. No wonder Jesus was sweating blood. No wonder He was screaming in torment. Can you imagine an individual such as Jesus who had enjoyed eternal fellowship with the Father, loved the Father with all His heart, spent every day communicating with the Father, obeying the Father, being part of the Father's love, and now because of our sins, He would have to abruptly be separated from that? I can well understand the blood that was flowing out of His pores. Can't you? Do you know any other human who has sweat blood over having sinned against God?

So many don't even think twice about sinning, not realizing that when we sin, we are drinking the cup of spiritual death.

But Jesus was screaming, "Father if there's another way." In other words, "I don't want the sin of the world on me. If there's another way, I don't want to be made to be sin. Why? Because I don't want to be separated from your life." Are you with us so far? Are we painting a picture for you? Do you see Jesus in the garden suffering, going through that torture, that torment, over the fact that He is going to be separated from the Father? Our heinous sins, our offenses, our trespasses, our disobediences, our rebellion, our lustful thoughts, our promiscuous ways, everything that you can think of, every single sin that has ever been committed by humankind-Jesus was going to get every last one of them dropped into His Spirit. He would enter, on our behalf, the state of spiritual death.

Then as we saw right here in Hebrews 2:9, <u>He tasted death for every men</u>. We found out that that word "tasted" meant that <u>He experienced it.</u> He partook of it. We said also that it wasn't just a figment of His imagination. It wasn't just an ugly thought of death that seemed to pass through Jesus momentarily. Jesus literally became sin, and His spirit experienced total spiritual death-total alienation from the very life of God. No communication, no communion with God, the moment our sin was dropped into Jesus. And Jesus didn't take that lightly.

We've all used this expression, "Man, did I sweat blood over that!" Well with us, it's just a figure of speech. Or we just simply say, "Boy did I sweat over that problem! Did I ever sweat over that circumstance! Man, I'll tell you, I was sweating bullets over this and over that!"

We make all kinds of statements as figures of speech. But Jesus Christ our Lord literally did sweat drops of blood. Think about this for a moment. Picture a convicted criminal, who has come under the judgment of our state laws for a crime he committed, and who faces the death penalty. Think of that for a moment. Here's a man who is about to be dragged down that corridor and strapped in an electric chair. Any moment they're going to pull the switch. You can bet that man is sweating on the way to that chair.

But in the history of mankind, never have we seen, never have we heard recorded, even under the most hideous of circumstances, any person sweat blood. But Jesus did. We're belaboring the point because we want you to see what Jesus thought of sin. We want you to see what the Father thinks about sin, and what Jesus knew spiritual death would produce.

Identifying With Us in Sin

Again, Hebrews 2:9 says that Jesus actually experienced death in His Spirit; and that spiritual death brought Jesus the same punishment that was due you and me. Remember, He was our substitute. He took our place. A substitute is one who takes another's place. And when He became our substitute, He was able to identify with us. There can be no identification unless there is first a substitutionary work. He was our substitute, and so He tasted death for all of us. That means He took our place. Now you're getting this!

So now, He can identify with us in our sins and in our trespasses, can't He? He's our substitute, so He can identify. God must place what was in our spirit right into Jesus' spirit, because, to identify means to make identical, to consider and treat as the same.

Now, God, by justice, is required to make Jesus exactly what each of us was. He must treat Him in the exact same way that He treated each of us. When sin was in our spirit man, think about this, how did God treat us? What did He do? He separated Himself from us. He removed His very life from us. We had no more communion with God, did we? We had no communication with God, did we? We were spiritually dead.

Again, spiritual death is separation from God. And when Jesus became our substitute, when Jesus took our sin (when the One who knew no sin was made to be sin for us), then God had to abandon Jesus, just like He abandoned us. Are you following this? If God was going to abandon us, then God has to abandon my substitute. If He's going to cut off communication with us, because we're spiritually dead, then He has to cut off communication with Jesus. If He's going to remove the life, His life, from us, then He has to remove His life from Jesus. That's why Jesus cried out in torment, "My God, My God, why hast thou forsaken Me?" Because God had to leave Him. God had to abandon Him. God had to remove His communication from Him.

Made to be Sin

Now Jesus was our substitute, our spiritual sacrifice. Jesus didn't do anything wrong. A lot of people say, "Well, you know, Jesus never committed any sin." No, He never committed any sin. He was made to be sin with our sin that the righteousness of God could come upon us. So Jesus was made to be a spiritual sacrifice. He didn't do anything wrong. He was simply made to be sin, with our sin.

Think of it this way. Under the old covenant, when they sacrificed animals, had those animals done anything wrong? They were innocent, weren't they? They hadn't done anything wrong. The people had the priest lay his hands on the animals, on their behalf. And what did the priest do? He confessed the sins of the people over them, and the animals became a sin offering. Then the animals were sacrificed or killed. They were innocent animals. This was done as a foreshadowing of the final sacrifice, Jesus, the Lamb of God.

Now spiritual death was due those sinning Israelites. Think of what took place. The Scripture says the soul that sinneth must die. Therefore,

> *And the goat shall bear upon him all their iniquities* unto a
> land not inhabited: and he shall let go the goat in the
> Wilderness *(Leviticus 16: 5-22).*

Finally, look at verse 30: "For on that day shall the priest make an atonement for you, to cleanse you that ye may be clean from all your sins before the Lord."

This atonement is pointing towards the final sacrifice on Golgotha's hill. Did you notice that it took two goats to fulfill the atonement? Two goats. This atonement, as we said, pointed to the final one on Calvary, and it took two sinless goats to complete this sacrifice. These goats were sinless. The first goat represented sinlessness. It was a pure, clean sacrifice. They did not confess their sins over that goat. But they killed that goat and he shed his blood. Jesus was the Lamb of God-sinless-and He shed His blood on Calvary's cross. That's part of our redemption. But there's more to see and understand.

What about that second goat? On the Day of Atonement, they killed an innocent animal. He shed his blood. But that wasn't all they did. They didn't send the people home after they had sacrificed the first goat, they then took the live goat, put their hands on him (to show identification with the sacrifice), and confessed all their sins on the goat. This represents Jesus as spoken of in 2 Corinthians 5:21: "He hath made him to be sin who knew no sin."

They then confessed the sins of Israel over the live, sinless goat and sent him out to the wilderness to die. This represented Jesus Christ as our sin-bearer, representing our separation from God. The goat went into the wilderness. The word wilderness, according to the dictionary, is a desolate place, an uninhabited place. In Hebrew, the word uninhabited, or not inhabited, as you might see in your Bible, is a place of separation. This goat was a type of Jesus bearing spiritual death for us. He went to a place of separation so we wouldn't have to go there. The two goats together, and what each did, were accomplished totally by Jesus. Praise the Lord. One goat shed his blood; the other went to a place of separation as does everyone who is in spiritual death. It took two goats, but Jesus covered both aspects all by Himself on the cross.

This might be a good place for us to encourage you to read Isaiah 53, from several different versions of the Bible. If you don't get it then, go back and read it again, then study it. As you can see, there are many things about our redemption that won't be seen unless we dig deeply. We have to understand what our redemption is all about.

How Did He Do It?

And so the question is: If redemption took place, how did He do it? Now keep in mind, we're not trying to establish some new doctrine because one day, a remote scripture appeared to say something about identification. No. There are numerous scriptures, and we need to search them out for ourselves. We probably won't get to them all. And we're not sure that we can find them all ourselves. But let's pursue this subject with an open heart and a diligent spirit. No doctrine should ever be built on one single verse of scripture. We must be very careful about that because that can be extremely dangerous. We must see what God says in several places and then allow the Holy Spirit to piece it all together for us, in order to see what God is really trying to reveal to us.

Scripture after scripture has shown that all of us, under the Adamic nature, were in a state of alienation from God-spiritual death. We had sin in our spirit, and the soul that sinneth must die. We were in spiritual death. It resided within us, not on us. Not on our bodies. But spiritual death resided in our spirits. Spiritual death had to be removed. How was it done? We all say that Jesus died for us, but why? What took place when He died?

If redemption is a major doctrine of the church, then we ought to understand it. Consider this: if something affected your life as much as Jesus' death, burial and resurrecton, then you would want to know the why's and the how's about it, wouldn't you? This is important. It affects your life. If our salvation depended on Jesus bearing our spiritual death, wouldn't you consider knowing this as being very important? If Jesus didn't die spiritually for us, we would have received our full judgment. Do you know what that judgment would have been for us? (And God had to do it out of justice.) We would have had to spend eternity in those everlasting fires. That was our punishment. That was our sentence.

The Son of Man Lifted Up

Look at John 3:14: "And as Moses lifted up the serpent in the wilderness, even so must the Son of man be lifted up." Jesus here is relating His crucifixion with Moses' lifting up the serpent in the wilderness. Jesus Himself is relating His being on the cross to that incident in the Old Testament when Moses lifted up that serpent. In other words, when Moses lifted up that serpent on a pole in the wilderness, Jesus was simply saying, "It's talking about Me. That scripture has a direct reference to me."

Go with us back to the Old Testament. Keep the above scripture in mind, however, as you look at Numbers 21:7-9. Now remember, the people of Israel have rebelled against God. They sinned against God. Isn't rebellion a sin? They spoke against God. They showed insurrection. They had idolatries in their lives.

> *Therefore the people came to Moses and said, We have sinned, for we have spoken against the Lord, and against Thee; pray unto the Lord, that he take away the serpents from us. And Moses prayed for the people.*
> *And the Lord said unto Moses, Make thee a fiery serpent, and set it upon a pole: and it shall come to pass, that every one that is bitten, when he has looked upon it, shall live.*
> *And Moses made a serpent of brass, and put it upon a pole, and it came to pass that if a serpent had bitten any man, when he beheld the [that word 'beheld' means he was occupied with and influenced by] serpent of brass, he lived.*

Brass is a symbol of judgment, and that serpent, not a lamb but a serpent, was made and put on a pole. It was made of brass. These people were dying as the live serpents were biting them. They were biting them because they had sinned. This was part of their punishment. Now God said that while they were being bitten, if they would look at the serpent of brass, they would be healed. Now that serpent on the pole was an Old Testament type of the atonement. We already saw in John 3:14, above, that Jesus Himself said, "as Moses lifted up the serpent in the wilderness, even so must the Son of man be lifted up." Jesus gave us direct relationship of Himself to that serpent on the pole. He said, "That's Me." You see, that serpent represented the curse. All that mankind had become through Adam was on that pole. And when Moses lifted up that serpent, God was giving a revelation of Calvary to the people of Israel. He was showing them that one day the entire curse would be put on one they would call the Redeemer.

Galatians 3:13 says, "Christ hath redeemed us from the curse of the law, being made a curse for us: for it is written, Cursed is every one that hangeth on a tree." Someone will say, "That symbol of the serpent on the pole doesn't represent Jesus. That's some old Egyptian symbol that means medical aid." People have said that.

179

So do they mean that if someone breaks his leg somewhere, waits for the ambulance, then looks at that symbol on the back window of the ambulance with the blue cross and the serpent on the pole that all of a sudden his leg is going to be healed instantly? Well, the ambulance pulls up, he looks at the symbol, and nothing happens. But they say that it represents medical aid. Do you believe that? We don't. That symbol can't heal anybody.

The serpent on the pole couldn't heal anybody either. It did, however help the people of Israel release their faith in what it represented. If they released their faith in the medical aid and got divine power to flow, then all we need to do is put that symbol up everywhere. Let's put it on the doorposts of our house. Let's put it on our schools. Let's put it on our hospitals. And let's just get the aid that we need. Listen; there are hundreds of people in hospitals who believe in medical aid. Hospitals dispense medical aid. But there is no divine power flowing through what the hospitals are dispensing. If it were, why are so many not getting healed?

There is no healing apart from Calvary. That serpent was only a reminder of the crucifixion that would take place, a type of Jesus taking the curse upon Himself and away from us.

CHAPTER

14

DID JESUS DIE SPIRITUALLY?
(PART 4)

In Numbers 21:7-9, we read: "Therefore the people came to Moses, and said, We have sinned for we have spoken against the Lord, and against thee..." [Now notice that these people said they had sinned against two people, the Lord and the Lord's anointed. And the way they had sinned was in their talk against both. So we're letting you know that God does not take lightly our conversations, especially when they're negative toward His leaders. And if He doesn't take this thing lightly for His leaders, then how does He view it when it comes to speaking negatively against Him?]

Verse 7 continues,
...pray unto the Lord, that he take away the serpents from
Us. And Moses prayed for the people.
And the Lord said unto Moses, make thee a fiery serpent
and set it upon a pole: and it shall come to pass, that every
one that is bitten, when he looketh upon it, shall live.
And Moses made a serpent of brass, and put it upon a pole,
and it came to pass that if a serpent had bitten any man,
When he beheld the serpent of brass, he lived.

The word "behold" there, as we said, means to be occupied with and influenced by. It's not just a glance. It's a *steady* glance with an understanding of what you are looking at and what you are occupied with and influenced by. What does that say to you? It doesn't simply say, "I'm looking at a brass serpent on a pole." We all should keep in mind that it's more than just a glance. It's an <u>understanding</u>. And when we talk about Calvary, Calvary is more than just a glance. We don't just simply say, "Oh, well, yes, we understand that Jesus died on the cross. Thank You, Lord." Most denominations think of it in those terms, but we should know better.

But for the past 13 chapters, we have been gathering an understanding of what took place on Calvary's cross. We found out that more than meets the eye took place up there. And the only way we are going to have a full understanding of what took place on Calvary, is to behold Calvary and be occupied with Calvary. We have to be influenced by Calvary. Our hearts must be open to understand what God accomplished on the cross that awful day 2,000 years ago.

The Symbol Is a Reminder

We ended Chapter 13 by speaking about the serpent that Moses lifted up in the wilderness. John 3:14, states, "As Moses lifted up the serpent in the wilderness, even so must the Son of man be lifted up." Jesus was relating the incident of Numbers 21 to Himself. He's talking about Himself. We said that even though that symbol of the serpent on the pole came out of Egypt, and even though the medical profession has adopted that symbol as a sign of medical aid, no one can look at that medical-aid symbol and release the power of God in the area of healing. We said that if you break your leg, and somebody calls an ambulance and you look on the back window at the serpent-on-the-pole-symbol, you're not going to get healed. You're not going to release the power of God by looking at that symbol.

When Moses lifted up that serpent, it was to cause the sinning people of Israel to release their faith in the Redeemer who would become a curse for them at some future date. That symbol reminded those people that a curse was on that pole. It was to remind them of the Redeemer, the Lord Jesus Christ, who would one day come and become a curse for all the people of the world. We said that there was no healing apart from Calvary, because healing is a part of the atonement. We want you to know that. There is no healing apart from Calvary. Moses was getting the people to release their faith in the atonement of Calvary when one day the Messiah would come to become a curse for them.

As we've already studied in Galatians 3:13, Jesus became a curse for us. That's what God was trying to bring across in Numbers. No symbol can heal you. There is only one place you can get healed, and that's at the cross of Calvary. There's only one place to which you can look for a release of the power of God into your bodies. Healing, again, is in the atonement.

It's absolutely ridiculous to think that because the Egyptians had the symbol-a serpent on a pole-that God had to take it out of Egypt, out of their witchcraft or sorcery and bring it into the present time so believers could take hold of it for healing. That is absolutely asinine to think about. We don't believe that for one minute, and we hope you don't either. God never, ever uses anything of the devils as part of His tool in any way, shape or form. A lot of people say, "Well, God uses the devil to get people saved." God doesn't use the devil for anything! You'd have to know nothing about god to think that God would go to Egypt, pull something out of their witchcraft or sorcery, and bring it over to benefit believers. You don't believe that, and we don't believe that. We must learn to believe the Word of our Lord Jesus Christ. Amen?

Jesus said, "As Moses lifted up the serpent in the wilderness on a pole, so must [I] the Son of man be lifted up." Not medical aid, but the Son of man must be lifted up. Let's take it a step further. Go to 1 Timothy 3:16: "And without controversy great is the mystery of godliness: God was manifest in the flesh, justified in the Spirit seen of angels, preached unto the Gentiles, believed on in the world, received up into glory."

Declared Righteous

What we want you to zero in on is the part of this verse, which says that God was manifested in the flesh, justified in the Spirit. One of our modern translations says, "Jesus became righteous in Spirit." Another says, "Jesus was declared righteous in spirit." Still another says, "Jesus was pronounced righteous in His Spirit." Now the word "justified" is used in the New Testament a total of 21 times, and every time the same Greek word is used. The Greek word is *dikaioo*. In every case, the meaning is exactly the same. Twenty-one times the meaning is the same. It means to render just, to render innocent, free and righteous. To render free and to render righteous. Now here's the question: how could the Holy Spirit render Jesus innocent, just, free and righteous, if He never was guilty, unjust, captive and unrighteous?

In short, how could Jesus be rendered righteous, unless He was at some time unrighteous? Second Corinthians 5:21, states, "For he hath made Him [Jesus] to be sin for us, who knew no sin; that we might be made the righteousness of God in him." Does that sound like substitution and identification? Sure does. God made Him to be sin for us. Remember when we said every time you look for identification you look for the "in Him", "for us", "through Him"? These expressions, in most cases in the New Testament when referring to Jesus, are referring to a substitutionary work and our identification with that substitutionary work. In other words, the innocent, just, righteous One was made to be sin for us. Jesus knew no sin. Jesus never committed sin. He was without sin; but our sin, the sin that was ours, was placed on the Lord Jesus Christ. Remember Jesus had to become everything that we were in order for us to become everything He is through His resurrection.

Where Does Sin Go?

Now, what were we before Jesus came into our lives? One word-sinners. We were spiritually dead. Death reigned in our spirits. That death had to be taken out of our spirits. But where was that spiritual death to go? If it were in us, then it had to be taken out of us somehow. So where did it go? Jesus said to His Father, "Father, I'll take it as the substitute for every man and woman that lives on the earth." We call Jesus our substitutionary sacrifice. But, where did it go in Jesus? Did it go into His head? Did it go into His torso? Where did the sin that was in our spirits go on Jesus? In Jesus spirit. Why? Because sin is spiritual, not physical. So our sins had to be laid into Jesus spirit. What then happened to Jesus' spirit? It died, didn't it? Spiritual death took over Jesus' spirit.

When spiritual death entered Jesus' spirit, did Jesus cease to exist? No. He was still alive; He was on the cross; he hadn't yet died. Physically, He was still breathing, and from time to time, He was talking to the Father. He did not cease to exist when spiritual death took over His spirit. But He was spiritually dead, alienated from a conscious communion with His Father, God. Is that not correct? He was alienated from a conscious communion with the Father, God, and we know that for two reasons.

Number one: the scripture in Romans 6:23 says, "The wages of sin is death." But why did Jesus, when our sin was laid upon Him, cry out to the Father? Why did Jesus cry to the Father? Because the Father was turning

His back on Jesus. Just as when we were sinners He turned His back on us. Jesus was paid the wages of sin as our substitute. He took our sins into His spirit, and what was His pay? Death. Death where? In His spirit man. He bore our unrighteousness in His spirit, and God then had to justify Him, because if we were going to be justified, Jesus had to be justified first.

Look again at 1 Timothy 3:16: "And without controversy, great is the mystery of godliness." On the subject of whether or not Jesus died spiritually, God says there is no controversy. No controversy. Of the very thing that many fume and fight over, and say we have as controversy, God says there is no argument. So it's about time we, as believers, say what God says and stop walking around saying, "Boy, this is a controversial subject." God says, "No, it isn't. There's no argument about it." If we'll only read the Scriptures and try to understand it the way God sees it, instead of trying to see it the way man sees it, there will never be a controversy.

Jesus Had to be Justified

God said Jesus bore mankind's unrighteousness, man's sin, man's spiritual death in His spirit. And then Jesus was justified. He was made free and righteous once again. Now the Greek says, "He was justified in Spirit." And the word "Spirit is capitalized, did you notice that? Well we want you to know there were no capitals in the Greek language. No punctuation. So the translators had to make a decision. But what difference would it make whether or not the Holy Spirit did the justifying or the justifying took place in Jesus' spirit? The fact still remains that He was justified. That's one of the arguments you'll get. It doesn't make any difference whether the Holy Spirit was doing the justifying, or Jesus was justified in His spirit. If you want to keep a capital letter on the word Spirit, it doesn't make any difference. Either way Jesus was justified.

It was necessary for Jesus to be justified so we could be justified. Scripture also states that God was manifest in the flesh. That's the incarnation. It's clear that God took on flesh. But we have a big controversy over that, too. God says there's no controversy over either issue. So what are we fussing and fuming about? There are people who say, "Oh no, there's no Trinity." God says, "I was manifest in the flesh." There's no controversy. Again, if we'd only see what God says, there's no controversy. If we want to listen to other men, then we argue, fuss and fume over it. God says there is no controversy. If there is no controversy over the incarnation of deity, and no controversy over Jesus having to be justified, then it ought to be easily understood by all. But most people don't want to understand it. If Jesus never experienced spiritual death in the spirit, then He never would have to be justified, would He? What we're saying here is only common sense.

The Father's Plan

We want you to look at Luke 23:46, because this is something you're going to hear as an argument: "And when Jesus had cried with a loud voice, he said, Father into thy hands I commend my spirit." Now this is the scripture some use when trying to prove that when Jesus died, His spirit went straight to Heaven. They'll give you this argument. You see, they say," Well, He commended His spirit into His Father's hands, didn't He. After all, what would the Father have done with it?"

Well, that's a good question, isn't it? Let's not just assume because He commended His spirit into His Father's hands that His Father reached down with some great big vacuum cleaner and sucked Jesus' spirit right up to Heaven. Can we assume that? Some do. The word commend means (write it down) to deposit, to entrust and to commit to. Jesus simply, by faith, was entrusting the Father with His spirit. In other words, Jesus is saying to the Father, "I've borne this sin in My spirit. I know I'm judged by You, Father, to take their punishment in Hell. When justice is completely served, when justice is completely satisfied, Father, I've entrusted You to make My spirit alive again. I'm trusting You to justify My spirit. Therefore I deposit My spirit into Your hands." Jesus was simply committing His spirit to the Father so that the Father could do with it as He pleased. But don't you think for a moment that Jesus, when entrusting, depositing His spirit with the Father, thought that the Father would do His spirit any harm. The Father had a plan.

Let's prove all this out. Now the people who say this word "commend" means the Father just took His spirit right to Heaven, should look at Acts 14:23 at the story about the elders being ordained. Now lets look at what is says: "And when they had ordained them elders in every church, and had prayed with fasting, they commended them to the Lord, on whom they believed." Now, if we follow their reasoning and take the word commend to believe that it means to be taken immediately to heaven, then what good did it do to ordain these elders if the Father took them right up to heaven? Are you following this? *They commended them to the Lord.*

Now let's go to Matthew 12:40. You all know this particular story. Jesus related it Himself, and He also related Himself to this whole story. "For as Jonah was three days and three nights in the whale's belly; so shall the Son of man be three days and three nights in the heart of the earth." Now, if Jesus went straight to heaven when He commended His spirit into His Father's hands, when He deposited His spirit, by saying, "Father into Thy hands I commend My spirit," then when did Jesus spend three days and three nights in the heart of the earth? Jesus said that just as Jonah spent that time in the whale's belly, He would spend time in the heart of the earth. If He went straight to Heaven, when did He spend that time in the center of the earth? Let's find out about all this.

Made Alive in the Spirit

Look at 1 Peter 3:18: "For Christ also hath once suffered for sins, the just for the unjust, that he might bring us to God, being put to death in the flesh, but quickened by the Spirit, by which also he went and preached unto the spirits in prison." Now the word "quickened" there, as you know by now, means to be co-yoked and to make alive. If He were not dead then why would He have to be made alive? Now the words "quickened by" are incorrect in that statement. It should be in the spirit, not by the spirit. Let's look at some other translations, and you'll get it. The *Berkeley* says, "That Jesus underwent physical death, but in his spirit, he was brought to life." *Beck* Says, "He was made alive in his spirit." *Knox* says, "Endowed with fresh life in his spirit." *Jordan* says, "His spirit was made very much alive."

Let's keep in mind the principal of identification. If Jesus were not made alive spiritually, then we could not be made alive spiritually. What we got, He got. What He got, we got. We could not be born again unless Jesus Christ was first born again in our place. The bible says Jesus was the firstborn from the dead (Colossians 1:18). The principal is that if there is no substitution, there can be no identification. We've said that throughout this book. Keep in mind that it was the incarnate Son of God who was our Redeemer, not God the Father. It was Jesus, the One who emptied Himself of the fullness of the Godhead, and became as a servant, even unto death on a cross. Jesus died for us. He bore our spiritual death, and it is He that 1 Timothy 3:16 is speaking of. There should be no controversy over this. This same scripture says that God was manifest in the flesh. So we must conclude that Jesus was a God/man. He couldn't die as God alone, because God can't die. So

He didn't redeem us as God. He couldn't redeem us as man, but He could redeem us as a God/man. The Father didn't die. The Holy Ghost didn't die. The incarnate Son of God did.

First Timothy 3:16 tells us that this is a great mystery, but we should accept what he says and not start any controversy over it. We know the Trinity exists. That is, there is one God manifested in three divine persons. But we can't really explain it adequately, can we? In a sense, the Trinity is a mystery.

All God/All Man

We know that Jesus is all God and all man. Yet, we can't explain it. First Timothy says that God was manifest in the flesh. We have termed this the incarnation, but we can't fully explain it. You don't have to argue with people over it. Let's not major in the minors. We study, as God says in His Word, to show ourselves approved unto *God*, not unto man. If someone else doesn't want to understand this particular doctrine or wants to stir up a controversy with you, don't argue with them. Just keep studying to find as much benefit as you can from this study. You can't help other people who don't want to study it and just want to argue about it.

Let's explain some of these things. Go to Luke 23:43: "And Jesus said unto him [he's talking to the penitent thief on the cross], Verily I say unto thee, Today shalt thou be with me in paradise." This is another scripture that they use in arguing the fact that Jesus commended His spirit to the Father, Jesus said, "This day you're going to be with Me in paradise." They'll use this scripture for argument. Remember, if there's no substitution, there can be no identification. Also, while we were in Adam, a punishment was due us. You know what that was? We were to go to Hell. If there's no substitution, there can be no identification.

Paradise Explained

The word "Paradise" used here literally means a garden. It is one of the names of the places in the next world, before the cross of Calvary took place, which is reserved for the departed spirits of the righteous. Before the cross of Calvary, there was a place called Paradise. It is also called Abraham's bosom. It was a place reserved for the spirits of the righteous, or in other words, those who looked by faith with anticipation towards the cross. It was a place for them to remain and wait until Jesus went to the cross, or until redemption took place.

This is borne out by the story of the rich man and the beggar spoken of by Jesus in Luke 16:19-31. Two men died; one went to Abraham's bosom, the other to the place of torments. The rich man called up to Abraham. Remember, it says, he lifted up his eyes and being in torments (in Hades) asked Abraham to send Lazarus to touch the tip of his finger into some water and put it on his tongue. Do you remember that story? In this story there were two compartments or places for the departed spirits. One compartment, which was the upper compartment, was referred to in the Scriptures as Paradise. It is a literal garden. There is no torture or torment there. Abraham was there.

This man, who was rich during his lifetime, who fared sumptuously, died and went to a place called torments. Torments is not where Abraham was. It was a compartment below the place where Abraham was. The rich man looked up with his eyes and called to father Abraham in the upper compartment and said, "Abraham, send Lazarus to touch his finger in some water, and put it on my tongue, because I am tormented. So the lower compartment was a place, before the cross took place, where people went who died outside of the realm of faith, those who did not believe in the crucifixion, as spoken of prophetically that would come one day. They were in a place called Hades.

Abraham's bosom, as we said, was called Paradise. These spirits, who departed and went to Paradise, were righteous. Abraham was there, so we can conclude that when Jesus said to this man, "This day thou shall be with Me in Paradise," He meant Paradise, not Heaven, as we often think. The Scriptures make this clear.

The thief died after Jesus, didn't' he? Jesus died, and then they looked upon the thieves and broke their legs. The thieves' bodies collapsed on them, and they suffocated and died. Because he believed in Jesus, the penitent thief asked Jesus to forgive him. And the Lord said, "This day thou shall be with Me in Paradise." He assured this man that he would go to one of those two places. He said, "Today you will be with Me in Paradise." That does not mean up to Heaven, as you now understand.

Look at Ephesians 49-10: "Now that he ascended, what is it but that he also <u>descended first</u> into the <u>lower parts</u> of the earth? (Notice the word *parts*-it's plural. Jesus was involved with two separate places in the lower world.)

He that descended is the same also that ascended up far above all heavens, that he might fill all things.)"

Jesus Descended, Then Ascended

Look closely here. Jesus first *descended*, then *ascended* far above all heavens. Now why did Jesus descend first? Because the Scripture said so? We're looking for a reason. Go to 1 Peter 3:18-19 again:

> *For Christ also once suffered for sins, the just for the unjust*
> *That he might bring us to God, being put to death in the*
> *Flesh, but quickened by the Spirit:*
> *By which also he went and preached unto the spirits in prison, which were once*
> *disobedient..,*

The place for the disobedient spirits would be in torments. That's where the rich man was in torment. This was the grave of the wicked. He was in torment because it's a place of torture where there's endless weeping and gnashing of teeth. And that's where each of us was scheduled to go had not Jesus become our substitute, Glory to God! He went down there for us. He paid our penalty as our substitute.

We would have had to suffer for all eternity in Hell, but Jesus went down there and spent just three days. In three days, God said justice was served. And the Father called upon the Holy Spirit to make Jesus alive again. Jesus then, when He was made alive, came back up from the lower compartment, stopped at the second compartment, took captivity captive, and went on up, back into His body, and came alive once again. Now He's alive forevermore. That's our Jesus!

The upper compartment, Paradise (Abraham's Bosom), is now completely empty. There is no more use for that place since Jesus' redemption. Now, it's either heaven or Hades (hell). If someone accepts Christ and dies, he goes to heaven. But if he rejects Christ, he goes to Hell and remains there until the final judgment, at which time, Hell will be cast into the lake of fire for all eternity.

15

DID JESUS DIE SPIRITUALLY?
(PART 5)

It's very important in our confession of faith to recognize that we treat God's Word the same way we treat God. So many people today have neither a love nor an understanding of God's Word. If they only knew what Jesus said in John 6:63: "The words that I speak unto you, they are spirit, and they are life." We must understand that when we study God's Holy Bible and the words contained therein, we should be recognizing that this is God Himself speaking to us. This, after all, is called the Word of God. It is not the word of man. It is the Word of God. And so, when we read the Bible, we should have the highest respect for it. In fact, the respect we have for God Himself, is the respect we should also have for His Word. You cannot take some respect away from the Word and say, "I still have respect for God." They're one and the same. God is the Word. Jesus is the living Word. So, when we study the Word, we're studying about God. God wrote it for our benefit.

When you start telling people that Jesus did die spiritually, they have an argument for you. Someone may say, "Well, wait a minute now, I can tell you that Jesus couldn't have died spiritually because of what the penitent thief said on the cross to Him and also because of Jesus' response to the penitent thief."

Let's look at Luke 23:39-42:
And one of the malefactors which were hanged railed on

him [railed on Jesus], saying, If thou be Christ, save thyself
and us.
But the other answering rebuked him, saying dost not thou
fear God, seeing thou art in the condemnation?
And we indeed justly; for we receive the due reward of our
deeds: but this man hath done nothing amiss.
And he said unto Jesus, Lord, remember me when thou
comest into thy kingdom.

Here's what we want you to zero in on, because here is the argument; "And Jesus said unto him, Verily I say unto thee, today shalt thou be with me in Paradise."

Portrait of Hell

Let's look at the whole picture. Turn back a few chapters to Luke 16:19-31:

There was a certain rich man, which was clothed in purple
And fine linen, and fared sumptuously every day;
And there was a certain beggar named Lazarus, which was
laid at his gate, full of sores,
and desiring to be fed with the crumbs which fell from the
rich man's table: moreover, the dogs came and licked his sores.
And it came to pass that the beggar died and was carried by
the angels (notice the beggar died and was carried by the
angels) into Abraham's bosom. (You can circle that-
Abraham's bosom-or write it in your notes. This is important.)
The rich man also died and was buried;
and in hell...

There are many people out there saying there's no such place as Hell. Jesus Himself is speaking these words, and He says there is a place called Hell. He said, "... and in hell,"

[Talking about the rich man who died] "...and in hell he lift up his eyes..." Notice what he did. He lifted up his eyes. In other words, he looked upward. It is important that you understand this. God doesn't put these words in the Bible because He wants to fill up spaces. Look at that again with me now. The beggar went to Abraham's bosom, carried there by the angels. But the rich man died and found himself all of a sudden in Hell.

"And in hell he lift up his eyes, being in torments…"

Someone may say, "Well, I don't mind going to Hell, all my friends will be there. Ha, ha, ha. We'll just have a big party down there." Are you kidding? There's no party in Hell. This scripture says <u>the rich man was in torments.</u>

"…and seeth Abraham afar off, and Lazareth in his bosom, "And he cried and said, "Father Abraham, have mercy on me, and send Lazarus, that he may dip the tip of his finger in water, and cool my tongue; for I am tormented in this flame."

Notice what he said. Dip your finger in cool water; put it on my tongue. Why would he want cool water on his tongue? Because he was burning from the inside out. Let's not discount the fact that there were flames there. *There were flames there*, because it says so. He was burning from the inside out. He was tormented because he was burning inside his head, and the flame just went down through his body to his feet. When it got down there, it started all over again in the head. And this goes on for eternity.

What do *you* think, can there be any partying going on in Hell? How foolish are these people in the world who put their hands up and mock God by saying there's no Hell! Who do they think they are? Jesus says there is a Hell. It's a place of torment. Notice Abraham's response in verse 25: "But Abraham said, Son, remember that thou in thy lifetime receivedst thy good things, and likewise Lazarus evil things; but now he is comforted, and thou art tormented." Now watch this.

> *And beside all this, between us and you there is a great gulf fixed: so that they which would pass from hence to you can not: neither can they pass to us, that would come from thence.*
> *Then he said, I pray thee therefore, father, that thou wouldest send him to my father's house:*
> *For I have five brethren; that he may testify unto them, lest they also come into this place of torment.*
> *Abraham saith unto him, They have Moses and the prophets; Let them hear them. [He was saying, 'They have God's Word and that should suffice.']*
> *And he said, Nay, father Abraham: but if one went unto them from the dead, they will repent. [Notice, even in Hell, he's giving an argument that God's Word is not enough.]*
> *And he said unto him, if they hear not Moses and the prophets neither will they be persuaded though one rose from the dead.*

Now, here's the argument they'll give you. Jesus could not have died spiritually because spiritually dead people go to Hell and not to Paradise. Now we're here to tell you in the New Testament the word *paradise* is only used three times altogether. Just three different times. One is used in Luke 23:43. The other place is 2 Corinthians 12:4. Remember when Paul the Apostle went up to Paradise and heard unspeakable things? And the last place it's used is in Revelation 2:7, when Jesus Himself is speaking to the Church of Ephesus. He's talking about Paradise.

There is a place, of which Jesus is speaking, where there is continuity of thinking, thoughts, life going on, which we have just seen, have we not? Then where do some of the cults get the doctrine of soul sleeping? Please, somebody answer this! In other words, Jesus, when He died, and the penitent thief, Abraham, the rich man, the beggar and everybody else down there, all seem to be pretty conscious of life around them. And if, when we die, we go into soul sleep, why didn't they? Jesus said that man down there, that rich man, was in torments. You can't tell me he's in soul sleep. Go ask him, because he's still in torments today, more than 2000 years later.

Let's go back to Luke 23, and look again at verse 43. It's from here they pick their argument. Again, here's Jesus talking to the penitent thief, who says, "Hey look," to the other guy who didn't change his mind about his lifestyle, "we deserve what we're getting. We're hanging up here because we did something wrong. This man didn't do anything wrong." And he turns to Jesus and says, "Remember me when thou comest into thy kingdom." And Jesus said, "Today shalt thou be with me in Paradise."

Before the cross, before Jesus redeemed us, there was a place called hell-*Hades* in the Greek

Hell or *Sheol* in the Hebrew language. It was a place where the spirits of people who died were confined. Now, within this place called Hades, or Sheol in the Hebrew language was a place that had at least two compartments. There was an upper chamber and a lower chamber. Remember, the rich man lifted up his eyes. Why did he have to lift up his eyes when he spoke to Father Abraham? Because Father Abraham was in the upper chamber, and he was in the lower chamber. It says in Luke 16, that there was an impassable gulf between them. He said," I can't come to you and you can't come to me."

Why? Well, the man who died in sin was in Hell, and that's where he was going to stay. It was a fixed place where no one could get out. But the man who was the beggar obviously had looked to Jesus Christ, towards the cross which was in the future, just as the penitent thief, hanging up there on the cross with Jesus (tied up there) says, "Lord, remember me when You come to Your kingdom." Jesus said, "Okay, today you shall be with Me in Paradise."

Where was Paradise? Paradise was the upper chamber. All paradise means, in every place that you see it written in the Scriptures, is just simply a wonderful garden, a park-like atmosphere. Okay? It's just a park. Central Park in New York, that's the thought. You could call that a paradise. Probably not today, but you know what we're talking about. It's a park. That's all it means-a park, garden-like atmosphere.

So let's put this in perspective now and see what happened here. One man died in sin. He just rejected the Lord Jesus Christ. Now of course, the man on the cross, he's right there in the midst of redemption. But redemption isn't completed yet. Jesus is still alive, right? He's talking to this thief who is saying, "Please remember me." And Jesus says, "I will. I'm telling you Today, you will be with Me in Paradise." If I said to my wife, "Honey, I am telling you today that you are going to be with me at the mall," that doesn't mean that I am going to the mall in the next 24 hours. It simply means that at some point we will both be together at the mall. I'm just letting her know today about my future plans.

Now if you take out the punctuation, which was not in there originally, it could be read two different ways, couldn't it? In other words, Jesus could say to him, "Today, this day, you're going to be with Me in Paradise. I'm going there today, and you're going there today." It could mean that, couldn't it-*If* you punctuate it differently? Or, it could mean, "I say to you today, this day, the day I'm talking to you, that sometime in the future you'll be with Me in Paradise." We believe that it is the latter. When Jesus bore spiritual death for us, He had to first go where we would have gone, and we were not going to Paradise. After He paid our penalty for sin, He came back up through Paradise and set the Old Testament saints free (one of them being the thief on the cross).

Paying Sin's Penalty

Now, the people in Hell,or torments will never ever come out of that chamber. The Bible says that all of Hell itself will one day be picked up and thrown in to the lake of fire (Rev. 20:13-15). They'll just never come out of there. Because they never looked with faith towards the Lord Jesus Christ and Calvary's cross. We made this pretty clear in the last chapter, but we want to drive this point home.

Are you following this so far? Jesus goes down into Hell, spends three days there. Now, our punishment was eternal. But remember, He's the Son of God. And so God, after three days, says, "Enough, justice has been served." So what happens then? Jesus, before He leaves, makes a proclamation. "And how do you know that?" Because in 1 Peter 3:18, it says that He went down and preached to the souls in Hell. And the word "preached" simply means to herald. In other words He made a proclamation.

We don't know what He said to them, but He heralded something, which means He made a proclamation. He probably just declared who He was and why He came there. And after three days and three nights (*And how do we know He spent that long there? Because Jesus Himself said He would: "As Jonah was in the belly of the whale three days and three nights, so shall the Son of man be in the center or the heart of the earth three days and three nights." Jesus said it Himself.*) The Holy Spirit gets His orders from God the Father who says to the Holy Spirit: "<u>Quicken Jesus.</u>" In other words, <u>make Him alive</u>. He suffered long enough. Justice has been served for all humanity. <u>Make Him alive</u> (Rom. 8:11). The power of God goes into Jesus, and He comes up to the next chamber.

It's Either Heaven or Hell

Watch now-everybody who was down in Hell stays there; they can't come with Him. But it says in the Bible that He comes up and leads captivity captive. To all those who were captive in the place called Paradise for all those years, all those centuries, days, whatever it was, since their death, He says, "Now you can all come with Me." And they dismantle the upper chamber. It no longer exists today. There's no need for it anymore, because Jesus died for us. So when you die now, you either go to Heaven or Hell. We said it was dismantled-but it's probably just an empty chamber.

You see some churches have this Purgatory idea. Well, it's not in the Bible. It's ridiculous. Absolutely ridiculous. It would make a mockery of the death of the Lord Jesus Christ if there was another way for you to sneak into Heaven, wouldn't it? In other words, how can a person go through life-sin, sin, sin-and at the last minute, somehow sneak in, with the Lord saying, "Oh, you haven't been too bad. Go to Purgatory for 1,000 years. After you've suffered there, you can go to heaven one day." That would be earning your salvation, and no one can do that (Eph. 2:8,9). That's man's wishful plan of salvation, but it's not God's.

Now think about that for a moment. Even in the natural that makes no sense at all. If God the Father said there's only one way to Heaven, and that's through His Son, Jesus Christ, then there's only one way. There's no other way. You're not going to sneak in. People aren't going to pray for you and after you spend 10 or 20 years then you're permitted in.

The Scripture says in the Book of Ecclesiastes *that where the tree falls is where it will lie.* In other words, the state you're in when you die determines your eternity. There's no second chance. You had every opportunity while you were living, walking, breathing on this earth. Just like the rich man. Just like the rest of them down in the torments of Hell who had an opportunity to hear the Gospel of Jesus Christ. Romans 1:18-21 declares that such a one is "without excuse." So this argument for Purgatory cannot possibly be true, can it? It's a man-made doctrine. It's not Bible.

When we say that Jesus Christ went to Hell, friends, we are not cursing. Hell is a place, not a curse word. The reason Jesus went there is because His spirit had taken our sins into it. As our substitute, he then took our punishment. Hell was our punishment.

Now, let's go on a little bit further. Did you know that when Jesus came up, met the people in the upper chamber, at that point, other resurrections took place along with Jesus? Look at Matthew 27:52 It says in Matthew 27:52-53: "And the graves were opened; and many bodies of the saints which slept arose, and came out of the graves after his resurrection and went into the holy city, and appeared unto many."

Partakers in His Resurrection

Do you know whose graves opened? Those people. Some of those people in the upper chamber came out of the graves and walked around the city of Jerusalem. And then, later on, went all the way up with Jesus to be with the Lord in Heaven. That's what it says right there, doesn't it? But we have all the hope we can have through Jesus Christ that one day all of us are going to be raised from the dead, also because Jesus did it. We're going to get to that part of our identification with Christ.

In any event, the point we're trying to make is that Jesus did go to Hades, because He bore spiritual death in His Spirit. Then He was made alive again. Thank God, He was made alive. If He were not made alive, we would still be dead in our sins and trespasses. He had to be taken out of Hell, because everything He got we got.

Are you following this? You see, a lot of people get upset with you when you say that Jesus died spiritually. "Oh," they say, "not my sweet Jesus. Oh, Jesus never went to Hell." Well, you don't know the Bible if you say that. Remember when Jesus told His disciples that He was going to be dragged through the streets of Jerusalem and spit upon and killed, Peter says, "Not so, Lord, not my sweet Jesus." What did Jesus say to Peter? "Get behind me satan." He used the law of double reference on Peter, didn't He? He said, in other words, you're being influenced by the devil.

Yes, that was Peter, the apostle, to whom Jesus told, "Get behind Me, satan." Listen, when we say that Jesus went to Hell for us, we are not attacking the deity of God. In reality, we are exalting the love of God for us. Think about that. God so loved the world, that He gave His only begotten Son. The word "gave" in the Greek language is *ditome*. That word means to deliver, to yield, to suffer, to offer and to smite with the palm of your hand. God turned His face on Jesus and walked away from Him. Why? Because God so loved the world that He gave His only begotten Son. God's love for us made Jesus into a substitutionary sacrifice for us. He became a sin offering.

What love God has for us that He would send Jesus, the innocent Lamb of God to Hell for us! Jesus didn't have to go there, did He? Jesus didn't have to go there. But it was your sin and my sin that sent Him there. We transferred, as it were, the sins that we had on us, on to Jesus, and He received the punishment due us. He took our place.

Let's go a little bit further now and look at Acts 2:22-23. Now you really have to follow along. We don't want you to miss anything because this is very important. This subject is going to help you teach other people. But more importantly, what we're teaching is going to help you stay free from the lies of the devil.

Because the devil lies to more people about that than anything else. The devil wants to keep you thinking, "Well, I'm just no good. I've done this." And he'll keep you thinking all the time on the wrong channel.

But when you know who you are in Christ, your identity with Jesus Christ, the devil can't lie to you anymore. That's the only weapon he has. He's a liar from the beginning. There's no truth in him, the Bible says. Isn't that right? So everything he tells you, you've got to figure just the opposite. Isn't that right? If he has no truth in him, every time he opens his mouth he lies. If he says you're no good, it must be just the opposite. You're pretty good. Isn't that right? Pretty simple deduction.

What Are the Pains of Death?

Acts 2:22-24:
*Ye men of Israel, hear these words; Jesus of Nazareth, a
man approved of God among you by miracles and wonders
and signs, which God did by him in the midst of you, as ye
yourselves also know:
Him being delivered by the determinate counsel and foreknowledge
of God, ye have taken, and by wicked hands, have crucified and slain*

Now pay very close attention to the words in verse 24: "Whom God hath raised up, <u>having loosed the pains of death</u>: because it was not possible that he should be holden of it."

Look at the wording in there, "the pains of death." Circle that in your Bible.

Some will say that this is not talking about spiritual death here, this is physical death. Are you sure? Are you positive that this is just simply physical death? If this is speaking about physical death, then let's ask a very important question: Do you know of anyone who, after he has died, was in any pain? I said *after* he died. Do you know of anybody? Do you have pain while you are physically dead? If we do, then those signs on those gravestones saying R.I.P. are sadly mistaken. Acts 2:24 says that God loosed Jesus from the pains of death. Is there any pain in death? Can we go to the graveyard? Can we find somebody and look up his name on the gravestone and say, "Here's poor old ED. He died in 1950. Boy, he must have been in pain for a long time"? Do we think in those terms? No, of course not. That's ridiculous. That's ludicrous. We wouldn't think in those terms, friends. Since 1950, when this man died, he has been in no physical pain. Why not? He's physically dead. Now follow this. So, what does God mean, when He said He loosed Jesus from the <u>pains of death</u>? It appears that as God raised up Jesus, simultaneously He loosed Him from the pains of death. So when was Jesus raised up? After being in the grave three days and three nights. Was Jesus in any physical pain in those three days and three nights while He lay there in the grave? Of course not. He had no physical pain. So what does God mean that He loosed Jesus from the pains of death?

While Jesus' body lay three days and three nights in the grave, His spirit was in pain in Hell. It's called a place of torments. Jesus' spirit was suffering from the torments associated with being in Hell. Perhaps much of this suffering is the realization that He has been totally cut off, no communion, and no communication, with God the Father. No life of God in Him. Just simply a hopeless, helpless, alienated person from all that's good, perfect and desirable. That may be much of the torment in Hell-knowing you have no life of God in you anymore, and no chance of ever changing that circumstance. Once you go to Hell, friends, that's it for all eternity.

Have you ever let your mind just kind of run a little bit wild with you in terms of thinking about what Hell is like? We couldn't help but think about relatives and fathers who died years ago now. See, we don't know whether they were saved or not. And you know, we're thinking in terms of just 20-30 years, a little better than 25 years since some of our relatives died. We don't want to think about it, but if they weren't saved, they've been in that torment already for almost 30 years. It's hard to fathom 30 years in Hell, never mind the people who died hundreds and hundreds of years before Jesus came and went to the cross. Some of those people who went to Hell could have been in Hell now for as much as 5,000 years.

Doesn't it disturb you when you hear people talk about Hell like it's some kind of a game? And when you try to tell them about Jesus, doesn't it disturb you when they talk to you like they do? You know it's totally out of ignorance, but you can't seem to penetrate their minds no matter what you say to them. They just think that everything they're doing here and now is well worth the chance they're taking. They have no concept of what Hell is like.

Your Sins on Him

Some people say, "Well, you know, a lot of preachers are preaching that doom and gloom stuff." But you know something, Jesus preached it. He talked more about Hell than He did about Heaven. Did you know that? He tried to spare people from going there. He knew what Heaven was like. He was trying to get you to Heaven. But He told you what Hell was like to get you to figure out that maybe you're on the wrong path. Yet people rejected the Lord Jesus Christ. In addition to all the pain Jesus suffered while He was in Hell, thinking about His being completely shut off, cut off, from the life of God, He also had all our sins on Him. Can you imagine having the sins of the world bearing down on one person? Lying, stealing, deception, adultery, and we're talking about lesbianism, homosexuality. Just go through the list. It's endless. And we're not just talking about one time each. God only knows how many times people have fornicated since the world began, but every one of those sins was on Jesus. And God looked at Jesus, and all He saw was detestable. Could you try to picture what all the sins of the world looked like on Jesus in His spirit? They were so hideous that God said, "I can't look at You, Jesus," and He walked away. "I can't look at You, Jesus." Why do you suppose Jesus was screaming, "My God, My God, why have You forsaken Me!"? Because of sin.

Don't tell us that God doesn't love you! Don't tell us that Jesus doesn't love you! He was willing to have the Father turn His back on Him for you and for us. The most hideous torment. Picture Jesus after He was up on that cross for a while. He was covered with Blood; His back split wide open. The thorns were three inches long-not those little things that you get on your rosebush outside your house either. Those things were three inches long, pushed into His skull because of our sins.

We don't want to dwell on things like that, do we? Remember, we already said a couple of chapter's back, as we looked at Isaiah 53:9 that Jesus said he had made His grave with the wicked and with the rich in His deaths. Two deaths, plural-physical and spiritual. If He made His grave with the wicked, then His grave could not be as we understand it, in Paradise, could it? If he made his grave with the wicked, then He couldn't possible have gone to Paradise. He had to go to Hades on your account and on my account, and He spent three days and three nights in torment. Now we can't figure anything else that these scriptures could possibly mean, if it doesn't talk about spiritual death. There is nothing else.

Let's go to Matthew 27:46: "And about the ninth hour Jesus cried with a loud voice saying, Eli, Eli, lama sabachthani? That is to say, My God, My God, why hast thou forsaken me?" Now, here is Jesus, the Son of God, crying out to God the Father because He's been forsaken. Some have said that Jesus cried because He was going through the torments of physical death. It couldn't have been physical death that scared Him. "Why Not?" Because He said He had within His authority, within His power, to call 12 legions of angels, if necessary, to set Him free. He could have done that at any time. Besides that, in the garden, Jesus had already submitted to the will of the Father. He said, "Father, if there is any other way, please do it. But not My will, but Thy will be done." It was not physical death He was screaming about, it was spiritual death that made God turn His back on Jesus.

First Man to be Born Again

Let's go a little further. You need to understand this. Hebrews 1:4: "For unto which of the angels said He at any time, Thou art my Son, this day I have begotten thee? And again, I will be to him a Father, and he shall be to me a Son." Ever notice that before? "And again…" Why did He put that in there? "And again I will be to him a Father, and he shall be to me a Son." Notice three things in here: "this day: I have begotten thee: and again." A definition of "to be begotten" means to be born of. You can see this in the genealogies of the Bible, where Adam begot Cane; Joseph begot: and Abraham begot… The word "begot," again, means to be born of. God said about Jesus, "This day You have been born of Me."

Don't let us lose you now, because if you lose this, you're going to miss it. Follow along. God said about Jesus, "This day You have been born of Me." Some say this is a physical birth, when Mary delivered Jesus. No! It's talking here about the Son of God. Jesus was always the Son of God. The eternal Son of God, who took on flesh. But here it says, "This day, I have begotten thee." So, if all of us can figure out which day this was, it would surely tell us whether or not this was when Mary had Jesus, or if this was some other situation at another time. And of course there just happens to be a verse in the Bible, which tells us which day it was. So, before we take you there, look at verse 6. Notice that Jesus was the first begotten. Look what it says, "And again (*why again?*), when he bringeth in the first begotten into the world (*notice, He's called the first begotten into the world*), he saith, And let all the angels of God worship him." Notice that Jesus was the first begotten. It says so here, doesn't it? He's the first begotten. If Jesus were the firstborn (physically), what about Mary and Joseph, Abraham, Adam, Eve? Didn't they come into the earth before Jesus? These people were born physically long before Mary had Jesus. And if Jesus was the firstborn, then Mary couldn't have had Him, could she? So this is not referring to Jesus becoming the Son of God (He always was the Son of God), nor is it speaking of the incarnation of Jesus, that is, His physical birth through Mary. Colossians 1:18 & Revelation 1:5 call Jesus the first born from the dead. The first to be born from the dead. Jesus wasn't born from physical death to physical life, just like you were not born from physical death to physical life through your mother. Think about this. When a woman delivers her first child, she doesn't refer to him as her first born from the dead. The child wasn't dead right before she gave birth. The child was physically alive inside of her. The living baby just changed locations when the mother gave birth. You see, Jesus wasn't born from physical death, but from spiritual death. He was the first person to pass from spiritual death to spiritual life, or to be born again.

Look at Acts 13:28-33:

And though they found no cause of death in him, yet desired
they Pilate, that he should be slain.
And when they had fulfilled all that was written of him, they
took him down from the tree, and laid him in a sepulcher.
But God raised him from the dead:
and he was seen many days of them, which came up with
Him, from Galilee to Jerusalem, who are his witnesses unto
the people.
And we declare unto you glad tidings, how that the promise
which was made unto the father,
God hath fulfilled the same unto us their children, in that he
hath raised up Jesus again; as it is also written in the second
Psalm, Thou art my Son, this day have I begotten thee.

What day are we talking about here? The day He was raised up was the day He was begotten. When God raised Him from the dead. This is not a physical birth, but it was the first begotten (spiritual birth) of many brethren. In Hebrews 1:6, Jesus was the first man to be born again. And now that He has been, all of us can identify with Him, and we can be born again.

CHAPTER

16

MADE ALIVE WITH CHRIST

In the beginning, we gave you a definition of "to identify" which we've used over and over again. We said it means to make identical, to consider and treat as the same. When we first gave you that, we emphasized the importance of memorizing that definition, because what we're talking about is identification with Christ. When discussing identification, we should constantly be aware of certain words that come up. For example, as you're reading in the Epistles, you'll find the expressions, "with Christ" and "in Christ." Every time you see "with Christ" or "in Christ", that pertains to you, because Jesus Christ was your substitute. When He became your substitute, He went to the cross on your behalf. Not only did He go to the cross, but in order to complete redemption, Jesus had to go through a total of seven phases of redemption.

When people looked at Jesus on the cross and heard Him say it was finished, they really had a shallow understanding of redemption. Jesus did not mean that redemption was completed when He said, "It is finished." There were many, many more things that Jesus had to do, and He did them all for you and all for me. Whenever you see this expression, "with Christ," know that you were joined, you were there with Christ in God's eyes. And everything He did, He did not do for Himself, but for you. You were involved in that part of redemption.

Up to this point, we've only looked at crucified, died and buried. We are going to continue to go on to look at four other areas that are very, very important. Next we're going to be looking at being "Quickened with Christ" or made alive with Christ. That's what we're calling this chapter, "Made Alive With Christ."

This chapter is very important. Grasp this and you're going to really start taking a hold of something extremely important. After this study of being quickened with Christ, we're going to go into an area called "Conquered With Christ." Did you know that you became a conqueror with Christ? You conquered with Christ. After that we're going to look at "Being Raised Up With Christ." That's an important one. And the last one we're going to look at is "Seated With Christ."

So, there are seven areas that make up our entire redemption. If any one of these were left out it would not be a complete redemption. So once again, it's <u>crucified, died, buried, quickened, conquered, raised and seated with Christ.</u> There are seven important phases to our complete redemption. As we said, if you leave any one of these out, it will not be a whole, complete redemption. There is no doubt that we have probably spent more time with the first three issues we've mentioned than we'll spend with the others, but they are all very important, and make up our complete redemption.

One of the things we tried to bring across to you over and over and over again, and we wanted you to be settled on this fact, was that the old man, the Adamic nature, was killed. He's dead, and he's buried. You have to understand that the old nature is dead. If you don't grasp that, the devil will continue to come along and try to tell you that you're still bound to those old vices, those old habits, that old way of life, and you can't be set free. But you know as well as we do that the Scripture says in 2 Corinthians 5:17: "Therefore if any man [anyone] be in Christ, he is a new creature: old things are passed away; behold all things are become new."

We are going to look at some new things but will continue to keep this important fact in mind-the old man and his Adamic nature is dead. We don't have to succumb any longer to the lies of satan. At one time you were dead in your sins and trespasses; you didn't know Christ then. You were doing what your father told you to do. Since Christ came into your life, you've become a new species, a new creation, a new creature. You don't have to follow after those old vices, those old habits, those old things that kept you in bondage, because whom the Son sets free, is free indeed (John 8:36). You have to know that. The devil comes along all too often and says, "Oh see, you're just doing that because it's just the way you are. You have two natures.

You have the old nature and the new nature." No, you don't have the old nature anymore. God told you all things have become new in the spirit realm for you. Your spirit man has been made new in Jesus Christ. You don't have the devil and the Holy Spirit living on the inside of you simultaneously. The old nature is gone. The Adamic nature is gone. It's dead. Its' buried; reckon it so. The old man is dead. Buried. Flowers-on-top dead. Graveyard dead.

With that in mind, let's look at Ephesians 2. We're going to be studying about being made alive. You see, you can't be made alive until you're dead. That sounds ridiculous, doesn't it? Many people don't understand this, and that's why they say the things they do about Jesus Christ. You have to die before you can live again. You can't be resurrected unless you're dead and buried. You have to be quickened. When we talk about that word "quickened," we're talking about being made alive, having the very life of God put into our spirit man.

Resurrection Power

Think about this. The power that raised Jesus from the dead had to be more powerful than the power that God used when He created the earth. Did you know that? It had to be. Do you know why?

Because when God created the universe and everything in it, there was probably no one opposing Him. He just spoke it out. He just had a thought in His mind, in His heart, and He spoke it out of His mouth and everything came to be. But when Jesus was dead, down in Hell, down there on our behalf, sin was in the world. There was a law called sin and death, which is in opposition to life. And there was a devil in opposition to all that God was doing in Christ. With everything the devil had he was pushing against it and pushing against it, trying to stop the resurrection. So we want you to know something. The power that God used to raise Jesus up, the power He used to give Jesus fresh life was much greater than it was when He spoke creation into existence.

Ephesians 2:1 Says, "And you hath he quickened [and we know that word quickened now means made alive], who were dead in trespasses and sins." You were quickened when you were in trespasses and sins. He quickened you. You were dead and He made you alive. If we look at that quickly, we may say that it really may not fully pertain to Jesus and us or Jesus and you or me in particular. But God isn't going to leave us hanging. He says, "Let's go to verse 5 where it clears it all up."

In verse 5, He says, "Even when <u>we</u> were dead in sins, hath quickened <u>us together</u> [here it is] <u>with Christ</u>, (by grace you are saved)." It says we were quickened together with whom? With Christ. Now listen, "with is a preposition, and a preposition links two things or two persons together. Listen to me. We were dead in trespasses and sins, it says. My question is: Is this a physical death or a spiritual death? It's a spiritual death. It has to be a spiritual death. This can't be physical.

Think of it now. What if we decided to go out on the street to witness? We walk down the street, and let's say we happen to come upon a lost person, any unbeliever. We walk up and begin to talk to that individual, and we say to him, "Listen, we would like to talk to you about the Lord Jesus Christ." And he says, "Lord who? I don't think He's lord." "Well let me tell you about Him anyway. You know you cannot be saved unless you invite Jesus Christ, who is the Redeemer, Messiah of the world, into your heart."

He says, "Well, I don't believe that He's Messiah. I don't believe that He's the Redeemer. In fact, the only thing I know about Jesus is that He was a great prophet, maybe a great teacher of His day. But I don't believe that you have to know Jesus Christ to get saved."

Now this person totally rejects the Lord Jesus Christ. Do we turn to him and say, "Well, you see now, you're physically dead?" No, we wouldn't say that to him, would we? After all, that would be pretty stupid. Here he is breathing, looking at us, talking to us, and we'd say, "You're physically dead?" No, but we would be accurate, if he rejects the Lord Jesus Christ, if we said, "You are spiritually dead." You can be walking around, breathing, eating, working, talking, playing, sleeping and yet be spiritually dead, because we found out that spiritual death is not cessation of life, is it? You now know that when you become spiritually dead, you don't cease to exist. Spiritual death is really an alienation-we've said this over and over, and we are saying it again because we want you to get it. Spiritual death is nothing more than an alienation from Life itself, that is, from the very life of God. There's no more communion. You are out of the pathway of life. God has turned His back on you because you see, sin, the Bible tells us, separates you from God. But again, you don't cease to exist if you are spiritually dead.

So Ephesians 2, when it says we were <u>dead in trespasses and sins and quickened with Christ, it means that we were spiritually dead</u>. We, Jesus Christ and us, were given spiritual life by God. That's what quickened means-to be made alive. Quickened together with Christ. We were both in sins and trespasses (and both needed a quickening, even though Jesus did not commit sin), so God quickened us together.

Death Before Life

Please be sure that verse one and verse five are put together. The quickening took place together with Christ through God the Father and the operation of the Holy Spirit. If some oppose the idea that Jesus was ever spiritually dead-and you know that we've gone over that very, very carefully- how could we be made alive (spiritually) together with Him, if He were not spiritually dead? He wouldn't need to be made alive if He weren't dead, would He? But as long as we were made alive together, it tells us that together we were spiritually dead and had to be made alive. If He were never dead spiritually, He wouldn't have to have been made alive. Therefore, there would be no correlation there for us.

So we were made alive from spiritual death, but Jesus was made alive from physical death? No. That doesn't make any sense. Identification means to make identical, to consider and treat as the same. There's our definition again. It keeps being woven in and out of what we're talking about. It couldn't have been physical because we haven't received our glorified bodies. That promise is yet to come to pass for us. If I have been made alive together with Christ, it has to be spiritual. He can't get one thing and we another. We are identified together. The only difference is the glorified body. We haven't received it yet, but it's promised to us and we will get that.

Now let's go on. Jesus made Himself identical with us. He became sin, he who knew no sin, that we could be made the righteousness of God in Him. There's that "in Him". Notice "in Him" gives us another or a further identification. In Christ, we were taken from spiritual death to the very righteousness of God. How did we get that? Because we were in Him. When He got it, we were in Him. This took place through a quickening process. When Jesus was made alive, we were made alive with Him. You see, God saw us, right there with Jesus through the whole thing. Through all seven phases of redemption. There we were with Jesus. God saw us crucified on the cross. He saw that we died with Jesus. He saw us buried with Jesus, and He sees us quickened. He sees us being made alive with Jesus. If Jesus didn't die spiritually, then we could not have been made alive spiritually. And woe to us; we would still be dead in our sins and trespasses. Can you see this clearly?

We're trying to make this as simple as we can. There can be no identification without substitution. Never. It can't happen. Do we not call Jesus' sacrifice substitutionary? That means He took our place. When He took our place, God saw us in Him. It's very important that you see yourself in Jesus. Had

Jesus not been quickened spiritually, as we said, we would still be in our sins and trespasses. But thank God, the power of God was given to Jesus. He was raised up with fresh life. And when He was raised up, you can see yourself right there with Jesus, being raised up with fresh life. Both Jesus and we got God's fresh life together through the quickening power of the Holy Ghost.

Raised Together

At the same time that God gave Jesus fresh life, when He was made alive, we were made alive. At that very same moment, we were quickened together with Christ. It wasn't ten minutes after; it wasn't ten minutes before. It was exactly at that same time. It says we were made alive together. There's unity there. I'm in Christ, So when He got it, I got it. At the same moment He had life put in Him, we had life put in us. You had life put in you. This is important. You say, "Why are you belaboring this point?" Because we are doing just that. We are making a point, because we are leading you to something that's very important. Together means identically-at the same time. We were pulled out of the kingdom of darkness at the very same time Jesus was. And at the very instant Jesus was placed in the kingdom of light, all of us were place in the kingdom of light. Exactly at the same time because we were with Christ. We were with Christ on the cross. We suffered with Him. As those nails were pounded into Jesus' hands, it was as real to God as if we were on that cross with Him and the nails went through our hands. When Christ died, it was as real to God as if we died with Him right there. He saw every one of us, every single one of us, every single human being that would ever live on the face of the earth. God saw them on the cross with the Lord Jesus Christ.

We were with Him in His death, and then we were buried with Him. It was as real to God as if we were right there. As they took Jesus' body off the cross, there was your body, every single person on the face of the earth that ever lived. God saw our bodies being taken down from the cross and put into the grave.

We want you to understand this. We were with Jesus. Everything that happened to Jesus has happened to us simultaneously. We were pulled out of the kingdom of darkness, as we said, at the very moment Jesus was. Not ten minutes later. Not ten minutes before. When He was pulled out, we were pulled out.

Concerning Ephesians 2:5, listen now to the translation from *The Way*: "Thrilled us with the same new life, wherewith he quickened our Messiah."

Twentieth Century says, "Gave life to us in giving life to the Christ." The *Amplified* says, "He gave us the very life of Christ himself, the same new life with which he quickened him." *Jordan* says, "God in his overflowing sympathy and great love breathed the same new life into us as into Christ." Now we want you to get that. Notice in all those translations it says, "The same new life." The same fresh life. The same life that Jesus got, we got with Him. When the Messiah got new life, we got new life. Are you hearing what we're saying? Because Jesus was our representative man, God sees us in Christ, and everything Jesus got, we got simultaneously.

Legally Speaking

Romans 8:2 says there is a law that caused all this to happen: "For the law of the Spirit of life in Christ Jesus hath made me free from the law of sin and death." This is telling us that there's a law. There's a law that we all were compelled to keep when we were in Adam, or when we were under the dominion of satan. That law said that no matter what you tried to do, you were going to commit sin and sin is going to end up in death, unless the law of the Spirit of life in Christ Jesus is infused into you. Are you following this? So we could say there's a new law now.

Legally speaking, we were born again 2,000 years ago. The legal act took place on the cross. The law of the Spirit of life in Christ Jesus, 2,000 years ago, legally freed us from the law of sin and death. We did not experience the results of that legal quickening until the day, or the moment we asked Jesus Christ to be our Lord and Savior. When that moment came, when you and I asked Jesus to be Lord and Savior of our lives, then the legality of what took place 2,000 years ago became <u>vital</u>. (Did you get that word?) – vital to us the moment Jesus came in. In other words, it became real to us, it affected us right then and there!

When Jesus became our personal Savior, at that very moment each of us said, "Jesus come into my heart," death was canceled. In other words, life swallowed up death. Can you imagine what kind of power had to be in that life? It swallowed up death. Death disappeared out of us. We've become alive in Christ Jesus. It canceled death in us. Totally canceled it out. We became alive. The law of the Spirit of life in Christ Jesus began to rule and reign in our lives!

There's something about this subject that we need to know and understand and this is what we've been leading you to. If we were quickened together, then the very same life that was put into Jesus went into us. We didn't get less life than Jesus. God said to the Holy Spirit, "Quicken Jesus, make Him alive." And whatever power it took to do that, to cancel out the law of sin and death and replace it with life, the Holy Spirit did it. There was a great opposition, as we said earlier. Satan was fighting this with everything he had. Darkness was fighting this with everything it had. Sin was fighting this with everything it had. There was an enormous pressure of darkness, sin and all kinds of opposition, but the Holy Spirit said, "Life!" Darkness was swallowed up; sin was swallowed up. Bang! Just like that. And new fresh life went into the Lord Jesus Christ. At the moment Jesus got that life, you got it! You didn't get one ounce less than Jesus because you were <u>quickened together with Him</u>. What He got, you got!

Eternal Life Defined

Is something beginning to stir in you? You got the same measure of eternal life that Jesus got. You got God's zoe life. Zoe was put into you, and we're telling you that when we say you have eternal life, it is not just a promise to go to Heaven someday. Eternal life is the God-kind of life. It's the life that Jesus said, "I have come that you may have life." He didn't stop there. He said that you might have it more abundantly(John 10:10). The life that has been put into Jesus and us is for now, not just when we get to heaven.

You see, when we talk about eternal life, we seem to get religious. We hate to keep using this expression, but we get religious. You say to someone, "Do you have eternal life?"

"Yes, I'm going to Heaven, someday."

Friends, if that's what you think eternal life is, you have a shallow understanding of eternal life. <u>You have eternal life in you</u>. It was given to you when you accepted Jesus. And that same life God put in Jesus has enormous benefits to it, benefits that can be used here and now as you live on this earth. If eternal life only means that you are going to Heaven, if that's what you think it is, you have a limited understanding of eternal life. Don't feel badly, most of us do. That's why we don't live the kind of life God wants us to. The devil has put blinders on our eyes. He has held from us what eternal life really is. We tell you it's a shame that more pastors, preachers and teachers are not pulling that veil off and telling the people what eternal life really is all about.

Do you recall when the disciples were released from prison, the angel said, "Go back into the temple and tell them <u>all the words of this life</u>" (Acts 5:20).

Let's look at another translation, because it makes it even clearer. It says in this other translation, "Tell them about the life of God and what it means to them." That was a command from the Holy Spirit to let people know, that when you get eternal life, it's not just a reservation in Heaven. Eternal life begins right here and now and should carry you through the rest of your life in a more abundant fashion than you could ever dream of, if you really understand that you have been given the same life that Jesus Christ was given. It is God's life in us. It's the very substance of God. He is life. Jesus was given that life, and we got it in the exact same measure. What He got, we got, because we were quickened together with Him. We got the portion of God's life that He got-no more, no less. We got it.

This eternal life that we are speaking about, as we said a moment ago, is called *zoe* in the Greek language. It's God's very own nature and life. That should begin to turn a few lights on inside you.

Vine says that "zoe" is used in the New Testament as a principle- "Life," as he says, "in the absolute sense." Life as God has it. That which the Father has in Himself, which the Son manifested in the world. The life that we got when we were quickened was the very essence of Almighty God. Let's put it this way. The life that makes God, God, was put into us as God put that life into Jesus. It's just not a confirmed reservation in Heaven, as we said. It's not just a guaranteed ticket to Heaven someday, or to spend eternity in Heaven. Jesus said, "I have come that you might have life, and that you might have it more abundantly."

Now you have a little better grasp about what Jesus is talking about when He said, "I've come that you might have life." You see, He's walking the earth and saying, "When you take Me, you're going to take everything that God is. God is life. When we have God's life in us, the very essence, the very nature of God, then that life cannot be classified anything other than abundant, or life in the fullest sense."

Life in the Fullest Sense

What does that mean to you? Life in the fullest sense. When we were in Adam, we had the satanic nature in us, didn't we? What was that nature? Death. You had death in the fullest sense. You couldn't get any more dead. You had abundant death abiding in you, didn't you? Now we have God's nature in us (II Peter 1:3,4). What is that nature? Life. "For the law of the Spirit of life in Christ Jesus hath made me free from the law of sin and death."

213

We have God's life in us. So many people think of eternal life as just living forever. But we have found out that sinners, those living in spiritual death, will live forever, won't they? But they'll live forever in a different sphere. The word 'eternal" throws us all off. We all think in terms of a time duration, eternal meaning time unending or time forever. Of course it means that.

Let us take you to another contemporary translation. For the Greek word *zoe*, it says that "eternal life is that kind of life which is given to all true believers in Christ." The word eternal "draws attention to the quality of that life, not to its duration in a temporal sense." Thus, eternal life can be experienced by believers even while subjected to the temporal conditions of earthly life. "Translators of the Bible should be very careful," it goes on to say, "to avoid expressions, which mean no more than a timeless continuation of life after death." This statement is quite self-explanatory. However, with what this translation says, we can now affix quality to our statements of eternal life. Here's what we can say, "If I am in Christ, it's one type of quality, isn't it? If I am in the devil, it's altogether another type of quality. Both qualities have a never-ending time to them."

We also want you to note that the word "eternal" gives a type of quality to the realm in which one spends his everlasting life. In Christ, the realm is everlasting happiness.

In satan, the realm is everlasting tormenting flames of fire. You all understand this, and now you can realize that this abundant life that Jesus came to give is still in all of us right now. As soon as you accept Jesus Christ, the quickening power that went into Him 2,000 years ago, legally done, can now become vital to your life. It becomes a fact in your life, but you learn to experience that life as you continue to believe God's Word. What it's going to do is affect every area of your existence-your spirit, your soul, your body, and your finances. This "zoe" life should keep our bodies healthy, our spirits free, and our minds on the highest level of understanding and wisdom. Jesus lived this kind of life. Sickness and disease couldn't touch Him. He never got sick. He didn't come home at 13 years of age and say to His mother, "Mary, do you have an aspirin? I have a headache." He didn't get headaches. Nothing touched Him. Depression couldn't take hold of his mind, and temptation had no effect on Him to make Him get into disobedience to His Father's laws.

When we were quickened together with Jesus Christ, we were translated out of the power of darkness and made free indeed. The devil doesn't want us to know that. We'll say it again because in the next chapter, when we go into the conquering aspect of our being in Christ and as we look at the seated-with-Christ aspect, this has to mean something to us. We kept going over the fact that our old man is dead. He's been buried. You were crucified with Christ. You died with Christ. You were buried with Christ. You know that you were quickened with Christ. The life that's in you is not just any kind of life.

It's like our going back to the beginning in the Garden of Eden. The Father reached down and picked up some dust of the earth, formed a man and breathed into that man the breath of life. What kind of life was that? The God-kind of life, the kind of life that says sickness and disease can't touch you. "The kind of life that makes God, God, is in you!"

Is it becoming real to you now? It says right here in Ephesians 2, we didn't have to go any further than that "And you hath he quickened who were dead in trespasses and sins." That's spiritual death. Verse 5: "Even when we [Jesus Christ and us] were dead in sins, hath quickened us together with Christ." God said to the Holy Spirit, "Pour out Our nature into our new sons and daughters." Where were we when that happened? We were right there. As God looked down, He saw us there. We got what Jesus got. Don't tell us that we should be walking now in sickness, in disease, in poverty, in lack. We are filled with the "zoe" kind of life-God's life. Not only should it affect our lives, it should affect people's lives all around us. Everywhere we go we should be exuding with "zoe." The devil has kept the church blind and deaf of these important Biblical facts.

Friends, this is Bible. That's what it says. You have been given the very life of Almighty God. The life that makes God, God, is in you. Don't let anyone talk you out of what Jesus bought and paid for so you could have an abundant life.

Let us tell you what happened years ago to a Pastor who was a layperson at the time. It happened to him and his wife. He was all excited. He heard about healing. He was young in the Lord. He heard that God heals people. He got all excited. He saw that in God's Word-God heals people! Jesus Christ, the same yesterday, today and forever, heals. He and his wife were in this church, and they ran up to this poor, old lady that was in a wheelchair, and they said to her, "You know, Jesus will heal you and raise you out of that wheelchair." Somebody grabbed them, pulled them aside, and said, "We don't talk like that in this church."

"Like what?"

"Don't give that poor old lady false hope."

False hope! They were telling her what Jesus died for- what Jesus wanted her to know. Are you hearing what we're saying? That's going on in churches all around you. The pastor of that church was all excited about Jesus Christ. He'd come from another country. He was a man who ended up in an Ivy League divinity school. There he practically cried all four years that he was there, cried his heart out. They told him, "Don't speak in tongues while you're here; don't talk about Jesus. You're just here to get an education and then get out."

He finished at this Ivy League school, and then was made the pastor of that church we were talking about. You know something-they ended up kicking him out of that church because he was enthused about the things of God. Can you guess who kicked him out? The deacon board. There's no other organization in the world like the Body of Christ. We wound each other; we kill each other; we step on each other; we prevent ourselves from growing in the things of God. Then we walk around with pious looks on our faces, like we've got it all together, puffed up because we've convinced others that we are spiritual.

You know what that man said to this young Christian? He said, "Don't you give that poor woman false hope." He said, "Look you young whippersnapper, I've seen guys like you come up and down the pike. I've been in this business a lot longer than you have. Just learn to shut your mouth and flow with the stream." Oh really? Some can flow in that stream, but that young man and his wife didn't want to!

The young man knew that one of these days that Pharisee was going to get caught. He got caught. It took a few years more, but he got caught. He was trying to fake out the Body of Christ with his phony prophesying; trying to make everybody think he was spiritual-Mister Spiritual. He didn't know what he was talking about. These kinds of people never grow up in the things of God, and they hold others back too. That's a sad story and it happens all too often.

You see, it's like those that shut up the kingdom of God. They put heavy burdens on people, and they don't lift a finger to help them. That poor lady needed somebody to help her. She hadn't heard this message in her entire life. She probably had been in that denomination, probably a Christian, for 50 years, and nobody ever said to her, "You can be healed."

You see. We don't know what ever happened to the old lady in that church. For all we know, she could still be alive today in that wheelchair. You say, "Well, what if she didn't come out of the wheelchair?" What harm did it do to tell her that she could? She was told the truth of God's Word. Is that a false hope? That's the truth of God's Word. She can take it or leave it, believe it or deny it, or whatever she wanted. Let someone at least tell her what the Word says. This kind of stuff goes on all over the Body of Christ. You know the Word of God tells me, if you promote the Word of God, God will promote you.

God's Word is full of wisdom and good advice. It's peaceable and easily to be entreated and we all should speak the truths of God's Word as long as we have breath, even if we go down coughing, sputtering and die, the Word of God is still truth. You can be healed. Just because your healing may not have come to pass, doesn't mean you can't be healed.

Don't deny God's Word. Don't deny its free course in your life, because it's life. Jesus said, "The words I speak are spirit; the words I speak are life (John 6:63). That's the kind of life that raised Jesus from the dead. You have it in you. Fresh life. God's life. The 'zoe' abundant life. We should be walking around with a kind of spring in our feet. We should be walking around with a smile on our face. We should be going to people and saying, "Boy, we have something we want to tell you about. You know, when you witness, you shouldn't be able to stand still. You have great truths in you. You should say "How about letting me tell you about it? I have life in me. I have the life of God in me. I have God's life in me." You know what we're saying? But we go around and we witness like, "Oh, did anyone ever tell you about Jesus (flat and unconvincing voice)? My goodness. Are you listening to this? You have the life of God in you! Just let it work in you! Reckon it so, and act like you know it, believe it, and they'll see it! They will soon ask you what's different about you.

You need to say every morning, "I have the life of God in me. I'm the temple of the Holy Spirit. I have God's wisdom. I have the mind of Christ. I'm more than a conqueror. I'm seated in heavenly places with Jesus Christ. I've been raised up from the dead. The old man is dead! I'm alive! I'm alive! Devil, you can't touch me. I belong to Jesus; I have God's life in me. You used to have me, but you don't anymore. I'm a new creation. I'm alive! Alleluia! I'm alive! Amen! Alleluia! Praise the Lord! Thank you Lord. I'm alive! We've been quickened with Christ. We've been made alive. Alleluia! I'm alive! Alleluia!" That's just every day simple confessions of God's Word.

"Sure, I've been crucified with Christ. Nevertheless, I'm living now." That's what you have to tell the devil. "I'm the temple of God. I've been bought with a price. Get your hands off me!" (That's right. He can't touch the property of God.) "I'm a new creation, devil. Take a good look at me. I am not the same guy I used to be. He's dead and buried. He's down in the graveyard pushing up daisies. You don't have any power over me! You're nothing but a liar. I'm alive! I'm living in the truth that Jesus has set me free!"

What we just confessed is called, in the Greek language, *homologeo*. That means we say the same as God says about us. What He says about us, we say about ourselves. In the Greek language the word "confession" or "profession" is *homoleogeo*. We say out of our mouths what God says out of His mouth. And we're told in God's Word to hold fast our confession of faith for He that has promised is faithful (Hebrews 10:23). Did you know that Jesus is the high priest of our confession? (Hebrews 3:1) What we confess out of our mouth in line with God's promises, Jesus brings to the Father. And as we believe it and confess it, not wavering, it will come to pass.

Our next chapter will deal with conquering and being raised up with Jesus. There's a lot to identification, isn't there?

CHAPTER
17

CONQUERING AND RAISED WITH HIM

As we have studied *the mystery* of our identification with Christ, we've said over and over (and we believe if we keep saying it will finally register) that this is one of the most important teachings any Christian can ever learn. We want to emphasize again that many churches never teach on this subject. And if you look at the people within such a church body, you'll find most of them languishing and in need of some sort of deliverance. Their lives are inadequate. They seldom experience victory in their daily lives. And in general, they just barely make it from day to day.

We want you to know that the devil will try to keep this teaching from coming forth as much as he can. He does not want you to know who you are in Christ. He does not want you to have an understanding of the "in Him's "and "with Him's "of the Bible.

We said that there are seven important phases or parts of our redemption that Jesus Christ had to go through. And listen to this, as He went through each phase, each of us went with Him. There are seven phases that Jesus had to go through in our redemption. Many people think he just died on the cross, and that was it. No friends, that's far from being it. What He did on the cross was extremely important, but there were six other things He had to do before redemption was complete. As He went through every single one of those things required By God Almighty Himself, we were with Jesus and went through each and every phase of redemption with Him. Every single one. And God saw us going through it with Jesus. It's real to God. It ought to be real to each Christian on the face of this earth. You ought to understand what it means.

Receivers of Life

We're going to talk about two more of these phases of redemption—conquering with Him and being raised with Him.

After Jesus was quickened, the Bible tells us that Jesus conquered death, Hell, the grave, and satan. Death, Hell, the grave, and satan. We also know that Jesus couldn't have done that while He was on the cross, because on the cross, Jesus was the sin bearer. The One who knew no sin was made to be sin. When sin is in your life, you will walk a continually defeated life. And don't tell us that Jesus wasn't defeated physically on that cross, because He died through that defeat. So, the quickening of the Lord Jesus Christ did *not* take place on the cross. It couldn't have. It took place at another time. Jesus had to have been made alive before He set out to conquer satan, Hell, death, and the grave. So we can conclude that Jesus' conquest took place after the Holy Spirit made Him alive.

Put Your Name in There

Look at Colossians 2:15: "And having spoiled principalities and powers [we like that], he made a shew of them openly, triumphing over them in it."

When we begin to read that Jesus Christ has spoiled principalities and powers, we have to do one thing: we have to learn this and learn it well, right from the beginning of our Christian walk. Every time you read in the Gospels anything about Jesus' death, burial, and resurrection, you must learn to insert your name in there with Jesus' name. Because over in the Epistles, you will find a parallel scripture that says you did it with Him. You were crucified with Him. You died with Him. You were buried with Him. You were raised up with Him. You were quickened with Him. You triumphed with Him. You are seated with Him. So every time you look over there in the Gospels about the death, burial, and resurrection of the Lord Jesus Christ, and we might add, when you go about to tell people about the good news of the Gospel, you should say, "Let me tell you what happened to me 2,000 years ago!"

It's that real! And when you get it down to that kind of illustration (*that you were there*), someone's going to say, "You were there?!" "Yes, I was there."

"Let me tell you about it."

You'll get people's attention. You need to learn to do that.

So, when Jesus spoiled principalities and powers, we have to recognize that we were there. We spoiled them also. When He triumphed over the devil, when He conquered the devil, we conquered the devil, through Jesus, at the exact same time.

What Colossians 2:15 is saying isn't totally accurate in the *King James Version*. What Paul is speaking about took place in the abyss, in the place where the demons were. Notice it says there in the last part of verse 15, "in it." And most people are thinking, when they see "in it," that it's referring to what took place when Jesus was on the cross; but it's more than that.

The Greek word there *en auto* does not mean "in it," but rather means "in Him."

So the fifteenth verse goes with the thirteenth verse. Look at verse 13: "And you, being dead in your sins and in the uncircumcision of your flesh, hath he quickened together with him, having forgiven you all your trespasses."

Now in verse 14, it becomes merely parenthetical. In other words, verse 13 says we were made alive together. Verse 15 took place after we were made alive, after He was quickened. We were alive together, and together with our new life we became conquerors. We were triumphant together in Him.

Let us give you a few other translations on this and you'll get even more excited. *Knox* says, "The dominions and powers he [God] robbed of their prey, put them to an open shame, led them away in triumph through him." *Conbear* says, "And he [God, that is] disarmed [listen to this, disarmed] the principalities and the powers which fought against Him and put them to an open shame leading them captive in the triumph of Christ." *Weymouth* says, "And the hostile princes and rulers he shook off from himself and bodily displayed them as his conquests." Here's the one we really like" *Noli* says, "He spoiled the infernal dominions and realms. He dragged their rulers as captives in procession." Don't you like that one, too? Can't you just picture that?

Triumphant With Him

Let's develop a word picture of what's happening here. You know, in olden times when a man went out and conquered his enemy, he captured the ruler. He would parade that ruler, that leader, in open shame. The victor would get on his white horse and ride down the street, and in chains behind him was the one he had captured. Now that's what Jesus did in the spirit to the devil and all his demons!

You see, you have a decision to make. All that Jesus did, He did for us. All He did, God gave credit to our account. Jesus was given all the glory for what He did, there's no question about it. Jesus was given all the glory for it, and we still give Him all the glory. But we were given the credit for what He did. It was just as if we were there with Him. God saw us there. God sees you there. Jesus sees you there. The devil knows that you were there with Jesus. But we're telling you, he tries to keep this the best-kept secret in Hell.

But the secret is out. We triumphed with Jesus. We conquered with Jesus. The triumph was with our Lord Jesus Christ. And if words mean anything, we conquered with Him. That's what the Bible says. We triumphed with Him. He made an open show of the devil, publicly dragged him down the street and said, "I beat you to a pulp. See all my saints riding with me? They got the victory," Jesus did this all for each of us.

Jesus-The Final Sacrifice

Well, some will say that it all took place on the cross. There are always those who will insist on that, because they don't understand what took place, where it took place, how it took place, and with whom it took place. When Jesus said, "It is finished"-listen to this, this is the argument-when Jesus said, "It is finished," that was it. If that were it, why did God then send Jesus to Hell for three days? That would have been an injustice to Jesus. When Jesus said, "It is finished," and everybody says that's when it was all done, then God really put Jesus through some torment for nothing, didn't he?

Well, it wasn't finished on the cross. It wasn't all taken care of on the cross. That was not sufficient. It was truly finished in the sense that Jesus became the final sacrifice of the Old Testament. He was saying that the Old Covenant was finished, and I am about to start a New and Better Covenant. He was also prophesying with His last physical breath what the Father was about to bring to pass through His Son's death and resurrection.

In fact, let's look at Hebrews 10. We want to show you something there. Jesus was the final and supreme sacrifice, friends. The sacrifices of the Old Testament were through. Jesus was now about to establish a new covenant. Look what it says in Hebrews 10:9-14:

*Then said he, Lo I come to do thy will, O God. He taketh
away the first, that he may establish the second.
By that which we are sanctified through the offering of
the body of Jesus Christ once for all.
And every priest standeth daily ministering and offering
oftentimes the same sacrifices, which can never take away sins:
But this man, after he had offered one sacrifice for sins forever
sat down on the right had of God;
from henceforth expecting till his enemies be made his footstool.
For by one offering he hath perfected forever them that are
Sanctified.*

Jesus was our passover and now He is our eternal redemption. First
Corinthians 15:17 says, "And if Christ be not raised, your faith is in vain:
ye are yet in your sins." Jesus had to be raised from the dead before our
sins were remitted, if words, again, mean anything. Did you get what it said
there? If Jesus was not raised, your faith is in vain; you're still in your sins
and trespasses. So, the cross and the resurrection, and all the 7 areas we are
studying are involved in our eternal redemption.

Freedom Through the Resurrection

What this says is that we would not have been set free from our sins if Jesus
wasn't raised from the dead. The plan of redemption was not completed
until Jesus sat down on the right hand of the Father. And from the cross
until He sat down, He had to be buried, quickened, He had to conquer, and
be raised. So we want you to understand fully what the Word of God says,
not what man may think or say.

Let's go a little bit further and look at how Jesus conquered the devil.
How did Jesus conquer the devil? You see, if His conquest is our conquest,
if what Jesus did in conquering the devil belongs to us, then we better know
what Jesus did for us and what we did with Jesus so we can remind the devil
of it. If we don't know that, then we can't remind the devil of it. He doesn't
want you to know this. He'll do anything to keep you from knowing this.
But the more you know, the more you can live in the victory. Do you agree?

Look at Hebrews 2:14: "For as much then as the children are partakers of
flesh and blood, he also himself likewise took part of the same; that through
death he might destroy him that had the power of death, that is, the devil."

223

Jesus took on flesh; He became as we were. He couldn't take on the task of redemption as God alone. He couldn't do it just as a man, because he would have been in Adam. Or, putting it another way, He would have been in spiritual death, wouldn't He? Jesus was all God and all man. But God became incarnate man. He emptied Himself even unto death, according to the Bible (Philippians 2:5-8). And through death, we read, "He might destroy him that had the power of death, that is, the devil."

Satan's Power Made Void

Now remember, what Jesus got, we got. So, Jesus destroyed the devil. Jesus destroyed the devil, then we destroyed the devil in Jesus. Now, the devil has no more power over us; he has no more power over you. Are you with us so far? Yes, the devil still exists, but we have all authority and power over him in Jesus Name!

The word "destroy" in the Greek means "to make of no affect, to bring to naught," and (we should all like this one) "to make void." Now follow this, the devil's power has been made void. When he threatens you, just tell him to look into the mirror. There's a great big word-VOID-in capital letters on his forehead. Tell him, "I stamped that on you with Jesus 2,000 years ago. Devil, your power over me has been voided."

We said everything that Jesus did, you did with Him. You have to understand this. You see, if your mind is checking out right now, it's because the devil's checking your mind out. Don't let him check it out. Look carefully at what we're saying here, because this could bring victory to you.

Let's look at what some of the other translations say about Hebrews 2:14. You'll get a kick out of these. *The Way* says, "He did this that he might be able to die and by his death might annihilate the power of him who sways the scepter of death terrors, that is, the devil." The *Jordan* translation says, "That he might break the grip of the one who controls death." *Berkley* says, "He might neutralize the one who wields the power of death." The *Plain English Bible* says, "By death he might bring to nothing the lord of death." And *Julius Smith* Translation says, "That by his death he might leave unemployed him having the strength of death."

The devil is without a job. He's unemployed. He has no job anymore. Jesus said, "You're voided out." When Jesus was made alive from spiritual death, He passed out of the grasp of satan who rules over spiritual death. We passed out of death with Jesus. You passed out of death with Jesus, and thus, out of satan's sway and dominion for all eternity.

We'll give it to you in a nutshell. Satan has been dethroned, defeated, put to naught, made of no effect, overthrown, neutralized, paralyzed, crushed, and unemployed! Alleluia!

Isn't that good? Wow! We conquered with Christ! You must get a hold of this. This is not just a hip, hip hooray. This is a fact of the Scripture. It's wonderful that we say, "Alleluia!" but make sure you get an understanding of this. We're not just saying this to get you pumped up and excited; we're telling you a fact of Scripture. His victory, Jesus' victory, was our victory. We were made alive with Him and were raised up with Him.

"Well, listen, you don't understand what the devil's been saying to me. The devil talks big to me." For example, let's assume we write you a check for $10, and we are about to give it to you but decide, "no, we don't think we'll give it to you." So, we take a stamp and stamp the word "void" on it. Let us ask you a question: if we give that check back to you and you go down to a bank and hand it to a teller, will the teller cash it for you? That person would come back and say, "The teller wouldn't cash it."

We say, "Oh, well, let us write you another one."

This time, we write a check for $10,000, after all 10,000 speaks louder than $10, doesn't it? This time, she'll cash it, won't she? We stamp it void and you go to the bank with it. Will the teller cash it?

We don't care how big or how loud the devil talks to you; he has a void on his head. He's powerless. He can't cash in on anything. He can talk as loud as he wants to, but he's still voided out. Don't listen to his big talk. Just say, "Turn around and look in the mirror, satan. You've been voided out; you've been crushed; you've been neutralized. You're unemployed, jobless, because of my Lord Jesus Christ. Alleluia!"

Our Fight Is the Good Fight of Faith

Someone may still say, "I just can't seem to get the victory. I just can't seem to get the victory." You don't have to try to get something you already have. That's the problem. You've been trying to get something that's already yours. You're struggling for nothing. Why can't you just turn around, look at Jesus, and say, "Thank you."

It's that simple. Our fight is not for the victory. Jesus already conquered the devil, and we conquered the devil with Him. *Our fight is the fight of faith.* Most people don't understand what our fight is. It's a fight of faith. We know that we have the victory by what the Word of God says. <u>It's our faith that keeps the victory.</u>

How do you do that? Friends, you do it by learning all you can about what took place at Calvary's cross. What took place when you were crucified with Christ? What took place when you died with Christ? What took place when you were buried with Christ? What took place when you were quickened with Christ; when you conquered with Christ; when you were raised up with Christ; and later on, as we shall see when we were seated with Christ. You had better know all that. The devil knows it very well, and he keeps that secret, if he can, from every Christian for as long as he can. After we conquered with Christ, it says, we were raised up with Christ.

We could say that being quickened and being raised up are almost the exact same thing. But let's look at a couple of points about being raised up. Colossians 3:1 says, "If ye then be risen with Christ [now listen, people seem to miss this] seek those things which are above, where Christ sitteth on the right hand of God." Now, to also look at this from a different angle would be quite helpful. Let's see what it meant to Jesus to be resurrected. Do you think Jesus understood why He was resurrected? You see, if Jesus is our representative man (and He is, we know that now) and we are identified with the Lord Jesus Christ, to find out what resurrection meant to Him would mean finding out what it should mean to us, shouldn't it? Because what He got, we got. Are you following this?

To identify, as we've said so many times, means to be identical, to consider and treat the same. Remember, we were crucified, we died, we were buried, quickened, and we conquered with Him. And now we are raised up together with Him. He represented us. We got all that He got through Him. Colossians 3:1 says that we were raised with Christ. When we find out what it meant to Christ, then we'll know what it means to us.

Walking in the Resurrected Life

When Jesus was raised, He went to a realm, which was altogether new, didn't he? A place where sinners cannot go, where sinners cannot walk. This realm is simply called the Kingdom of God. So as Jesus was raised up onto this higher plane, we were also. Remember, we're in Christ. Everything that He gets, we get. He is our representative man. And so, if we were raised up to this plane, this higher level of living, that's where we have to learn to walk. Isn't that correct? We could call that *walking in the resurrected life.*

Some say that we are to live a crucified life. If you mean let the new creation you are in Christ rule and reign over your soul and body, then you are right; but if you think that you are an unworthy worm and must crucify the old nature, then you are wrong. To take up Jesus cross and follow Him, means to take up His cause, and to do like He did in John 6:38. The Lord Jesus said that He came only to do the Father's will. Yes, we're to crucify the flesh. Don't let your fleshly desires rule over you. Be led by the Holy Spirit through your reborn spirit. Jesus is no longer on the cross. Death no more has a hold on Him.

So why should we live a crucified life? If death has no hold on Him, then it has no hold on us. He is in a state of having been resurrected so He walks on a higher plane. Let's get Jesus off the cross, and when we take him off the cross, let's get ourselves off the cross as well. Let's start thinking Bible, instead of a kind of "goose bumps" religion.

Death no more has a hold on Jesus. That's what we just read. It no more has a hold on you. We are now on the plane of the One who walks in the resurrected life. In this life, on this higher level in the Kingdom of God, all our needs are met according to His riches in glory by Christ Jesus (Philippians 4:19). That is eternal truth!

Here and now, we are walking in the resurrected life, on the plane of the resurrected life, and everything that Jesus gets on that plane, friends, we're here to tell you again, we get.

We are taking you through this slowly. We don't want you to miss anything. Here and now the resurrected life should be the same as what Jesus is enjoying. As He is, so are we, *in this life(I john 4:17b)!*

Now, is Jesus depressed? Is Jesus broke? Is Jesus poor? Is Jesus sick? Is Jesus worried about paying the rent on the throne room next month? Then, if we have been resurrected with Him, and our adversary the devil has been defeated, paralyzed, made of no effect, overthrown, neutralized and crushed, what's holding *us* back? The lie of the enemy. When we swallow his deceptive lies, we cannot get to the place God wants us to be.

"Be not deceived. I wish you'd not be ignorant brethren," Paul said so many times. That's why we've been telling you over and over again, "Look at what the Word says."

Don't listen to people. Your worst enemy is sometimes the person sitting right next to you in church every week. Have you ever been told by people in the world that you're not seated in heavenly places with Christ Jesus? No, it's the person sitting next to you who says, "Well, I can't believe that. I don't think that Pastor's right. He doesn't know what he's talking about."

Listen to what the *Bruce* translation says in Colossians 3:1: "But you not only died with Christ, you have been raised up with him too. Go in then, for the higher things, those things which belong to the realm which Christ is seated at God's right hand." *Andrews'* translation says, "If you were resurrected with Christ, live on that plane."

"Well", someone will say, "how can I live on that level, on the plane of the resurrected life? Is it easy?"

Like anything else that's new, we're here to tell you it's going to take time to adjust to that new life. Don't say it's not true. Don't say it's impossible, because over and over the Apostle Paul, in every one of his prayers, prays that the eyes of your understanding would be enlightened. He said, "Open your eyes and see what is yours." He keeps praying that prayer over and over for the body of Christ. "Open your eyes open your eyes. Get an understanding." As we quoted earlier, "Therefore I commend myself to God and to the word of his grace, which is able to build us up and give us an inheritance among all them that are sanctified."

You have an inheritance. But how many of you have received it and are living in it? Very, very few. Look over Christendom as a whole. How many are living a resurrected life? What is holding us back? The lies of the devil and our stinking laziness, that's what.

Let's be real with one another. Why? Because you don't believe it. My goodness, it would be like our coming out with millions of dollars and just handing it out. "Here, who wants a million?"

You'd look at us and say, "Is that real? I mean, I don't know if that's real. I don't know if I can trust you." Smell it, taste it, eat it, then go down the street and try to spend a little of it in any store. We're trying to be real with you.

If you look again at Colossians, chapter 3, verse 1, it says, "If ye then be risen with Christ…". You will realize that the reason we <u>can</u> do everything else the Lord commands of us in that chapter, is because we are risen with Christ. That's where our power comes from. It's not in out own abilities. We need to learn how to tap into God's resurrection power within us.

The only way we are going to be able to walk in the resurrected life is if we understand it. And the only way we're going to understand it, is if we study it. As we begin to study it, we'll begin to rid our minds of all the lies; and we'll begin to understand that God is speaking some truth to us that we ought to grasp. Then, when we begin to say it out of our mouths, we'll begin to believe it. When we begin to believe it, we'll begin to walk in it. When we begin to walk in it, we'll leave the old life behind. We will go to a higher plane where the devil can't defeat us. Yes, he can attack us, shoot darts at us, but we will quench them with our shield of faith Ephesians 6:16)!

We dare you to believe it, walk in it, and speak about it. Isn't it about time for you to come out of defeat? Isn't it time to start enjoying the abundant life Jesus paid for?

Talk About It

We should constantly be talking about what Jesus did for us. That's the only way we're going to get it imbedded in us. Talk about it to one another. Say to one another, "You were crucified, 2,000 years ago. Do you realize that today you're now living on a higher plane because you were buried with Jesus, raised up with Jesus, and quickened with Jesus?"

We ought to say that to one another. "I'm alive because Jesus is alive. I have fresh life in me because Jesus has fresh life in Him. I got it the same time He did. What He got, I got." Oh, if we could just understand this!

The devil's out there right now, hoping that you don't get it. He's standing in the corner, looking you over, saying, "Oh, there's one who's half asleep. He doesn't understand a word."

Come on now, it was such a marvelous thing Jesus did against the devil. Such a victory. Such power in there. We got it. We got it. Say it!

You now know that He had to die spiritually. That didn't mean He ceased to exist anymore than we ceased to exist when were spiritually dead. We were just alienated from the life and power of God, alienated from life itself. But Jesus gave us new life. What are we doing with it? We're letting a nation go down the tubes because we don't believe the power that we have right within us. We could change things.

Just think, if all of us walked in that knowledge day after day, the devil couldn't touch us. Then, we could go out and teach this to others. They in turn, would teach others. Do you understand what we're saying? It's called making disciples of all the nations (Mathew 28:19,20).

One way we should talk to God is, "Give me more, I want more, I'm not satisfied. I'm grateful and very thankful for what I have already experienced, but I want to experience complete victory in my life. I don't want a victory now and then. I'm in Christ. I'm in His will."

We want to walk in complete victory every day of our lives. We want to enter into the rest of God. Don't you? We have to get serious about God, don't we? And if we really want the victory, we'll stop playing games and wasting time.

We'll start being better stewards of our time and of the mystery (Ephesians 3:9). We'll get our minds opened up. "That the eyes of understanding will be opened," should be our prayer every morning, that the eyes of our understanding be enlightened, that we would know the hope of our calling.

"What's your calling? What's your purpose for our lives?"

He says, "That you'll be conformed to My Son, Jesus Christ" (Romans 8:29). That's what He'll always answer.

"Oh, my, what a big job that is." Conforming to Jesus? Yes. Did you ever think of that? Just think about being conformed to His Son, Jesus. Then, He begins to talk to you about how you can be conformed to Jesus. Then, it expands and gets bigger and better. And the more you talk to Him, the more He says, "You can do it; you can do it."

It's grace. His grace is sufficient for us. Grace for the inner man (Ephesians 3:16). Strength for the outer man. All you need to do is call upon Him. You know, we ask God for things like He doesn't want to give them to us. Our God-He's ready. Can you almost picture His hand coming down through the ceiling, just filled with all kinds of gifts and saying, "Who's ready to ask Me for it? Here it is."

Yet we don't ask. Or, if we ask, we just walk away from it after we ask, and God says, "Well, if you don't care, I won't give it to you. Tell Me you care about it."

You have to start talking to God like He's real and He cares about us, not like He's twenty million miles away. Now, God has a two fold purpose for our lives on this earth. First, as we said, to be conformed to the image of His Son. Second, that His manifold wisdom might be made known by or through the Church to the principalities and powers in the heavenly places, the eternal purpose which God accomplished in Christ Jesus our Lord (Ephesians 3:10,11). As Christians, that's why we are still here! Let's get our job done so that Jesus can come back and receive unto Himself a glorious Church!!

CHAPTER

18

SEATED WITH CHRIST

As we go through this chapter on being seated with Christ, we're going to take it from the viewpoint of a covenant. A covenant is the most sacred thing that any two persons can enter into together. It's sacred. We're going to find out how we got into Christ. We're going to find out what God thinks about it and how this all came about. And when you finish the next two chapters, you're going to see it so clearly. It's going to come together. It's going to mesh together. It's all going to be real to you. And every time you read these things in the Bible, you're going to begin to say, "That's me. I was there. I know I was there.

I realize I was there. I don't have a doubt about it. I was there with Jesus. I was in Jesus. When He was crucified, I was crucified. When He was raised up, I was raised up. When He was given new life, I was given new life. When He conquered, I conquered. And when I was raised up and ascended, I was seated with Jesus in heavenly places. I don't have a doubt about it. God, the Father, sees me there in victory."

WE have to know what we're all about, what Jesus did for us-in short, who we are *in Christ*.

Jesus didn't do anything for Himself on that cross. He didn't' do anything for Himself. He did it all for us. And the whole purpose behind Jesus doing this was to get us back to God's original purpose, God's original plan. At one time, God came to a man whom He created called Adam and said, "How would you like to cooperate with Me on this earth? I have a plan. I have a purpose. My will is that certain things be done on earth. Adam, would you like to be My man, My partner? Would you like to cooperate with Me to bring about what I have up here in My heart for all eternity, down onto the earth that I just created? Would you like to be part of that? How about it, Adam, what do you say?"

Adam blew the whole deal for mankind. Because Adam was our representative man, when he said no to God, he lost the blessing of the Lord. He gave in to the devil. But listen folks. God never changed His original purpose. He wants to bring His will down to this earth (Mathew 6:9,10). And we'll show you a little bit of what God's will is.

But we're going to talk about being seated with Christ. What does that mean to you now before we even begin? In what terms do you think, when we say you're seated *with Jesus Christ* in heavenly places? What does that conjure up in your mind? What do you visualize? What do you think about when we say you're seated *with Jesus Christ* in heavenly places? Is that real to you? Is that fantasy to you? Is that just some good preaching to you? What does it mean to you? Because the Bible tells you that you're seated with Jesus Christ in heavenly places. What does that mean?

Quickened With Christ

Ephesians 2:1-6 says:
And you hath he quickened, who were dead in trespasses and in sins;
Wherein in time past ye walked according to the course of this world, according to the prince of the power of the air, the spirit that now worketh in the children of disobedience: among whom also we all had our conversation in times past in lusts of our flesh, fulfilling the desires of the flesh and of the mind; and were by nature the children of wrath, even as others.
But God [Don't you like that because it sounds like He had a purpose in mind for us? And no matter what we were, no matter how spiritually dead we were, He could make us alive.
***But God...]** who is rich in mercy, for his great love where with He loved us*

*even when we were dead in sins, <u>hath quickened us together</u>
<u>with Christ</u>…*

Oh, there's a wonderful phrase-<u>quickened us together.</u> <u>Gave us life together.</u>
<u>When He gave Jesus life, new fresh life, His breath of life went into us also.</u>
When God breathed in that life, He breathed power into Jesus. And we
were in Jesus. Wherever He was at that moment when God gave Him fresh
life, we got it because we're in Jesus.

"Even when we were dead in sins, hath quickened us together with Christ,
(by grace you are saved ;) [Now watch this.]

'And hath [past tense] raised us up together, <u>and made us sit together in</u>
<u>heavenly places in Christ Jesus.</u>"

Seated With Him

When Jesus was raised up to be seated at the right hand of the Father at
that very moment, not five minutes later, not five minutes before –as Jesus
was raised up and the Father says, "Come now, My Son, My beloved Son,
You have fulfilled My will. Come now to Your reward and sit at My right
hand" –<u>we went right there with Him</u>. Exactly at that moment we were
seated with Him, and that's what the Word says. It has been done. In God's
eyes, it's done. It's not *going* to happen. It *has already been done* in God's eyes!

Now remember something we talked about earlier. In Hebrews 2:14, we
are told that Jesus destroyed the devil's power of death. We all read that. The
Jordan translation says, "That He, speaking of Jesus, might break the grip of
the one who controls death." *Weist* says, "He might render inoperative the
one having the dominion of death." Now we said this, and we'll say it again.
We want you to get it-when Jesus defeated the one who had dominion and
took the dominion away from him, He didn't just slap him on the cheek.
<u>He crushed him</u>. <u>He annihilated him</u>. <u>He rendered him inoperative</u>. It was
as if He forcefully put the word "void" on his forehead. He said, "You are
unemployed; you no longer have any power whatsoever over God's people. I
have it all." Now understand that. When Jesus did all that, where were you?
You were in Him. His victory, His crushing of satan, was your crushing of
satan. Whatever He did to satan, you did to satan. And we're here to tell you
that satan knows that fact more than you do. Every time he looks at you,
he becomes spitless. He's scared of you, but you see, he also knows about
something else that you don't know. He knows about the very power that

resides inside you. And he knows that you don't understand the full victory that Jesus gave to you. So he plays games with you and keeps you blinded to the facts of the Gospel, the truths that will make you stay free. Satan was and still is the prince of death. He rules in the realm of death. He doesn't rule over you anymore, the believer. He rules in the realm of the spiritually dead. But you are alive. Remember? You were quickened together with Jesus. You have spiritual life in you-God's life…and now you reign with Jesus!

Jesus was made to be my sin, and He tasted death in His Spirit. Jesus became what each of us was, that is, sin. He became what you were, that is sin, and in effect took you into satan's domain. There, when He was made alive in His Spirit, He passed out of satan's grasp, who ruled in death.

Death is the instrument of satan's sway over mankind. When Jesus conquered death, He conquered the instrument of satan's sway over mankind. When Jesus conquered death, He conquered the instrument of satan's sway. We passed out of death with Jesus, and thus conquered with Jesus over all the realm of satan. We're no longer under satan's control. For those that like using their computers, we could say it this way. Jesus broke the link or connection between the computer of our lives and the devil's computer. Spiritual death was satan's link that kept us connected, but Jesus destroyed it! Each of us now has inside us, that same life that made Jesus the master of Hell and the master of satan. We have that same life in us. Satan has been rendered powerless over all of us by Christ's victory. We were in Christ; it was our victory. Satan has been dethroned, paralyzed, crushed and put out of commission. He has been made an open show of by Jesus Christ. You conquered with Christ. His victory is our victory because we have been made alive and raised up with Jesus.

Now that we recognize we've been raised with Him, we are now able to live on a new level, a new realm of life. We have now been transported out of the realm of darkness, out of the Kingdom of Darkness. We are now in the Kingdom of Light, a new level for us to live on in total victory. And we want you to know this-it's a level, if you choose it to be, <u>of continual victory</u>. It can be. It should be, and it will be if we do everything the Bible tells us to do.

Enthroned With Jesus

Ephesians 2:1-6 says that we were raised up together and made to sit together. We were made to sit together. God's purpose from all eternity was that each of us would sit in heavenly places with Jesus Christ. That's one of

His purposes. It's one of His pursuits, one of His plans from all eternity. Now, where is Jesus seated right now? On God's right hand. When Jesus sat down, we sat down with Him. Now let that sink into you.

"Well, you might say, I'm sitting in my chair on the earth."

That's right. But you're also seated somewhere else and that place is more real to God than where you're seated right now. In God's eyes, you're seated right next to Him. Even while we remain on this earth, God sees us seated at His right hand with the Lord Jesus Christ. Would you say that the right hand of God is a very high place of authority? Where are you seated? At the right hand of the Supreme Authority. You're seated with Jesus. Now *the Translators New Testament* says, "He raised us together with him and causes us to share his place of honor in the supernatural world." *Knox* says, "Raised us up too [also] enthroned us too, above the heavens in Christ Jesus." Did you know that you've been enthroned by the Lord Jesus Christ? You're not a nobody. You're somebody special. You're seated on the right hand of God, the Father, in Christ Jesus. Do you know that we share Jesus' place of honor? We have been enthroned with Him?

Do you fathom the kind of honor that Jesus carries in the supernatural world? Have you ever thought of what kind of honor, what kind of respect He is given in the supernatural world? We sing about it. We say, "Angels bow before Him." Angels are bowing before the Lord Jesus Christ. And we want to tell you, the devils see this; they know this; and they're panicking over it day by day.

Well, you may find this hard to believe, but we rule with Him in the supernatural world. The devils should be scared spitless of us. They should be. Do you know something? They are. But you see, they've convinced you that you ought to be afraid of them. The *Good News Bible* says, "In our union with Christ Jesus, he raised us up with him to rule with him in the heavenly world."

Even while you're on this earth, your position of authority is at the right hand of God in Christ Jesus. God says you're seated with Jesus. He sees you in His Son, Jesus Christ. And that's the position of highest authority. Jesus was given authority over Heaven and earth and beneath the earth, we are in Christ. Therefore, we have been given authority in Heaven, in earth and beneath the earth. In Christ Jesus we have full authority. While you are in that position, God expects you to rule and take dominion, take full dominion while you're on this earth, because this was His original plan.

Do you remember back in the garden? God said, "Adam, take dominion." And Adam said, "No, thank You." So what did God do? He spent some arduous years bringing Jesus Christ through the righteous line into this earth to get that dominion back into His hands so He could once again give it out, as His original purpose was, to those He created; and He has given it to us and expects us to use it this time. He doesn't want to go through that again. He won't go through that again. Jesus Christ was not the second Adam. He was the last Adam. It's not going to be done again. He said, "This is it, folks. You blow it this time, and it's all over for you. I've given you dominion." You have full authority in Jesus' Name (Mark 16:17,18; John 14:12-14).

> Look at Ephesians 1:18-21:
> *The eyes of your understanding being enlightened; that ye*
> *may know what the hope of his calling is, and what the riches*
> *of the glory of his inheritance in the saints,*
> *and what is the exceeding greatness of his power to us-ward*
> *who believe, according to the working of his mighty power,*
> *which he wrought in Christ, when he raised him from the*
> *dead, and set him at his own right hand in heavenly places,*
> *far above all principality, and power, and might, [did you notice that?]*
> *and dominion, and every name that is named, not only*
> *in this world, but also in that which is to come…*

His Power In Us

What is Paul saying in here? He's saying, "Look, I've been trying to get this across to you. Would you allow your minds to be enlightened?" He's saying, "These things are not going to come to pass. These things have already taken place. Just open up your mind and receive it as the truth of God's Word." He's constantly saying, "I want your minds to be enlightened to the facts of the Gospel.

I want you to understand what Jesus did for you." Paul often says-don't be ignorant. Your ignorance could destroy you. God said so in Hosea 4:6, "My people are destroyed for the lack of knowledge." That's ignorance. Never does Paul say, "This is *going* to happen." He says it already *has* happened. All you need to do is turn the lights on and understand what has happened on your behalf. The *Basic English Bible* says, "And how unlimited is his power to us who have faith."

Noli says, "And how immeasurable is his power in us who believe in him." Isn't that what he's saying in the *King James*? "And what is the exceeding greatness of his power to us-ward who believe." What is the exceeding greatness? He could just say it's a great power. He says, "It's an exceeding great power." And you know that power resides on the inside of you? Everybody says, "Send the power down; send the power down." God is saying, "You've got it in you; send it out of you." You see, we say these things out of ignorance of God's Word.

Isn't that what we always yell? "God, give me the power; give me the power."

God must be saying, "Haven't you read My Word? I've given you the power. It resides within you. Take it and use it." *Jordan says,* "May you experience the incredible outburst of his power in us, who rely on his might and his abundant energy. This same energy working in Christ raised him from the dead and gave him spiritual victory and authority over every ruler." That's Jesus. He received all that. Where were we when Jesus got all that? In Him. Did we get something when He got it? We got everything He got.

Listen to what *Lawbach* says, "I pray that you may realize that his power in us who believe is great beyond measure. It is the same mighty power that worked in Christ. By that power God raised him from the dead and had him sit at his right hand in heaven. There Jesus sits above all rulers, above all authority, above all power, above all lords."

We've given you several translations to bring across to you what happened to Jesus when He was seated next to the Father. What did God the Father give to the Lord Jesus Christ? Whatever it was, you ought to search out the Scriptures to find it. Because whatever He was given, you were given at the same time. It says, in the *Jordan translation,* "I want you to experience this."

In other words, don't let it just be something that you read off the page or hear in your ears. You read it here; you read it there; somebody told you this. He says, "I want you to experience this." How do you experience this rulership, this authority that you received through Jesus Christ? How do you experience it? By taking God at His Word, face value, and saying to yourself, "There's an exceeding great power that worketh within me. And that power is there for me to turn on and with which to take dominion, because God expects me to." So in order for me to experience it, I have to get out and do it. I have to get out and take what I have heard to be the truth and make it my personal experience to prove to myself that what God says is truth.

The devil is going to try to hold you back from that. He doesn't want you to go out and experience the power. He doesn't want you to go out and use the power. He doesn't want you to walk around and say, "I'm seated with Christ in heavenly places." He doesn't want you to know that you've been quickened with Jesus Christ, that the same power that went into Him, the same fresh life that went into Him, the same conquering spirit that's in Jesus, is in you. The devil doesn't want you to know that. And so he comes along as Peter said, as a growling lion. You know that's all he has (where Christians are concerned) is a growl.

Remember, the devil's been stamped void. You know a void can growl, but can it harm you? He's going about seeking whom he may devour. It didn't say he could. He's seeking those in the body of Christ who never listen when teachings come forth; who never think it's important to study the Word. The devil says, "Who hasn't picked up a Bible in a month? Those are the ones I'm going to devour. Those are the ones who will give in quickly when I start growling. Hah!"

"Oh help me, Jesus," each one yells in panic. But Jesus says, "The power is within you." Paul calls it the good fight of faith, doesn't he? Did you know the word "fight" is the Greek word, *agon*. We get our English word agony from it. It's an agony of faith, is it not? You've heard ABC call it the agony of defeat. The "Agon" of defeat. The fight of defeat. There's no fight when you get defeated. Paul calls it a good fight. A good fight is one that we win! You are going to have to resist the devil as James 4:7 says, but it also says that he will flee from you; not might flee. He will flee from you!

Attending to God's Word

We have a fight. You need to win that fight. If you believe God's Word, it becomes a good fight, and you win every time. You stand on God's Word no matter what comes your way. You completely do what Proverbs 4:20 says: "My son, [My daughter] attend to my words…" God's words didn't mean much to Adam because Adam didn't take the dominion that he was told to take. And look what happened. How did it happen?

Well, satan comes along and says, "Did God really say that?" You see, questioning God's integrity right from the beginning. Is anything different today? No. The devil's still challenging you with God's integrity: "Does God really say that? Does God really mean that? Not in your case, couldn't possibly be in your case. You misunderstood that. I mean, you're seated in heavenly places? You're crazy. Come on!"

You see, the devil is always checking to see if you know whether God is truthful when He said something to you in His Word. He's constantly challenging it. But you see, Proverbs 4:20 says, "My son, attend to my word…" The devil comes along with words, words and more words. Whose words are they? Are they God's Words? If not, then you don't pay any attention to them. Pay close attention to God's Word-there's where you will find life.

"Yes, but the devil's over there."

So what? You don't have to pay attention to him. Fix your attention on God's Word.

So the devil speaks some more words, "Yes, but doesn't your body feel pretty bad right now?"

"It doesn't make any difference; I'm attending to God's word. He said it would be health to all my flesh."

"Yes, but do you really believe that God means that in your case?"

"Yes, God said it; I believe it."

"Yes, but I don't think that word is truth-just look at your body. It's hurting, you're in pain."

"It doesn't matter, God said it; that settles it; I believe it." Do you understand what we're saying?

"Do not let them [God's Words] depart from your eyes."

The problem with us is we don't really take God's Word seriously, and we let our eyes roam everywhere. They go everywhere. Yes, but you know, Sister So and So, who was a pillar of the church, said she believed in Jesus Christ with all her heart, and she died of cancer.

What have you just done? You've taken your eyes off the Word. You're not attending to the Word anymore. You've let your eyes roam, and you looked at Sister So and So who died. So what if she died? Does that make God's Word void? She did something wrong obviously, didn't she? She made a fatal mistake, didn't she? Are you going to follow her pattern, because you think she was a pillar of the church?

Don't go by externals. Don't go by what you see. You don't know what Sister So and So did behind closed doors at home. You just saw her saintly look in church. She's a pillar of the church? How do you know that? By the way she looks? She could be home tormenting her husband every day of his life. You don't know that, do you? And besides that, you could love Jesus with all our heart and still die of cancer. Did you know that? Then, what's missing? You didn't know or believe Proverbs 4:20.

You really don't know what's in a person's heart, do you? Then get your eyes off people and get your eyes back on the Word, because the Word is there for you. I don't care what he's doing, she's doing, the Word's there for me to look at. Doesn't matter what they do. The Word's there for us, and we don't take our eyes off the Word. We don't care what the devil says to you. As we said, it's agony sometimes. It's agony to keep your eyes right there-agony. That's a fight of faith; that's agony, your flesh doesn't like it, but the benefits of obeying the Word are wonderful and far out weigh the agony.

What we asked earlier was why don't we do it? Because it's agony and we American, Western people are used to comfort. Instant everything. Instant coffee, instant food, instant this and instant that. We need to sit, feast and chew long on God's eternal Word. It's health to all our flesh. Do you remember what the word "Identify" means? To made identical, to consider and treat as the same. God looks at you, He says, "You're identical to My Son, and I'm going to treat you just as if you were Christ." What does it take on our part to get that exceeding great power, that same power that raised Jesus from the dead, to work in our lives? Faith in God's Word. That's all. Faith in God's Word. It's called the good fight, the good agony of faith. You see, we have to determine that sometimes it's going to be agonizing to stand on the Word. The devil's going to try to pull you like a magnet. He's going to pull on you, "come off that Word. Come off that Word. It's not working for you. Get off that Word; it's not working for you. See, it doesn't work. This Christianity stuff doesn't work. This faith stuff doesn't work."

How many times has he told you that this week? He wants you to give up and quit standing on God's Word.

Has the Word been totally fulfilled in your life yet? Then what are you giving up for? You stay with it until you get what you've asked for. You see, that's what God means by attend to My Word. It means, "Do not let your eyes depart from it," He says. "Store it in the midst of your heart. If you have to keep running to the Bible to read what it takes to get from God what you want, then you don't have it stored in your heart."

"Oh, I don't remember. I wish I had my Bible with me. Oh, my goodness, what was that passage? Oh, my goodness, God I need it right now. Where was it?"

He says, "Store it in your heart." You know how you store it in your heart? By meditating, reading and listening to it every day. Paul says, "The eyes of your understanding be enlightened that you may know what is the hope of His calling." You need to be enlightened.

There's no excuse for you to be ignorant any longer because if you read the Word, you'll find out who you are in Christ. And if you find out who you are in Christ, the devil will stop deceiving you. He'll know he can't any more, because you have an understanding of the truth.

The Bible says we were crucified with Christ; we died with Christ and were buried with Christ, quickened with Christ, conquered with Christ, raised with Christ, and seated with Christ. Our part is to believe that what the Bible says is true. That's our part. If God says, "This is true, you are seated with Christ," and we can't find anything in the Bible that contradicts the fact that it says over here that we've been raised up together and made to sit with Christ in heavenly places, then it's true.

Now we're going to tell you something. There are churches and preachers out there who will tell you, "That's nonsense. Don't you believe that stuff?" Won't they? You know why they tell you that? Because they don't understand it, and they don't want to bother to take time to study it. And so they preach the same old baloney that they preach week after week to people. We say baloney because that's what it is, because it doesn't change their lives. A Lot of them are not preaching the Word of God, just their opinions, trying to please men; not wanting or expecting true revival in their churches. In some churches the people are dying right there in the pews. They're getting sicker by the day. And if anybody dared to lay hands on them, and said, "I'm going to pray for you to get well, "they would say, "What are you doing? Take your hands off that person. Don't do that. Don't give them hope. What's the matter with you?"

The whole Bible is about hope. It says it right here. Let's read it again, "The eyes of your understanding be enlightened that you may know what is the hope." There's a hope in Jesus. But there's no hope for you if you don't believe what Jesus did for you. Oh, we're not saying that you won't go to Heaven. In fact, you might just go there a little earlier than you anticipated if the devil gets a hold of you. Are you understanding what we're saying?

Our part is to believe that what God says is true. That's it. When we do, the same power that raised Christ from the dead is at work in us. His resurrection power is overwhelmingly great, unlimited, immeasurable and tremendously mighty. His resurrection power is at work in us, because we were raised up with Christ, made to sit with Him. When we are raised up with Him, don't we get to share His benefits? One of His benefits is that He rules in authority. God gave that to Him because of His obedience. So now, all we have to do is recognize that we're seated with Jesus Christ. We are enthroned with Him in the heavenly realm. We share the authority of His throne. Jesus said so.

Raised to be a King

A lot of people say, "Well, I don't believe that." Well have you read Romans 5:17 lately? It says that you reign in this life as a king. Kings are not subject to other people. They rule. You're a king in the kingdom of the Almighty. You've been raised up to be a king. You're a king. You're meant to rule and reign in this life with one Jesus Christ. We are to rule with Him over sin, poverty, sickness and demons. And all our circumstances, all that is under His feet is under our feet because we are seated with Him. All principalities, powers, dominions, forces and all demonic forces are under my feet. Sickness and poverty are under our feet. Satan is under our feet. We have authority to tread on scorpions, on serpents and over all the power of the enemy because now we're rulers with Jesus Christ (Luke 10:19).

Follow now as we show you how simple this is. By admitting Christ into Heaven as my head and representative, the Father made me to sit with Him in those heavenly places. Exactly where Jesus is seated, we are seated. We have been admitted into those heavenly places in the person of Jesus Christ. We share His resurrection. We share His ascension. What the Father did for the Son, He has done for us. We are now in Christ, Who is in Heaven, and therefore, the heavenly realm is where we live. See yourself there reigning and ruling as a king. Share His place of honor in the supernatural world. Be established with Him in the heavenly realm. It's real to us. It's real to God. It's real to the devil. It's real to Jesus. It ought to be real to you. All authority invested by the Father in Jesus, has also been invested in everyone of us. To paraphrase it, when Jesus received the full authority over Heaven and earth, He said, "Now I can put it back into the hands of man as it was originally intended." (Mathew 28:18-20) In other words, He's talking about dominion. What was God's original intent in the garden with Adam and Eve? That His will would be carried out through His appointed representative, who at the time was Adam. Adam said, "No thank You, I think I'll just believe the serpent. He says I can be like you, if I do what he says." You already are like God-made in His image.

God says, "I want My will to come forth in the earth. I still have that purpose. It is my will. It is my utmost objective to bring My will into the earth."

God told Adam, "Take dominion." God wanted man to rule this earth under Him, bringing into this earth the very will of God in all its respects. But satan came along and challenged God's integrity, as he still does today. And he said, "Does God really say this?"

"Yes, He did say this," That's what Adam should have said, "I believe Him. That's what God said." Many of us are just like Peter who took his eyes off the word Jesus gave him and sunk into the water. The devil made waves for Peter; he became fearful and he sank!

God wants to take dominion back to bring His will into the earth. That's always been His purpose, as we've said. We do have dominion. After Christ's Spirit had been freed from Hell, He then entered His body and was raised to immortality. That's what the Scriptures tell us. Acts 2:31 says, "He seeing this before spake of the resurrection of the Christ, <u>that his soul was not left in Hell,</u> neither His flesh did see corruption."

Now before His ascension to sit at the right hand of the Father, He gathered His disciples together in front of Him and He told them: "All authority in Heaven and earth has been given unto Me." He told His disciples that. As a man, He was given authority over the world and over the world rulers of spiritual darkness. With that authority, He sat down at the Father's right hand. He did it for us. That authority has been now given to us in Jesus' Name!

> Let's look at Ephesians 1:20-23:
> *Which He wrought in Christ, when he raised him from the dead,*
> *and set him at his own right hand in the heavenly places*
> *Far above all principality, and power, and might, and*
> *dominion, and every name that is named, not only in this world,*
> *but also in that which is to come:*
> *and hath put all things under his feet, and gave him to be*
> *the head over all things to the church,*
> *which is his body, the fullness of him that filleth all in all*

Jesus is the head of the church, is He not? Do you agree with this? We are His body, is that correct? Well, if we are His body, and He is the head, and all dominion, power and might are underneath His feet, who else has it under their feet? We do. We just read that all things were put under Jesus' feet. Under His feet would have to be under His body also. That's us. Then we are seated with Jesus Christ. We were raised up together with Him and made to sit in heavenly places in Christ Jesus-that's what is says in Ephesians 2:6. And in Romans 5:17, as noted earlier, we read "for if by one man's offence death reigned by one; much more they which receive abundance of grace and of the gift of righteousness <u>shall reign in life by one, Jesus Christ.</u>" Are we to reign when we get to heaven?

Reigning Now

Where do we reign? In life. Right here and now. You don't have to think about when you get to Heaven. You have to think about now. Right here, as you're living, you need to reign. You've been given the gift of righteousness, and now you can reign in life by one Jesus Christ. The word "reign" is *basileuo* in the Greek language. It means to rule, to rule from a sovereign foundation of power. If we reign or rule in this life, it is from a foundation of power that has been given us by the sovereign King, Jesus Christ. So what are we going to do with it? Jesus is waiting for us to take, in a vital sense, what was made ours legally. In His name, we must put every enemy under our feet that we might reign as kings with Him. As we rule with Him, we are to see that the Father's will comes about on the earth. Jesus said, "The works that I have done, you will do and greater works, because I go to my Father." (John 14:12-14)

What were the works Jesus did? First John 3:8: "For this purpose the Son of God was manifested, that he might destroy the works the devil." What were the devil's works? Sickness, poverty, spiritual blindness, disease and a long list of things that were not normal. What did Jesus do in fulfilling His Father's will on earth? He took all these abnormal situations and made them normal.

It's simple folks. The woman who bled all those years, that was abnormal. Jesus said, "Be made normal." We're just going to give you what the Father's will is now, because everybody seems to think that it's some big crazy thing out there that we'll never understand. The paralytic who was let down through the roof of the house, was unable to walk. That was abnormal. Jesus said, "Be made normal. Start walking." Blind Bartimaeus is another abnormal life. He couldn't see where he was going. Jesus looked at him and said, "Have your sight back. That's not normal being the way you are. I want to make you normal. Start seeing." The woman caught in adultery had led a life of sin. Jesus said, "I forgive you. Don't live abnormally anymore. Go and sin no more. Live a normal life of righteousness." Jesus ruled over all abnormal circumstances and made them all normal. If we are to do the works that He did, then ruling with Him from our seat of authority would mean that all abnormal situations are against the Father's will. Because Jesus said, "I came to do the Father's will." It's simple, isn't it?

"But I don't know what the will of the Father is." Just find something abnormal and make it normal. The poor demoniac at the Gadarenes was so abnormal that he had a legion of demons living inside him. Jesus kicked out that legion and said to that man, "Be normal." So it's abnormal to have demons in you. Being poor is abnormal, because the Apostle John said that he wished above all things that you have a normal life of prosperity. "Be prosperous," he said. That's normal (III John 2).

We are seated with the One who was dead but is alive forevermore. He faced death and conquered it. Spiritual death is abnormal. He said, "I'm going to be normal and so are you." He was given fresh new life, raised up and seated in a position of the highest authority in Heaven and earth. And guess what? We are in Jesus Christ. We have been raised up together with Him. Made to sit with Him in heavenly places. To rule over every abnormal situation and make every abnormal situation normal. That's our position and that's what God expects us to do. This is the Father's will. Did you get this? It's not difficult. Make all abnormal things normal, and you will be pleasing the Father as you do His will. It's God who does all of the works through us in Jesus Name! Now in the next chapter we're going to discuss "in Him" by a loyal covenant. The words "loyal covenant" are translated throughout the Bible as God's loving kindness, God's mercy, God's love. When we start talking to you about this covenant that God has made, it's going to all come together, and you're going to see clearly who you are and why you are *in Christ*.

19

IN HIM THROUGH COVENANT LOYALTY

As we begin the nineteenth chapter on this subject, we've been saying over and over again that this is probably one of the most important subjects from the Word of God that we could ever endeavor to study.

Let us say this to you. If we would decide to remove all these key phrases-"in Him,""in Christ," and "together with Christ" – out of the Bible, in particular, out of what Paul has been writing, then there would be very, very, little left. There wouldn't be a story there for us to relate to. Because if we took out that we've been crucified with Christ, buried with Christ, died with Christ, quickened with Christ, raised with Christ, conquered with Christ, and seated with Christ, what would be left of the Epistles of Paul? Think about that now. God sees us "With Christ," "in Christ," and "together with Christ."

Now what we are talking about are eternal realities.

It all breaks down to this: if we were not in Jesus Christ, we would be absolutely nowhere. In fact, these phrases express our real relationship with Jesus. Everything He did, everything He got, we were right there with Him and all of it became ours when it became His. In fact, even though Paul wrote about these key phrases as we see them in the Epistles, Jesus Himself was suggesting that this was the only type of relationship that would produce for you things of a lasting eternal nature. Here is an example of this. If you look over in John 17: "That they all may be one as Thou Father art in Me and I in

Thee, I in them and Thou in me." And over in John 15, Jesus said, "<u>I am the</u> <u>vine, you are the branches, Abide in Me for without Me you can do nothing</u>." Can you see this *in Him* relationship? Can you see what's being said here?

He said, "You can't bear fruit without being in Me. There will be no fruit-bearing aside from Jesus. You cannot produce anything without Me." Jesus was one with His Father, and so He produced fruit. The Father was in Jesus: Jesus was in the Father. And John 17 says Jesus wants us to be one with Him in the same manner. So He says to the Father, "I in them," suggesting that we realize that to be one with Him, we need to understand what it means to be <u>in Him</u>. The Word tells us how. Just reckon it so (Romans 6:11). We are alive unto God through (or in) Jesus Christ. We just quoted John 15, where Jesus speaks of the relationship of the vine and the branches-that in order to receive what goes through the vine, the branches must be one with the vine.

And in the last chapter, we saw the great and final phase of the redemption that Jesus took us through. We found out that we were raised up together and seated with Jesus Christ. When we talk about being seated with Jesus, we're talking about a position of authority. When Jesus sat down at the right hand of the Father, if you are in Jesus Christ, then you also sat down at the right hand of the Father.

Now this might not be real to you, you may not see this as real. It might be very difficult for you to understand this. But to God, it's real. When Jesus sat down at His right hand, you sat down with Him, because the Bible says so. You are seated in heavenly places in Christ Jesus. Notice, in Christ Jesus. Jesus has been given all authority in Heaven, in earth and beneath the earth. If you are in Jesus Christ and seated with Jesus Christ, where does that put you? In full authority in Heaven, in earth and beneath the earth.

Together With Him

Jesus wants our lives to be lived together with Him. "Abide in Me." He says again, "Abide-live-in Me." You are the branches that take sustenance from the vine. If you take yourself away from the vine, you have nothing; you can do nothing; you're unable to accomplish anything. Jesus wants our lives to be together with Him, <u>as one life living in unison</u>. So, if these words are the undergirding words of the New Testament, then wouldn't you say that above all other words in the New Testament, these words must be the most-understood words in the New Testament? "In Him," "In Christ" –shouldn't all of us have a real grasp on what they mean? We've used them over and over in this book. We've said to you, "you're in <u>Christ</u>; you're <u>crucified with Christ</u>; you <u>died with Christ</u>; you were <u>buried with Christ</u>; you were <u>raised up with Christ</u>; you were <u>quickened with Christ</u>; you conquered <u>with Christ</u>; you're seated <u>with Christ</u>."

If these words are so important to us, then we ought to understand them, because they undergird our whole life while we're here on this earth and mean so much for us eternally. Notice how the Holy Spirit places these phrases. He uses "in Him," "with Him," in such a way that we can plainly see, as believers, we have nothing except what we have in Christ. All our possessions, our position, our value, our victories, our abilities-all of these things (and the list goes on and on) are in Christ. Being in Christ also produces faith in us by which we can live.

Galatians 2:20 tells us something very important. Do you remember it says, "I am <u>crucified with Christ</u>: nevertheless I live, yet not, <u>I but Christ liveth in me: and the life which I now live in the flesh I live by the faith of the Son of God,</u> who loved me, and gave himself for me?"

You see, our faith comes from Him, too. We live by His faith. He has given us an example of what true faith is all about, and as we look at Him, we see what faith is all about, and as we look at Him, we see what faith is. And because He is the Living Word, the more we abide in Him, the more we have the Word in us, and it says faith cometh by hearing and hearing by the Word (Romans 10:17). Understand that if we're in Christ, then we should abide in Christ; we have the Word in us. He is in us; we are in Him; and together we are in the Father as one. We live in unity with the life-force of all creation. What flows through Him, flows through us. The authority and abilities we have are all from Him, and they operate through us as His channel.

If we live this kind of life, that is, allowing God's life to flow through us, then people all around me will get a correct view of what God is really like. What better way for people to come to know God than when we live like Christ? Jesus said, "If you have seen me, you have seen the Father."

When we begin to understand this, things are going to change in our lives. Yet, so many believers don't have the faintest idea what it means to be "in Christ." You can just go out among your friends, even ask your Christian friends, "Do you know much about your identification with Christ?"

Most of the time you'll hear, "I don't know what you mean."

"Oh, you know, the places in the Scripture where Paul, the Apostle, talks about being *in Christ.*"

"Oh, I've seen those in the Bible, but I don't really know what they mean."

"Well, you read where Paul says you were crucified with Christ. You know what that means don't you?"

"Well, I'm not sure."

The devil is defeating Christians because they don't know what this means. Many are being destroyed, as the Scripture says, for lack of knowledge. And if you're going to be destroyed for lack of knowledge, then you ought to be able to gain victory when you have some knowledge. And so, we have to get all the knowledge we can about being "in Christ," with Him together raised up, because these words are the undergirding, the hinge pins, so to speak, of the New Testament.

Now with our minds, especially here in the West, it is very difficult for you to imagine us, standing in front of you, and yet being *in Christ* at the same time. For Christ to be *in us* is perhaps difficult for some to comprehend. And it's hard for us to comprehend that Christ is in you. Now even more difficult to understand is that when Christ was crucified 2,000 years ago, we were in Him, 2,000 years ago.

The phrase *in Christ* is, as we said, the hinge pin for our understanding the entire New Testament. When you understand this, and you will, it will become solidified into your spirit by the end of the next chapter. All we've taught you up to this point, the 18 chapters of "Our identification With Christ," is going to come together for you.

The Blood Covenant

So how do we explain it? Is there a way of doing this? Yes, there's a way. There's only one way, and it's a theme that runs from the beginning of the Bible to the end, and it's called Blood Covenant. In fact, the blood covenant-although you may think it's only in the Old Testament, it's found in the New Testament, too-the blood covenant spans the whole Bible. You might say the blood covenant is the foundation of the Bible.

In the Old Testament, it was the way people thought; they didn't think any other way. They ate and they breathed the blood covenant. It was their way of life. The Bible comes to us framed in covenants. And when you get a hold of this, it just won't escape you anymore. Let's dig deeper.

When Paul brings us such phrases as "in Him," it comes right out of the Hebrew background. In fact, Paul, being a Hebrew of Hebrews, grew up in the knowledge of the blood covenant. So it was easy for him to write this. You see, he didn't have a doubt about what he was saying. He understood it fully, as the Holy Spirit gave it to him. All the Hebrews, who were saved in the early church, when Paul spoke about this, understood it without question and knew exactly what he was talking about. The Gentiles were having a time with it because they wouldn't have known much about the blood covenants.

Paul's whole background was immersed in blood covenants. These phrases are actually covenant phrases-"in Him," "in Christ," "together with Christ." These are covenant phrases, and every Jew knows what you're talking about when you talk about the "in Him's." They're easily understood when you begin to know what a covenant is. Of course, we in the west hardly even know about covenants or their significance.

Allow us to explain briefly what a covenant really is. We'll make it real to you. Let's say you're the nation of Babylon. Your ruler is King Nebuchadnezzar. He's strong and powerful;' and at times, quite a tyrant. He has ruled with an iron fist; so he is ruling over all of you as your master, ruler and king. There is also another nation, the tiny nation of Israel. And their ruler is a lesser king, not quite so powerful or well known as Nebuchadnezzar. His name is Zedekiah.

Nebuchadnezzar is moving across the nations surrounding Israel. And as he is moving, he is conquering, slaughtering and wiping out one nation after another. He is taking their kings captive and killing them. He's ruling the region and is on his way to Israel. (Does this sound a little bit like what the devil is doing to people worldwide?)

Zedekiah is sitting back there in that little, little nation, by himself thinking, "My goodness, what is going to happen to me?" He's probably thinking as the reports are coming in, "I'm going to get wiped out! I'm going to get killed! He's going to torture me and kill me!"

Imposing a Covenant

Nebuchadnezzar comes into the tiny nation of Israel, and he comes this time, not with a sword but with an <u>imposition</u>. Do you know what is meant by an imposition? He's going to impose something. You know what it means when you're imposed upon. But somehow let's believe that Zedekiah is quite thrilled that he didn't come in with a sword and instead comes in with an imposition of a covenant (II Kings 24:11-20).

In other words, Nebuchadnezzar says, "I can give you a choice here. I'm the ruler; I'm the king, the strong one. You know I can wipe you out, Zedekiah. I can wipe out every person in Israel. There's just no problem for me. I'm big. I'm powerful. I'm the most powerful ruler of the day. But you know something, Zedekiah, I've decided that I'm not going to slaughter you. I'm going to impose upon you a covenant."

Now get this, he imposes or forces something upon them. You can read this in the Old Testament books. King Nebuchadnezzar came to King Zedekiah and his people and said, "Instead of my slaughtering you, I'm going to obtrude; I'm going to force a covenant upon you. You understand what this means, Zedekiah? Nebuchadnezzar comes with a covenant that's been all set. He doesn't come in there and say, "Okay Zedekiah, get your lawyers; I'll get my lawyers. We'll sit down and write the terms of the agreement." No. He says, "I'm imposing this upon you. The rules are set. The terms are set. The conditions are set. This is the way it's going to be."

So he comes in there and obtrudes with a covenant upon the lesser king. In other words, here are the terms of the covenant. He said, "This is my part of it, and here's your part-here's what you will do." That's it. There's no choice. It's simply imposed. Nebuchadnezzar said, "I could have wiped you out, Zedekiah. I could have wiped out your whole nation. I mean, look at me and look at you. I'm big. You're nothing. But instead, I've chosen to impose upon you this covenant. Now Zedekiah, what are you going to do with it?" You see, Nebuchadnezzar sent Zedekiah back to Jerusalem to be his puppit king. Obviously, in this covenant, Zedekiah could live, but only as a slave to the dictates of Nebuchadnezzar. God has imposed a covenant on us, but it's a covenant of love, mercy and grace. We would have been crazy not to accept God's Blood covenant. We got the best end of the deal. We are now heirs of God and joint heirs with Jesus, and we are blessed with every spiritual blessing in the Heavenly places in Him (Romans 8:17; Ephesians 1:3).

But let's get back to our story. What would you do if you were in Zedekiah's shoes? What would you do if this covenant were imposed upon you? "Well," someone may be wondering, "what in the world is a covenant anyway?"

Binding Until Death

Let's answer that question, "What is a covenant?" Well, it is a binding oath that two people make which binds them together. This sacred (focus on these words we're using) *sacred* oath is sealed in their own blood. And both parties understand that this is absolutely unto death. It was not just a quick handshake-okay, we agree with this. No, this was serious and binding all the way to death.

This is what you'd say if you were in this covenant: "I will keep this covenant even if it kills me. And if I break this oath, you have a right to kill me." Once sealed, there was no exit. No way out of it. This was ongoing through life unto death. There was absolutely no way out of it once you entered into it. And I'm saying, "I'll let my blood flow and swear unto you that I'll keep this covenant even to the day that I die."

What particulars did Zedekiah and this other king enter into? Let us share with you from our studying of various blood covenants how people entered into them. Even through different groups of people, a lot of the aspects remain the same.

Well, here's a key to understanding covenants. They would get a representative. (That word is familiar to you now, isn't it?) They would get a representative man. In other words, we need a man. (Now take note, we're going to choose this word because we know it cannot be used in this case, but we want you to see the way God sees it.) They get a man who literally becomes the nation. He literally becomes the nation or the people whom he represents, and we acknowledge him as such, whether we're part of the nation of Israel or Nebuchadnezzar's group of people. We would both acknowledge him as our representative man. Once he's picked, that's it. He's our representative man. In fact, every person in that nation, if it became necessary, would vote for him. This is a fact of covenant.

Each would say, "I vote for him. He represents me, and I am in him. My very thoughts, my very being is in that man. He represents me. He's been selected as my representative man. What he thinks, I think. What he says, I say. What he does, I do. Where he goes, I go. What happens to him happens to me." Now, anybody making a covenant back in those days in the Near Middle East understood this to be a fact. Covenants were a way of life.

His oath unto death is your oath unto death. When he sheds his blood, so you shed your blood. He represents you. It doesn't matter if you're a big nation like Nebuchadnezzar ruled, or a little nation like Israel. No matter how many there were, he is still your representative man. What he does, you do. What he gets, you get. Are you with us? We become one with him.

Next the kings and their people would gather, perhaps in a large field, a place where this covenant can be acted out. Both kings would be brought in. Now Picture this; we want you to see it in your mind and know what's happening. They get in this large field. King Nebuchadnezzar gets on one side of the field with all the people that came from his nation with him. And on the other side is King Zedekiah with the people from his nation. They have selected one man from each nation to be the representative man. These representative men would then step out to represent their nation and walk to the middle of the field.

At that moment, at that very moment, they cease to be individual. And at that very moment, they become that nation. And that nation becomes one with them. Everybody there knows that. Everyone in that nation is in that representative man now. That man represents all of them. These representative men would step out into the center of this large field and in the center they would find an animal which was going to be sacrificed. Usually it was a healthy, strong bull, representative of strength and virility.

Now we're going to try to picture for you what takes place, because we want you to understand what would happen if you ever break such a covenant. (Look at how God cut a blood Covenant with Abraham, Genesis 15). They put that bull in the middle of the field, and would come out with strong heavy axes. First of all, they'd cut the head off the bull, and blood would be flowing everywhere. They would slice that bull right down the middle, and ax him right down the middle so that half of him would fall to one side and half would fall to the other side. And the two representative men would step into the middle of the animal with blood all over them. Blood on their feet, blood on their right side, blood on their left side, everywhere they turned, there was blood. They stood right in the middle of that. Blood everywhere. Can you picture this?

This truly was an oath unto death, and their vivid reminder that if they, either one, ever broke this sacred covenant, what was done to this animal would be done to the one breaking the covenant. Heads would be chopped off, cut down the middle, and the pieces thrown out in the middle of the field for the birds to eat. That's exactly what they said when they made the covenant. "Let my body be cast to the birds-cut up, chopped up, bloodied, if I dare to break this covenant."

Then the terms of the covenant would be read aloud with the two kings present and the two nations present. This is what Babylon intended to do with Israel. And these were the conditions which would be carried out. Terms and conditions. Then the representatives of Israel would say, "So be it." That's putting the final clincher on it-"So be it. As you have said, it shall take place. This is it." Remember, the word "Amen" means, so be it. Then they would raise their right arms and cut somewhere on their forearm, and with blood running from those cuts-just dripping down on them-they'd be standing in blood, there would be blood everywhere – those representative men would swear they'd keep every term and fulfill every condition. Then they would bring their bloody wounds together and declare themselves blood brothers. They'd touch their wounds and let their blood mingle right there. And they'd say to each other, "We are solemnly committed unto the terms of this covenant unto blood, unto death."

The Friend Closer Than a Brother

Here's another thing you need understand. And immediately they called each other friend. Did you get that? Now you can begin to put it all together.

In Proverbs 18:24, it says,"...there is a friend that sticks closer than a brother." Now we want you to understand this. "...there is a friend that sticks closer than a brother." This covenanted friend is even closer to you than your real blood kin or brother by birth. This friend is not just a close acquaintance, not somebody you just like who happens to be around. We're telling you that this friend has become obligated to you unto death to watch over every one of your needs and protect you if necessary.

For example, if this particular man were out somewhere (one of these representative men) and an enemy was coming after him, all he would need to do is simply raise his arm and show the scar. Immediately the enemy would back right off and say, "Uh-oh, he's not alone; he's covenanted with somebody else. I'd better be careful, because if I touch him, his covenanted partner will chase me until he kills me."

Do you understand what we're saying? It's more than just a casual acquaintance. He says, "I'll protect you unto death. I will stay with you forever." And in some of those Near Middle Eastern nations, they say (and this isn't meant facetiously) that blood is thicker than milk. Do you know what that means? In our Western mind, it just goes over our head. But do you know what that means to them? That blood is thicker than milk? Again, there is a brother, we might add, a blood brother, who sticks closer than a brother by natural birth. That is milk he's talking about here, meaning two brothers who were nursed from the same breast.

Blood, in covenant sense, puts two people closer than if they came out of the same womb. This is what's being said when he says there is a friend that sticks closer than a brother. The friend is the one who covenanted with you unto death. And the scar created by the blood covenant cut was the seal of that covenant (Remember, we are sealed by the Holy Spirit through Jesus' Blood!). They joined their wrists and said, "We are friends; we are blood brothers."

Look carefully at the next step. Then they would sit the two representatives, the king and his court on both sides, in this case, Nebuchadnezzar and Zedekiah. The people would gather around, and what was the next thing that they did? They had a meal together. And guess what they ate and drank. Bread and wine. That's what the meal consisted of.

Does this ring a bell with you too? Can you think of some other place where somebody sat down and had bread and wine with other people? They would then serve each other this bread and wine. And each would say as one fed the other, "All that I am, my entire being, my very essence, all that I have, all that is mine, is all now coming into you." Then the other person would feed the other one and say the same thing: "Everything that I have, everything that I am, everything that you see that is part of me is now coming into you. We are now becoming one; we are in this together. What's mine is yours; what's yours is mine." Then it was done. The covenant was sealed.

Marriage Is a Covenant

You know, we just might say at this point that if we really understood what takes place at a marriage ceremony, we would realize that it's not just a marriage contract. You run down to city hall and get your license. And people think of that as just a legal document, but in God's eyes, when two people come together, they are establishing a covenant. And if you really think about it, there's blood shed on the first night of the honeymoon. Is there not? And at the wedding ceremony, oh we take this so lightly. If we would only see what's taking place.

All kinds of symbolism are in the true wedding ceremony that was ordained of God. From the time that the father gives the bride away, what is he saying? When he picks up her veil and puts it back on her head away from her face, he is saying you're coming out from underneath my authority. You're now going to this man; he's your authority. What that groom is saying and what that bride is saying to each other is that "I'm coming into you with my whole being, and you're coming into me with your whole being. What you are is now in me," and so forth. (It's a covenant, and we take it so lightly.) No wonder the divorce rate is so high. We don't understand the covenant we are entering into with that woman or that man. It's a covenant. And from this point on, they should live in complete loyalty to each other unto death.

"Covenant loyalty," it was called back there in the East. In some of the Bible translations you'll find this covenant loyalty spoken of as _loving kindness. That's what God says. He says, "My loving kindness is better than life." He's saying, "You don't understand. I imposed a covenant upon you. And that covenant is My loving kindness towards you. Its' better than your life itself." The *King James* calls it mercy. Look it up. Mercy. And of course, it also is called love.

Love. The Word of God says lovingkindness is better than life. And then it says, "Thy tender mercies are over all Thy works." And God so loved the world that He gave His only begotten Son that the world would not perish but have life everlasting. Covenant loyalty friends, is love, mercy and lovingkindness, all bound together in terms of that sacred oath.

"I am bound," God is saying to us, "through Jesus Christ. I am bound to give you mercy. I am bound to give you love, and to show My kindness to you all the days of your lives." Friend, are you getting a hold of this? It is swearing unto death that you will keep all the terms of what you have sworn to. Remember, you have poured yourselves into each other. You have become one. You have become one with the Lord Jesus Christ.

In the next chapter, we're going to talk about David and Jonathan. And if you think as we do, the story of their covenant is going to bring tears to your eyes. Do you know something else? When you finish the next chapter, you're going to know more about Jesus Christ and the fact that you are genuinely, really in Him. And that He has promised, until you die, to show you lovingkindness, mercy and love, under any circumstance, and you don't have to do a thing to earn it.

CHAPTER

20

IN HIM

In this chapter, we're going to give you an illustration of a covenant relationship between two people taken from 1 and 2 Samuel in the Old Testament.

Let's first briefly review what covenant is all about. Because that's what we're going to talk about in our illustration-a covenant that was made between King David, when he was a young teenager, and Jonathan, the son of Saul. A covenant is a sacred contract. It's extremely sacred. It's extremely serious. We can look at one such contract, one such covenant over in 1 Corinthians 11:23, the scripture we use every time we partake of the communion table. We talk about Jesus Christ and what He did at Calvary's cross in remembrance. He said, "Do this in remembrance of Me. This is the New Testament in My blood." That was a covenant. It was serious, Jesus said. Many of us, because we don't think about it and meditate upon it, are sickly. Many of us die prematurely, before our time, because we don't understand the covenant that Jesus Christ has made and ratified with His shed blood. So we discussed a covenant and the cutting of the covenant in the last chapter. We talked about the act that when two people cut the covenant, they call each other friend. And we said we need to get rid of our Western thinking, our Western brain, so to speak, and throw it away for a moment or two so we can think like a Mid-Easterner would think.

When you talk to a Hebrew, a Jew, you will discover that people in the Middle East think, breathe and eat covenant. The "in Him's" of the Bible are covenant phrases. When you talk to those from the East and say, "with Him," "in Him," "by Him," "through Him", they know you're talking covenant. That's what they understand it to be.

God's Covenant with Us

Now we said that we were going to give you an illustration that will tie this together. I believe it's going to let you see how a covenant works and will give you a greater understanding of God's covenant with all of us through Jesus.

So, God did make a covenant unto death. If God broke His covenant with us He would have to destroy Himself. But, I'm so glad that it's impossible for God to lie and to break His covenant (Numbers 23:19; Titus 1:2; Psalm 89:34)! That's why in 1 Corinthians 11:23, when it talks about the communion table, it talks about coming there with an understanding of what's taking place. Jesus is saying, "I shed My blood. I made a covenant with you. Don't you understand what I did for you? I can't break it."

You see, when we go to God for healing, we have to go in with a different concept than what we normally have. Don't go in begging God to heal you. Instead, say, "God, You imposed a covenant upon me." Do you understand the word "imposed?" It's just like Nebuchadnezzar dealing with Zedekiah. In essence, he was saying, "I impose this covenant upon you. What do you want to do about it?"

And Zedekiah's actions said, "I'll take it." He was very smart. He knows that this covenant was going to afford him protection and all his needs were going to be met by the one he covenanted with. So when you go to God, point to His Word. A good place would be in Exodus 23:25-26, where He said, "…I will take sickness from the midst of thee…the number of thy days I will fulfill." Go to God and say, "you created the terms, I didn't." It means something different now, doesn't it? So when you go to God, just simply remind Him that He made the terms(Isa.43:26). He made the conditions. He just simply says, "Come and love Me and worship Me, and I'll take care of you. And if anybody comes up against you, they come against Me."

This is the covenant Jesus made with us. When we go to the communion table, we're to remember the covenant. Go in there with some thought. He said, "Do this in <u>remembrance</u> of Me." What are you to remember? The covenant. He's not breaking it. He never broke it. He said, "I'll protect you till the day you die. Anything you need I'll give to you. Remember, we're poured into each other. You're in me, and I'm in you. There's no difference. We're one together." In other words, God said, "We're in this together. You're not going through your life helter-skelter."

"Oh, I don't know what I'm going to do. I don't know how I'm going to get through this problem."

And God is saying, "What are you, some kind of person who doesn't pay attention? I'm with you. What is it that you need right now? I'm your covenant partner.

You see, the trouble with us is we have our religious head on all the time. We don't understand because religion has blinded us to the things of the most-high God. Get your religion out of your way. We've been saying that a lot lately. Get religion out of your life. Religion has done nothing but put people in holding tanks waiting for them to go to Hell. That's all it's done. Bondage, total bondage. We are not talking about religion, but a relationship with the Lord Jesus Christ. We have an awesome covenant now!

We want you to understand that God cannot break this Blood covenant!! Even though, physically, we were not there when Jesus died and arose from the dead, because it was about 2,000 years ago, we were still there in Christ. So God says, "Okay, that covenant is still good. You were born in this era. What are you going to do with My covenant?

Well, if we're smart, we'll take it. God says, "I'll take care of you. I promise you, I'll take care of you." Should anybody come against you, Jesus says, "There's My scar." Do you get what we're saying? When Jesus raises that hand up, the devil, we want to tell you, the devil becomes very quiet. But most of us don't allow Jesus to raise His hand and show the scar, because we go in with our religious head on. "Oh Jesus, if it's Your will." What an insult to Calvary- *if* it's Your will?

Come on now, think! Jesus says, "What do you think I did up there on that hill? Why do you suppose I shed My blood up there? Why do you suppose I did all that for you? So that you can come and beg Me for something that's already yours? Are you getting what we're saying? This is not religion. We don't teach religion as Christians. We teach covenant partnership. We're not into religion. We're into the truth of the Bible. If you want religion, you'll have to go back to being in bondage. We're not interested in religion or bondage. God's Word is His will. Since the Word (I Peter 2:24) says that by Jesus stripes we are healed; that's God's will. To ask God to heal you if it's His will is total unbelief. You only pray "if it be Your will" when the Word doesn't specify what God's will is. Faith can only be released where the will of God is known. So, we need to really study God's Word to find out what His will is.

All right, we're going to look at a situation. It's a covenant. We'll tell you where it is:

1 Samuel 8 through 2 Samuel. So don't try to read it all, just follow us. We're going to do it for you. We're going to take everything in those chapters and capsulize it for you. We're going to give you an overview and give you the characters in this situation. So first of all, we have King Saul. He's the one who came to power, came to office, and came to be king because the people of Israel wanted a king instead of God, just like all the other nations had. So Saul displaced God. It's as simple as that. He displaced God. The people chose Saul over God, and Samuel didn't like it at all. He was the prophet. He went to God and said, "Oh God, as the prophet, they've rejected me.

And God says, "No, they haven't rejected you, Samuel. They've rejected Me."

It went deeper than Israel just wanting a king. We want you to know that. The people didn't want God anymore, nor did they want God ruling over them. It's much like what goes on with people today. Don't you agree?

"I don't want God ruling over me. What do I have to know God for? If I have to know Him, I have to know what He wants; and I'm not interested in what He wants. I want to do my own thing." I want to do whatever I choose to do.

People are no different today than they were back then. They don't want God ruling over them. They don't want to hear all these do's and don'ts. They don't want to hear all the principles and precepts in God's Word. We're going to do our own thing. They were tired of God and all His rules. Secular humanism today is doing the same thing. "We don't need You, God. We have our own god and we are our own god."

Do you remember during the Iraq war when people went crazy at the thought of their sons and daughters going over there to possibly be killed? All of a sudden, the whole nation became religious. Do you remember?

"Oh God," everybody cried. Those heathen newscasters were probably choking as they were saying the word, "G-G-G-God." Throughout the nation, people were running back to church. What an insult to the Most High! They didn't care about Him. They were concerned about themselves.

"What will ever happen to me?"

And listen, we're not ridiculing this. Don't misunderstand. But these people were interested only in what would happen to their daughter or son if their child died. They weren't interested in God. This nation is a selfish nation, isn't it? Many people are only interested in themselves. But God is so good and so merciful, He wants to help us get free of our selfishness and learn to trust and serve Him. He wants to get involved in everything we are doing, and prosper us and make us a great blessing to others!

Rebellion Leads to Independence From God

Just as the humanists do today, the Hebrews wanted to make themselves their own kings and rulers. They are their own gods. "I'll determine what's right and what's wrong, what's good for me. I'm god, you see." That's what they were saying.

So Saul accepts the throne and the kingship which came out of rebellion. That's all it was. You can't put another name on it. It was insurrection against God! And not long after that, Saul himself rejected God. And so, through this massive move of insurrection came total independence from God. And, as in any case of insurrection and declarations of independence from God, Saul and his subjects opened themselves up to gross darkness and, listen, demonic activity.

Did you hear that? <u>When you reject God, when you declare your independence from God, you are about to enter into the darkest time of your life</u>. And while you walk in the dark, the demons will harass you and will ultimately destroy your life. Remember, the thief comes not but for to steal, kill and destroy (John 10:10). Your destruction will come from the lack of knowledge. When you use your own knowledge, you reject God's knowledge—and open yourself up to the evil powers of darkness. Please, remember this, any time that you reject the Truth, you automatically receive a lie!!

You see, most people don't know this because the demons don't walk up to your front door, ring the doorbell and say, "Here I am. My name is Spiritual Wickedness in High Places. I'm going to harass you for two months." No, it doesn't work that way, folks. It works other ways. You lose your job. You're always sick. You never have a penny in your pocket. Your bills are always overdue. They're repossessing your car. Your kids go on drugs. Your husband gets to be an alcoholic. Your wife becomes a prostitute. The devil just doesn't walk up and say, "here I am, and I'm going to give it to you for the next six months." No. He comes in all sizes and shapes, doesn't he?

Well, the demonic activity began to take place in the land. They began to be controlled by demons, but thank God for Jonathan. Jonathan was the son of Saul and heir to the throne. Thank God, he never declared his independence from God. He loved God.

Quite different from his father Saul, Jonathan loved God and liked to speak of the things of God. Not like the king. Yes, he's in Saul's family. He's the son and heir to the throne, but he's not of the family. He's *in* the family but he's not *of* the family. He's not partaking of their independence from God, but he's still a son. He's heir to the throne from the king. He still has a great heart for Almighty God, and his love for God is tremendous. Not like Israel. Now put this on hold while we take you further into this story.

Let's go to another character in this scenario, a young teenager whose name is David. He's just a young boy, but a vital character in this story. God sends Samuel. He says, "Samuel, I've got a job for you to do. Go and anoint David. Samuel goes and anoints David, pouring oil over his head. Not only did David get a bath in oil, but the Holy Spirit came upon him at the same time. At a very young age, he began to develop a love and wisdom far beyond his years. This young boy became the most loyal of all Saul's subjects.

Now, put yourself in his position. David gets a call from God that he's going to be the king of Israel one day. Yet, he did not get rebellious against the one who was in charge, even though Saul was in gross darkness. All he did was go about and promote Saul. He loved Saul. Never once did he try to get rid of him. He waited patiently. No insurrection. He waited patiently for the day that God would put him in the position he was promised by the anointing of the prophet. (Christians should take note of this. Let God do the promoting; be patient).

Mutual Commitment/Mutual friends

Then one day Jonathan meets David. A love develops between them, and before you know it, they are bonded together (not a sexual love -Leviticus 18:22; Romans 1:24-32: I Corinthians 6:9,10; Revelation 21:8). Almost instantly, they bond together. These two were so much alike. They both loved God. No question about it. Because of their mutual commitment to God, they were pulled together like two magnets. And the two of them one day found themselves talking about covenants.

"Let's make a covenant with each other," these two young boys said. And as these two teenagers stood somewhere in Judah, they became the representatives of their unborn families. You understand now.

In earlier chapters, we spoke about the fact that Jesus and Adam were representative men. That we were in the loins of Adam from the beginning.

In other words, we said, "If Adam died as a teenager, we wouldn't be here today, would we? We were in his loins. We were potentials, so to speak."

Well, the two families of these teens were potentially in these two young boys. Again, let's get rid of our Western mind. To the Hebrew, those families were there in those teenagers, in their loins. They knew exactly where they were potentially. And so, as they made the cut in their forearms and their blood began to mingle together, these two young men became representative men. Potentially, all their families were there, though as yet unborn. Do you understand this now? This is representation.

After a time, Saul realizes that he has been rejected as a king. And even in his shadow of darkness, as we've talked about, he realizes that God has placed the anointing on another, that David would one day replace him as king. Now, after Saul's rejection of David-because we want you to get a picture of where Saul was with this-bitterness, resentment, jealously, and all that demonic harassment overtakes him.

You can understand his pursuit to kill young David. He is relentless. I've got to kill him. I've got to get rid of him" As Saul begins to hunt David, he becomes a madman. You can read it in the Scriptures. He becomes obsessed. "I've got to kill David." And as time goes on, his desire to kill this young boy heightens, and he just can't control himself anymore.

In the meantime, Jonathan and David meet again. Jonathan knows what his father is doing. He's not blind to what's going on. And it's all so obvious to him now that God is dealing with David to be the king of Israel. And so Jonathan says to David, "We have to add another term to our covenant."

David says, "Okay Jonathan, what is it?"

He says, "One day, David, our families will be at war." You see, he's full of wisdom, this young boy. He's thinking ahead. "David, when that day comes, even when the Lord cuts all your enemies off the face of the earth, treat my family the same as you would treat me." Then they touched their scars together and swore to the covenant's added term.

In the meantime, Saul is going crazy to get rid of David. He begins to hate even his own son, Jonathan, because of his relationship with David and even tries to kill his own son by throwing a spear at him. With demons instructing Saul, they tell him, "If David ever becomes the king of Israel, you're going to be the first one he'll kill. He's after you. David's going to get you. If he's ever made king, Saul, you better look out, because he's coming after you first."

But you see, we know that David would never do that. He had many chances to kill Saul and never did, did he? More hate is poured into Saul's family by him against David. You see, his family was being told daily, "David is a murderer. David is a scoundrel. David is going to take the throne away from me. Your Dad is going to be ousted. I'm rejected because of David. I'm having a hard time controlling my subjects because of David. David's no good, you understand. He's a murderer. He's no good." Can you picture a family hearing that day in and day out?

Jonathan comes a third time to David and says, "We need to add another term to our covenant." This is Jonathan speaking to David; the heir to the throne of Saul is speaking to David. Jonathan is heir to the throne, and he realized that if something happens to Saul, he will be king. But he comes to David and says, "God has anointed you to be the king of Israel." He kneels at the very feet of David. Now picture what he did. He says, "I relinquish my right to the throne. I, through the act of my own will, am now bringing to an end the rebellion that is in the throne of my father, Saul. I will not be king. I simply will be a prince at your feet David. You will be king." He died to the right of sitting on the throne. He says, "I am not going to do it. You David will be king. I will be happy to kneel at your feet, and whatever you want me to do I will do it. Let's add this to our covenant, David." They hit their wrists together once again, and this term became part of their sacred agreement. Then he touched his scar, as we said, and he said, "It is done." The covenant is sealed.

A little later on in the story, Jonathan had a son, Mephibosheth. When Jonathan was making a covenant, Mephibosheth was in his loins. He wasn't born yet. When Jonathan and David were making their covenant; this son of Jonathan's was simply a potential in his loins, not yet born. Jonathan was heir to his father's throne. Mephibosheth, who had not been born, was in line for succession to the throne, if anything happened to Saul and Jonathan. Jonathan knew that if one day he had a son, that son would follow him to the throne.

Let's go a little further. When David found out that Jonathan had a son, all his thoughts turned toward that son in love. He understood his covenant with Jonathan. David loves the baby of Jonathan. Now, the Philistines invade Saul's kingdom and kill Jonathan. Saul is so demon-possessed by this point that he casts himself upon his sword and kills himself. The people of the house of Saul are afraid of the Philistines. And now, remembering that Saul said if David became king, he would kill all those people in Saul's household, they fled. They just took off. And in doing so 2 Samuel 4 says, the nurse picked up Jonathan's son, Mephibosheth, and drops him. He becomes lame; his leg so badly damaged that now he must drag it everywhere he goes. The family starts saying to him, "Mephibosheth, you know who did that to you? David did that to you. You had better hate David." Hate this man, David.

You see, Mephibosheth didn't know about the covenant his father Jonathan had made with David. Well, one might now ask, "David, what are you going to do?"

He replies, "I am going to try to treat Jonathan's son exactly as if he were Jonathan."

"Well, David, why would you want to find the son of Jonathan? Nobody knows you made a covenant with him? I mean, come on now, he's dead."

Do you know what David said? "Yes that's right. But I'm going to bless him. I'm going to keep the covenant."

Now, most people wouldn't believe him. Because they've been told many bad things about David. They're not believing that David really wants to bless him. They don't know of the covenant. No one told him where Mephibosheth was except he finally located one man who said, "I know where he is." So David gathers his chariots and men and heads out to find him.

"What are you going to do when you find him, David?"

He answers, "I'm going to forgive him. I'm going to pardon him."

"You're what? Then what will you do?"

"I'm going to reward him," David says, "As if he were Jonathan."

"You're going to reward this would-be murderer? This guy who's only looking to stick a dagger in your back?" "That's right, because of my covenant with his father." And if anyone argues with that, David now is going to raise his arm and show them the scar. "I've sworn to that by the shedding of the blood of Jonathan and myself."

Now follow along. So David sent out his chariots and a good sized army, and they drag back Mephibosheth. All the while they're dragging him back; this son of Jonathan hates David. "If I get my chance, I'll put a dagger in him." So they drag this cripple back to David, into the court of the king. This cripple, this would be murderer, this maverick of the desert who's been out there being told all these years that David was his enemy and his murderer, says, "I better get to him first." All of a sudden he stands face to face in front of David. Eyeball to eyeball for the first time in his life.

The king knows the covenant-the terms and the conditions, the cutting, the shedding of the blood, and the added terms to the covenant. But this rebel doesn't know that a covenant was ever made, even before he was born. He was still in the loins of his father, Jonathan, when David and his father locked their arms together in a sacred binding covenant. This rebel doesn't know this. He's walking in with years and years of hate. And every time he walks off on that leg he says, "Just let me get my dagger in David. I hate him!"

Pardoned in Love Because of Covenant Loyalty

The king, on the other hand, has but one passion in his life and that is to impose the covenant upon this poor, uninformed cripple. Mephibosheth is looking, waiting for David to give the word to tie him to a stake, torture and kill him. That's what he's thinking. But David opens up his mouth with love and says, "I accept you. You're pardoned." And then he continues talking to this young son of Jonathan. He says, "Do you remember all the land that your father Jonathan had and your grandfather before him? Do you remember all the land that they owned?" He says, "Well, we've been keeping it for you. Our gardeners have been keeping it all, and it's ever so beautiful. It's all yours, and all the gold and the jewels your father had are yours too. We've been watching over them for you. Here they are; they're all yours." Mephibosheth's head is spinning. He says, "A moment ago, I was calling myself a dead man. What's happening? I thought all those thoughts about you. Those terrible things I said about you, King David. I'm not worthy. I don't deserve anything."

David looks up and says, "It has nothing to do with your deserving all this. It's because of a covenant that was made before you were born. It has nothing to do with deserving or earning. It has everything to do with an imposition of love and pardon and blessing. You couldn't earn it. You weren't even alive. It happened when you were in your father.

We made a covenant together and swore by blood that I would treat you as if you were Jonathan. Yes, Jonathan's loyalty had swallowed up any anger that I might have had for you."

But one thing was left. In order for Mephiboseheth to receive this lovingkindness from the king, he had to acknowledge David as the rightful king to the throne. He must die to all that's in himself that's rebellious and to everything that would lead to his claiming the throne for himself. He must enter into the obedience of his father, stop all further personal ambitions and take his place beside the one that is the rightful heir to the throne. "Will I accept this imposition? Will I accept the covenant that was already made?" Yes. But you say, it will take weeks for him to sort this all out. But that's okay. Take as long as it takes to do this. But know that David accepts you right now. He loves you. He's pardoned you. You can understand the scar on his wrist later on. You won't understand it now. That's a long discussion. It will take months to understand what that means. Just accept his love.

Now this story, which is ever so small in the Ole Testament, capsulizes for us the whole New Testament reality of "in Him." All the "in Him" scriptures have just been told to you and now you can grasp what Paul has been telling us about being "in Christ". Someone may be saying, "I don't' deserve it."

That's right! You don't.

"I didn't earn it."

That's right! You didn't.

But Jesus said, "I pardon you. I made a covenant. Would you accept My imposition of the covenant terms? Would you accept my lovingkindness?"

"Yes, but what's that scar on your hand?"

"Don't worry about that now, Just accept Me, and when you accept Me, you become one with Me. We become one together. I accept the responsibility for your life. Do you need something? It's all in the covenant. Just ask. Do you want Me to protect you? Just say, 'Father, take care of it.'"

That's Jesus, our Lord and Savior. He has made a blood covenant with you. You weren't even born when He did it. You were *in Him* because He was your representative man. Everything He got, you got!! Amen?

About the Authors

Richard Mallette Sr. Th.d

Richard was born in Athol, Massachusetts into a Catholic family. He studied for four years for the priesthood in Seminary.

However, this was not God's call on his life. Twenty five years later, Richard and his wife Adrienne learned of Christ and received Him as Lord and Savior. Shortly thereafter they were baptized in the Holy Spirit. Under the direction of his Pastor and church, Richard began a ministry in his home. That ministry grew at a phenominal rate growth to two thousand members by the year 2000. The Ministry was called Living Word Ministries, and during those years, two church buildings were built. One in 1989 and the other in 2000.

The flock was well established in the Word of God, and in 2005 Pastor Mallette retired from Pastorial ministry. For five years he travelled extensively throughout New England teaching at seminars and in churches.

Richard is noted for his strong annointing in teaching and in healing.

He has been now led to establish another church, with the emphasis on "Who you are in Christ" and "understanding your righteousness in Christ"

Dwayne Norman

Dwayne Norman is a 1978 graduate of Christ For The Nations Bible Institute in Dallas, Texas. He spent 3 years witnessing to prostitutes and pimps in the red light district of Dallas, and another 3 years ministering as a team leader in the Campus Challenge ministry of Norvel Hayes. Soon the Lord moved him into a traveling ministry and he began teaching not only the principles of soul winning, but also the varied aspects of the authority and function of believers on the earth today.

He teaches with clarity, the work that God accomplished for all believers in Christ from the cross to the throne, and the importance of this revelation to the church for the fulfillment of Jesus' commission to make disciples of all nations. He strongly believes that we are called to do the works that Jesus did and greater works in His name, and that the prophetic ministry with healings, signs, miracles and wonders should be regularly demonstrated through believers as a witness to the resurrection of Christ, not only in church but especially in the market place.

To inquire for meetings with Dwayne Norman, please contact him at:

> Dwayne Norman
> Mt Sterling, Ky. 40353
> 859-351-6496 or 859-293-9572
> dwayne7@att.net

Breinigsville, PA USA
05 April 2010
235560BV00004B/2/P